£2.50

BK1850

Banking Certificate S[...]

Banking [...] UK Lendin[...] International Business

Audrey Davies ACIB and Martin Kearns ACIB

Series Editor: David Palfreman BA

The Chartered Institute of Bankers

Recommended reading for
the Banking Certificate

PITMAN PUBLISHING
128 Long Acre, London, WC2E 9AN
A Division of Longman Group UK Limited

© A Davies and M Kearns 1989

First published in Great Britain 1989

British Library Cataloguing in Publication Data
Davies, Audrey
    Banking operations – (Banking certificate series)
    UK Lending and International Business
    1. Banking
    I. Title   II. Kearns, Martin   III. Series
    332.1

ISBN 0 273 02879 0

Printed and bound in Great Britain

To our respective parents, and to Steve Cheetham, without
whose constant encouragement and perseverance this book
would never have been completed.

Contents

Agricultural Mortgage Corporation – Government
aid – Summary – Self-assessment questions

Also available in the Banking Certificate Series:

Banking: the Legal Environment
David Palfreman
ISBN 0 273 03112 0

Economics and the Banks' Role in the Economy
Geoff Lipscombe
ISBN 0 273 03156 2

**Customer Services – Marketing and the Competitive
Environment**
Phil Ford
ISBN 0 273 02883 9

Supervisory Skills
Brian Stone
ISBN 0 273 03111 2

Acknowledgements

Barclays Bank Plc for permission to reproduce specimens of documents.

The Chartered Institute of Bankers for permission to use past examination questions and the Chief Examiner's Advice to Candidates.

Cartoons were very kindly provided by Colin Swingler, ACIB, Barclays Bank Plc, who was asked to step outside his normal role of lending banker to display his other talent (*see* Chapters 1, 2, 4, 8, 10 and 11), and by Barry Jackson.

Preface

In this book we have attempted to provide you with the foundation – the building bricks – upon which you can expand your technical knowledge of international services and the principles of lending money. There is no substitute for your own practical experience, albeit sometimes a bitter one when a customer lets you down and you lose money for the bank. However, if you digest the material in this book you will equip yourself, not only to pass the examination *Banking Operations – UK Lending and International Business*, but to carry out your duties effectively and successfully.

If you are studying through correspondence or evening classes, please remember that the tutor cannot be expected to cover all aspects of the syllabus within the constraints of the time allotted. It is important for you to enhance your learning received through that medium by reading your own bank's literature covering the various subjects involved and by asking questions of your colleagues in the workplace. It has been assumed that you have already studied the legal aspects of banking operations in the syllabus: *Banking: The Legal Environment*.

You will find that some chapters we have written, notably Chapter 9 (General principles of security) and Chapter 12 (Interpretation of financial statements) have had to cover a wide range of information. Just because these resultant chapters are larger than others on, say, Remittance and receipt of funds (Chapter 1) does not mean that questions on these subjects will be featured in significantly higher quantity in the examination.

The Chief Examiner always looks for a balanced, practical approach across the syllabus as a whole.

The Chartered Institute of Bankers has recently published a booklet of general advice to candidates. We have received their kind permission to reproduce it here for your benefit.

Good luck in your endeavours. Confucius say: 'A long journey begins with the first step'. You have taken that step.

AMD
MJK

General advice to all candidates

As in all studying, students should undertake a disciplined approach to their examinations. Please remember examiners do not expect you to write solidly for three hours. They do, however, expect you to read the paper and individual questions carefully and then plan your answers to ensure that all the relevant aspects are covered. Before you hand in your paper you should check that you have answered the correct number of questions and that they have all been numbered correctly.

Read the paper through from start to finish – this includes the instructions on the front page.

Read through again and choose the questions to be answered. Choosing the questions that can actually be answered is perhaps the most important aspect of examination technique. The right questions can be chosen by spotting the key words which examiners put in each question to reduce the content to an amount that can be handled in the allotted time.

Strike out the questions that you are not going to answer.

Decide how long you will need to spend on each question and keep to that time scale to ensure that you complete all the questions you have elected to answer. A good idea is to keep a brief record. Ideally students should plan their campaign before they enter the examination room and allocate their time accordingly.

Always start with your best subject to build up confidence and trigger off points which may be included in outlines for the other answers.

Do not start writing immediately you decide your first question. Draft outline answers to all questions first.

Read again the first chosen question and highlight the main points to make sure that you include them in your answer.

Check how many marks are allocated to the answer. If there are only five marks for a part of the question then only a brief answer is required; if there are 20 marks then a more detailed answer will be necessary. Do not waste time writing long sentences of prose when short notes will be adequate.

Answer the question as set out in the paper. Too many students answer what they think the question asks. There will be an indication in the question (e.g. 'outline briefly. . .' or 'discuss. . .').

When the time that you have allocated to each question is up you should move on to the next question as more marks will be gained in the first 10 minutes of a new question than in spending a further 10 minutes finishing off an answer.

Allow time at the end of the examination to check your answers to make sure that you have not missed any important points or made any mistakes.

Conclusion

The Institute's book, 'Learning Banking' (free to members) gives other general tips for passing the examination and helps candidates identify areas where they will need additional knowledge. For instance a candidate working in an international division of a bank will need extra knowledge on UK lending. Similarly, domestic branch bankers will need additional knowledge on finance for export.

If you have gained a sound basic knowledge from attending evening classes, self-reading or correspondence courses then you have every chance of success in these examinations.

The examiners are instructed to be fair and to ask themselves 'Can we pass you?' rather than 'What errors have you made?'. Borderline candidates always have their answers marked again before being issued with their result.

It's up to you!

Good luck, you may even get a Distinction!

1
Remittance and receipt of funds

Objectives

After studying this chapter you should be able to:
1 understand the different methods of remitting funds abroad;
2 describe how each process works;
3 identify which is the most appropriate method for a given set of circumstances;
4 understand and describe the advantages and disadvantages of each method.

Introduction

There is a variety of methods of settling or paying for international transactions. These means of transferring funds around the world are available both to the individual and the business customer. This chapter looks at the more straightforward of these methods in order to help you understand their main features and the differences between them. We examine other methods in Chapter 4.

There are many reasons why customers might want to send money abroad, for example:

Personal customers

- Gifts to friends or relatives living abroad.
- Payments for holiday accommodation or for the purchase of property abroad.
- Urgent transfers to stranded travellers.
- Transfer of assets on emigration.

'Yes, sir, your dollar transfer is whizzing off to New York at this very moment.'

Non-personal customers

- Payment for imported goods.
- Payments to overseas employees and agents.
- Payments to overseas subsidiary or associate companies.

Whilst some weird and wonderful ways of settling international debts are being devised and introduced, by far the largest proportion of payments are still for cash. However, cash is a bulky item and therefore can pose significant problems if it needs to be transferred in large quantities between countries which may be thousands of miles apart. Cash transactions then become long-winded, very expensive, and completely impractical. In addition, of course, there is also the danger of the cash being lost or stolen.

Over many years, therefore, methods of transferring funds between countries have been developed which avoid the need to move cash and ensure that payment can be made quickly and effectively. These fall broadly into *two categories:*

(a) remittance by *post,*
(b) remittance *telegraphically/electronically.*

Remittance by post

Cheque

The simplest and most obvious method is merely to send a cheque to the beneficiary in the other country. This has advantages for the drawer of the cheque who only incurs the postage costs and bank charges when the cheque is debited. (*See* Figure 1.1)

However, if the cheque is in payment for goods, their delivery may be delayed while the payee of the cheque waits for it to be cleared. It is possible to issue a cheque in the relevant currency if the drawer maintains an account in that currency.

Now put yourself in the position of the payee who suffers the following:

- The cheque will often be drawn in the drawer's currency, thereby imposing an exchange risk on the payee.
- The payee's bank may insist on collecting the proceeds of the cheque before crediting the bank account, thereby delaying receipt of the funds by as much as a month. This delay, of course, favours the drawer.
- The payee will also incur some, if not all, of the expenses of the collection process.
- The cheque may not be paid.

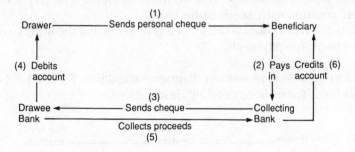

Fig. 1.1   The process for a cheque

In order to avoid some of these problems, beneficiaries can insist that:

- *cheques be drawn in their own currency.* This transfers the exchange risk back to the drawer but does not really solve any of the other problems highlighted.
- *payment be made by means of a Banker's draft.*

Banker's draft

This requires the remitter to give instructions to a bank to issue a draft, which is a type of cheque, drawn in the appropriate currency on a bank abroad. This may be one of its own subsidiaries or associates or a correspondent bank. For the payee this method solves the exchange risk problem, guarantees payment as the draft is drawn on a bank, and removes the delay in the collection process.

Consider the following example which illustrates *the process for a draft:*

Mrs Roberts wishes to send 100 000 French Francs to a property developer in the Dordogne as a deposit on a holiday cottage she wishes to purchase. She banks with the North Bank, whose correspondent bank is the Left Bank in Paris. The developer banks with the Perpignan branch of the Bastille Bank.

1 Mrs Roberts gives instructions to the North Bank and requests the issue of a draft.

2 North Bank draws a draft for 100 000 French Francs on the Left Bank in Paris.

3 North Bank debits Mrs Roberts' account with the sterling equivalent of FF100 000 plus charges, accounts to Left Bank for FF100 000, and hands the draft to Mrs Roberts.

4 Mrs Roberts sends the draft to the developers who pay it into their account with the Bastille Bank.

5 Bastille Bank collects the proceeds by remitting the draft to the Left Bank for payment.

This process is represented diagrammatically in Figure 1.2 (*see* Chapter 2 for a more detailed description).

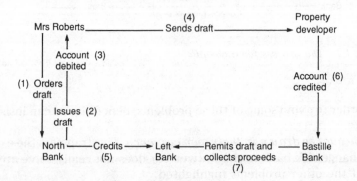

Fig. 1.2

Despite these obvious benefits, drafts are relatively expensive and can be delayed or lost in the post, causing considerable inconvenience and additional cost to all concerned, particularly as the customer will be required to give an indemnity to the bank. It is because of such problems that quicker, more efficient and less costly ways of transferring funds internationally have been developed.

International money order

One of the more popular alternatives to the cheque or banker's draft is the *International Money Order (IMO)*. It has the advantage of being immediately available once the customer has completed the application form and is often the cheapest method of sending money abroad. From Fig. 1.3 you can see that the IMO is drawn by the bank on itself and payment is, therefore, guaranteed.

International money orders are usually issued either in sterling or US dollars and are for relatively small amounts e.g. £1000 or US$2500, but can be for as much as £5000/US$7500. As they can be encashed throughout the world they represent a simple and effective way of remitting funds abroad, particularly as the beneficiaries can obtain the funds immediately on presentation to their own bankers.

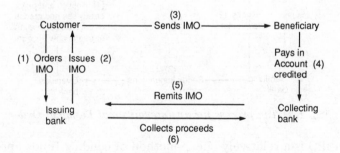

Fig. 1.3 The process for an International Money Order

If the remitter wishes to meet a commitment for an amount greater than the limit imposed by the bank for an IMO, then more than one IMO can be purchased, although it is likely to become impractical to use more than two. For the larger amounts it may be better to use an alternative method and particularly an international payment order.

International Payment Order

An *International Payment Order (IPO)*, also known as an *Airmail Transfer,* is simply an authority by a customer or non-customer to a bank to remit funds abroad in any available currency by air mail. Banks recommend its use for non-urgent transfers where the amount that requires remitting is above the limit for IMOs or the currency required is one other than sterling or US dollars. For example, if a customer wishes to send to Spain the equivalent of £10 000 as a stage payment in respect of the building of a villa, and there is no urgency, then an IPO is the better method.

The relevant instructions on a pre-printed form will be given to the bank in the UK. These instructions will then be sent to the bank in Spain nominated by the remitter or, failing this, chosen by the remitting bank. The Spanish bank will ensure that the beneficiary receives the funds as instructed and in the nominated currency.

The way the funds are transferred between the banks will depend upon which currency the payment is in and is further explained in the section on *nostro* and *vostro* accounts (*see* Chapter 2).

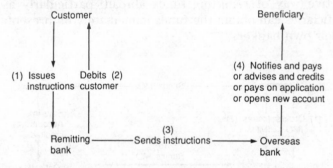

Fig. 1.4 The process for an International Payment Order

An IPO is a relatively cheap method of sending funds abroad but generally should be used for non-urgent payments. It is possible that some payments will be received within a week if the SWIFT system (*see* p. 8) is used but a more normal period would be three to four weeks, instructions being sent air mail.

There are several ways in which the beneficiary can receive payment. Instructions can be given as follows:

(a) *Notify and pay*–used if the beneficiary's bankers are not known. The beneficiary, once advised, will have to call at the bank to collect the money.

(b) *Advise and credit* the beneficiary's account.

(c) *Pay the beneficiary upon application* – used when the beneficiary wishes to collect the funds personally from a specified branch of a bank abroad.

(d) *Place to the credit of a new account* to be opened in the beneficiary's name – used when the beneficiary wishes to have a new account opened. In this case references and a specimen signature may be required by the bank abroad.

Whether the remitter or the beneficiary pays the costs involved will depend on the agreement between them. If the beneficiary pays some or all of the costs, then they will normally be deducted from the amount received.

Remittance telegraphically/electronically

Telegraphic transfer

A *Telegraphic Transfer (TT)* is the quickest way of sending money abroad and as such will often be used where the payment is urgent.

As with IMOs and IPOs, an order form is completed with the remitter's instructions, enabling the bank to authorise the bank abroad to make the funds available to the beneficiary. The beneficiary can receive the funds in most of the ways described for IPOs, i.e.

- *notify and pay*
- *advise and credit the account*
- *pay on application*

the exception being the opening of an account which is unlikely to be urgent. Furthermore, because instructions are sent by cable or telex it is not possible to send references or specimen signatures.

It normally takes two working days for the processing of TTs from receipt of instructions to payment to the beneficiary, unless payment is being sent to a remote part of the world, in which case it may take a little longer. The speed of payment is achieved by using cable or telex to transmit the payment instructions rather than sending them by air mail as with IPOs. The disadvantage is that this method makes the TT more expensive. Payment can be made in sterling or most foreign currencies, and TTs are particularly appropriate where large sums need to be transferred quickly to reduce interest charges or improve interest income.

Girobank/post office

Girobank offers several ways of sending money abroad, some of which are similar to those described already. Not all of the services are available to all countries, but should you wish to send money to a country not on the Girobank list, payment will be made by means of a bank cheque in US dollars, sterling, or an appropriate alternative currency at Girobank's discretion. The three main methods are:

- payment by cheque
- payment in cash
- payment direct to a Giro account overseas

There is a fixed charge for each method, but if the remitter has a Girobank account and the beneficiary overseas has a Giro account, then a transfer can be made between the two free of charge.

Finally, it is also possible to remit funds overseas by means of a postal order but there is a limited number of countries to which the system is applicable.

SWIFT

These initials stand for the *Society for Worldwide Interbank Financial Telecommunication* which is an international organisation whose membership consists of several hundred of the largest international banks. The Society, which was created under Belgian Law and is based in Brussels, was formed to accelerate the transfer of funds and other messages between the member banks.

The system works by means of a telecommunications link between the computer systems of the banks which allows the rapid transmission of messages. The system is used to execute telegraphic transfers previously sent by cable or telegraph and may also be used for international payment orders/airmail transfers at the discretion of the bank, making for a much faster execution of a customer's instructions. When instructions are transmitted in this way the bank is said to be sending a *SWIFT message* and for telegraphic transfers the phrase used is *urgent SWIFT message*.

Table 1 summarises the advantages and disadvantages of the methods we have covered so far. Study it carefully.

Table 1   Advantages and disadvantages of different forms of payment

Method	Advantages	Disadvantages
Cash	• Small amounts can be sent in note form very easily.	• Impractical and expensive if in large amounts. • Can be lost or stolen.
Cheque	• Remittance is quick and simple. • Can be inexpensive for the remitter where recipient covers collection costs. • Attachments are possible.	• Exchange risk unless issued on appropriate currency account. • Delay in receipt of proceeds by beneficiary where bank insists on collection. • Collection costs. • Cheque may not be paid.
Banker's Draft	• Issue process is straightforward. Remittance is quick and simple. • Available in most major currencies – exchange risk for recipient can be avoided. • No limit on amount. • Payment is guaranteed and quick if drawn on a bank in beneficiary's country. • Attachments are possible.	• Relatively expensive to purchase. • Can be lost or stolen – involves lengthy formalities including giving an indemnity to the bank. • Encashment overseas may be costly.
International Money Order	• Cheapest method, widely available and accepted. • Issue process is quick and straightforward. • Refunds/replacements available with little formality.	• Only appropriate for smaller amounts up to £1000 or US$2500, say, but possible up to £5000/US$7500. • Only available in sterling or US dollars.

Method	Advantages	Disadvantages
International Payment Order	• Instructions can be given in most currencies – exchange risk for recipient can be avoided. • No limit on amount. • Documents can be attached, e.g. specimen signatures. • Several payment instructions available. • Payment is inter-bank, therefore secure.	• Not appropriate for urgent transfers. • Relatively expensive.
Telegraphic transfer	• Quickest method of transfer. • Interest income on large sums can be saved – interest charges reduced. • No limit on amount. • Instructions can be given in most currencies – exchange risk for recipient can be avoided.	• Most expensive method.
Giro cheque	• Relatively inexpensive. • Issue process is straightforward. • Remittance is quick and simple.	• Possible collection costs. • Can be lost or stolen.
Giro transfer	• Simple and quick. • Free if from one Giro account to another.	• Recipient has to have a Giro account. • Number of countries is limited.
Postal order	• Purchase is simple and inexpensive. • Attachments are possible.	• Exchange risk for the recipient. • Can be lost or stolen. • Number of countries limited.

Summary

1 There is a variety of methods of settling or paying for international transactions.
2 They fall broadly into two categories: remittances by post and remittances telegraphically or electronically.
3 Payment by cash is impractical and payment by cheque can have significant disadvantages for the payee. Banker's drafts are an effective if expensive alternative.
4 The more attractive methods for non-urgent international payments are international money orders and international payment orders. Which method is used will be governed largely by the amount involved and the currency required, IMOs being for relatively low values in sterling or US dollars.
5 With IMOs the customer purchases the order from the bank and sends it to the beneficiary/payee. With IPOs the bank is responsible for the transmission of the instructions and the funds.
6 It is possible to send attachments/documentation with both IMOs and IPOs, and in the latter case a variety of payment instructions is available.
7 The fastest but most expensive method of transferring funds is the telegraphic transfer. These payments are sent by cable or telex but will sometimes be transmitted through the SWIFT system which enables funds to be transferred electronically.

Self-assessment questions

1 A customer wishes to send a birthday present of £50 to her daughter in Canada. Her birthday is not for two months. Which payment method would you suggest?
2 What can be the main drawback for a customer who pays in advance for goods from overseas by sending a sterling cheque drawn on a UK bank?
3(a) A retiring customer has decided to spend 6 months of the year in Spain and wishes to open an account there prior to departure. What method of transferring the funds would be the most appropriate?
 (b) What other requirements might need to be met before the overseas bank will agree to open the account?

4 The Managing Director of a haulage contractors needs to send £300 urgently to France where one of his drivers is stranded with a broken-down lorry. Which method of payment would the bank use?

5 An electronics manufacturer wishes to pay for some components from the USA costing $14 500. He needs to send some correspondence with the payment to the supplier. How might he best do this?

6 Why might an overseas trader be reluctant to accept payment in the form of a cheque drawn in sterling?

2
Interbank *nostro* and *vostro* accounts

Objectives

After studying this chapter you should:
1   be aware of the system for *nostro* and *vostro* accounts for the settlement of international transfer of funds;
2   be able to explain the operation of such accounts between UK and overseas banks.

Introduction

You will read in Chapter 3, covering rates of exchange, that the foreign currency market operates in some way like the UK clearing system. When a bank sells foreign currency to a customer, the bank must ensure that the funds are 'cleared' before the sterling or currency is paid away. Failure to do so would result in the bank lending to its customer the amount involved. You need to have a basic understanding of how the system works.

Operation of the system

Rather than sending cash physically across the world it is just the *title of ownership* that is changed when funds are transferred between accounts maintained by correspondent banks with each other. These accounts are called *nostro* (from the Latin meaning 'our'), and *vostro* (meaning 'your') accounts. The debit and credit entries are passed over the *nostro* account in the centre where it is maintained, and each bank keeps a 'mirror' account in its own books with an opposite balance 'reflecting' that account for reconciliation purposes.

Clearance is achieved by the banks sending requests via cable, telex, or SWIFT messages to those correspondent or branch offices overseas for the bank's currency account to be debited, and for the respective funds to be paid away according to the customer's instructions. For example, Barclays Bank in London will have a French Franc account with the Credit Lyonnais in Paris. To Barclays, that account is a *nostro* account (our account with you), to Credit Lyonnais it is a *vostro* account (your account with us). However, we always refer to these types of account from the *UK point of view*. So a *vostro* account is, say, the sterling account belonging to Credit Lyonnais, Paris, maintained in Barclays in London. Let us look at some examples.

Example 1

If your customer, Jane Jones, wants to transfer funds to Paris, it depends on whether:

(i) she wants to remit in sterling or currency, and

(ii) she has a French Franc currency account.

The alternatives are:

(a) If in sterling, her UK bank account can be debited.

(b) If in currency and she does not have a foreign currency account, the sterling equivalent can be debited to her UK bank account.

(c) If in currency and she has a foreign currency account, the currency amount can be debited to that account.

The correspondent bank in Paris will be requested to pay the funds away in Paris. If the funds to be transferred are, say, £1500 and the rate is FF8:£1, the entries would be:

• *Jane Jones Sterling Account*: for (a) and (b) above her account will be debited with £1500. For (c) her French Franc currency account will be debited with FF12 000.

• *Correspondent Bank Accounts*
(a) and (b)

UK Bank
Account of French Bank

	£		£
		Balance b/d (say)	15 000
Balance c/d	16 500	Cr re Paris customer	1500
	16 500		16 500

French Bank
Mirror of account with UK Bank

	£		£
Balance b/d	15 000		
Cr re Paris customer	1500	Balance c/d	16 500
	16 500		16 500

(c)

UK Bank
Mirror of account with French Bank

	FF		FF
Balance b/d (say)	80 000	Cr re Paris customer	12 000
		Balance c/d	68 000
	80 000		80 000

French Bank
Account of UK Bank

	FF		FF
Cr re Paris customer	12 000	Balance b/d	80 000
Balance c/d	68 000		
	80 000		80 000

Example 2

Your customer, John Smith, wants to send £2000 by telegraphic transfer to Madrid, Spain, in favour of his brother Ron who lives out there. The instructions are to advise and credit Ron's account. John must decide whether to send out sterling (which will be converted in Spain) or the equivalent in pesetas.

(a) *If sterling:* the UK bank will credit the correspondent bank's sterling account in the UK – *vostro* account (your account with us) – and will advise the correspondent bank, which will 'mirror' the transaction by debiting its overseas *nostro* sterling account abroad (our account with you) and credit Ron Smith's account.

(b) *If pesetas:* John Smith's UK bank requests its correspondent bank in Madrid to debit the UK bank's currency account (*nostro*) and pay the funds away to Ron Smith's account.

The entries will look as follows:

• *If sterling:* Day 1: debit John Smith's account £2000, credit Spanish correspondent's account £2000.
Day 3: (in Spain) debit £2000 to mirror account, credit equivalent to Ron Smith's account.

• *If pesetas:* Day 1: debit John Smith's account £2000.
Credit mirror *nostro* account (currency equivalent in pesetas).
Day 3: (in Spain) debit UK bank's *nostro* account, credit Ron Smith's account.

Summary

1 When payment is to be made in sterling, UK bank(s) credit *vostro* accounts in the UK.

The overseas bank debits its own *nostro* (mirror) account and pays funds to the beneficiary.

2   When payment is to be made in foreign currency, UK bank(s) credit *nostro* (mirror) accounts in the UK.

The overseas bank debits the UK bank's *nostro* currency account and pays the funds to the beneficiaries.

Self-assessment questions

1   Lloyds Bank, Birmingham, maintains a dollar account with Chase Manhattan, New York. What is it called?
2   Midland Bank, London, maintains a sterling account for Dresdner Bank, Frankfurt. What is it called?
3   A UK importer sends US$5000 to an exporter in the United States. Write out the transactions in both countries.
4   A Japanese importer wants to send US$5000 to an exporter in the UK. What are the transactions in the respective countries?

3
Rates of exchange

Objectives

After studying this chapter you should:
1 have exploded the myth that international exchange is a complex area best left to the experts;
2 have gained an understanding of the fundamentals of supply and demand of currencies and the factors which affect them;
3 have gained knowledge in the types of forward contracts and currency accounts and the procedures involved which will help you to understand how customers may protect themselves against exchange risk;
4 be able to explain the basics of the systems and procedures to a customer.

Introduction

At some time every business person involved in overseas trade, whether importing or exporting, will probably have to make or receive payment in foreign currency. The currency of the invoice can play an important part during sales negotiations and make a significant difference to the final costs or proceeds. This chapter highlights the risks involved and outlines how they may be avoided.

What is an exchange rate? An exchange rate is simply the price of one currency in relation to another. For example, if one pound sterling can be exchanged for four West German Deutschmarks in Munich, it will cost you £20 to purchase any article there priced at DM80. Should the rate move to DM4.25 for £1, then the article would cost £18.82; you will have more Deutschmarks for your pound.

'Look, we offered protection against exchange rates, not from your husband's reaction to your clothes bill!'

The foreign currency must be freely convertible, that is, you must be able to:

- sell it
- swap it
- exchange it for another currency.

Exchange rates are quoted in the Financial press at *middle rates*, i.e. the difference between the buying rate and selling rate, for acceptable currencies. Most banks have their own foreign exchange department and provide daily sheets or screens of up-to-date rates.

The foreign exchange market

Unlike the London Stock Exchange there is no physical centre for trading by the major foreign exchange centres. The market 'place' is the telephone and telex links worldwide.

All currency holdings reside in their country of origin; all sterling is held in the UK, all US dollars are held in the United States, etc.

Only notes and coins, insignificant in global terms, actually move from one country to another.

Participants in the foreign exchange market include central banks, commercial banks, other financial institutions, large commercial companies and a few wealthy individuals, as well as brokers who arrange deals between banks. The market undertakes trade in two distinct areas:

(a) *The wholesale market:* principally for inter-bank trading or very large commercial companies.

(b) *The retail market:* for normal trading and commercial customers.

Major currencies are traded; for example, US dollars, Deutschmarks, sterling, Japanese yen, Swiss francs. All quotations are made against the US dollar as the world's most available currency. There are few deals in the 'exotic' currencies, e.g. those of Malawi, Mauritius, Bahamas.

Each bank or broker must be authorised to deal in foreign exchange, and they are controlled by the Bank of England.

There are three kinds of business carried out in the market:

(a) *Spot:* for settlement after two working days;

(b) *Outright:* forward deals for settlement at some future date;

(c) *Swap:* the purchase/sale of a currency in the spot market combined with a simultaneous sale/purchase in the forward market.

Supply and demand

When there is a net inflow of funds to a country, say, for example, France, i.e. there are more purchases from France than sales to it, then the rate for French Francs will rise because of increased demand.

Interest rates

When interest rates are raised in, say, the UK, international investors may be encouraged to transfer funds into the UK, which creates a demand for sterling, and therefore its value in relation to other currencies rises.

Political and economic factors

Investors' confidence in a country may be shaken when, for example, unemployment becomes high, there is a fear of war, elections are due, etc. The forward rates will be affected by attempts to sell the currency to obtain better rates.

Central bank intervention

In the UK we have been free of exchange control restrictions since 1979. This means that we can buy and sell foreign currency freely and without restrictions. Some countries have regulations where exchange control measures may be introduced to regulate or restrict the flow of money, to ensure that the country has sufficient reserves of foreign exchange to pay its international debts. For example, travellers may transfer only a few drachmas into or out of Greece.

According to the type of underlying transactions, banks offer different rates of exchange, split into two categories:

Commercial rates

Unless otherwise stated, all commercial rates will be based on Spot. By convention, foreign exchange deals are arranged for settlement in *two working days' time*. The delay allows instructions to be given and received for the movement of funds between the correspondent bank accounts. These deals are called 'Spot' transactions.

The commercial rates will vary according to the *size* of the transactions. Some rates will incorporate interest costs during the period that the bank is out of funds, e.g. for negotiation of currency cheques. The rates are for paper-based commercial transactions and do not involve the movement of notes or coins.

Note rates

The rates of exchange for the purchase and sale of foreign currency notes and coins are loaded in favour of the banks to take account of the expensive cost of handling, transportation, etc.

Market forces

UK exporters and importers may prefer to conduct their overseas trade in sterling, in which case they are protected from the direct risk of exchange rate fluctuations. However, in the face of competition in the market place they may be forced to trade in a foreign currency. The alternatives need to be considered to determine the benefits and drawbacks involved from invoices drawn in:

(a) Sterling,

(b) The currency of the overseas trader,

(c) A third currency.

Sterling

From the UK trader's point of view the price of the contract is known at the outset and accurate comparisons can be made. Exchange risks are avoided. Bookkeeping is straightforward. On the other hand, business might be lost to competitors prepared to invoice in the foreign currency.

The currency of the overseas trader

By agreeing to invoices in the foreign currency a UK trader incurs an exchange risk until the funds are converted to or from sterling. Planned profit margins may be eroded. Additional bookkeeping will be necessary to monitor the situation.

Third currency

In cases where trade is conducted with a country which has a currency regarded as 'exotic', i.e. currencies in which only a small market exists such as the Kenya shilling, Greek drachma, etc, it is common to invoice in an international currency, for example, US dollars. Again, there will be exchange risk and planned profit margins may be eroded. Additional bookkeeping will be necessary to monitor the situation.

UK traders need to decide the best method and timing available to them for conversion between sterling and currency. There are four choices:

(a) To wait for the payment date and convert at the prevailing spot rate.

(b) To immediately set up a forward foreign exchange contract to buy or sell the specified amount of currency on the payment date.

(c) To purchase or borrow the foreign currency immediately. In the case of exporters they will make use of the borrowed funds immediately for working capital purposes, and the bank will be repaid from the proceeds of the invoice. In the case of importers, they will place the funds on deposit pending payment of the invoice.

(d) To maintain a foreign currency account.

Systems and procedures

Buying and selling foreign currency

When a bank gives a quotation, it will give two rates:
- *a selling rate*
- *a buying rate.*

The difference between these rates, called the 'spread', will be adjusted to attract or deter business and represents the bank's profit. All transactions are looked at from the bank's point of view. A bank sells low and buys high, which means that it will sell you less currency in exchange for a pound note, but will expect you to pay more than a pound note for the currency.

In order to avoid any possible loss for either of you on the transaction, because of the free pressure of market forces you will need to act promptly on a customer's instructions which involve foreign exchange transactions. When foreign exchange is bought or sold there is no physical movement of cash; it is just ownership which changes by means of paper transfer of funds between accounts in the counterparties' correspondent banks, the currency itself remaining in the country of origin.

The spot market

Rates are quoted for a variety of periods but the rate which serves as the basis on which the rates are calculated is called the *spot* rate, the rate for settlement in two working days' time. The currency has to be *cleared*, like cheques in the UK clearing system, to ensure that the bank has funds before the currency is actually paid away, hence the delay in settlement. Clearance is effected by cable or telex messages between the correspondent banks. The *spot* rate is sometimes called the *cable* rate. Since all major currency deals are made against the US dollar, even if the dollar is not involved in the transaction, the determination of the settlement (*spot value*) date will be affected when the New York market is closed. The date can be influenced also by the closure of other markets, for example during Bank/National holidays.

Exchange risk protection

Whenever someone is involved in a transaction in a foreign currency other than their home currency, an exchange risk occurs because one currency may move unfavourably against the other. Speculators may invest in a country with a weak currency where interest rates are high. An imbalance will occur between spot and forward rates, and the currency with the lower interest rate will be at a 'premium'.

An exporter has an advantage when currencies are quoted at a premium. Experience shows that, in practice, exporters do not bother to cover forward in a discount currency. The opposite is true for importers. If a forward contract has to be liquidated, i.e., when delivery is due but the customers cannot fulfil their part of the forward contract, there will be either a profit or a loss on exchange for the customer's account. If there is a loss the bank is at risk, since at that stage it may not be possible to debit the customer's account; it may, for example, be in receivership. Some banks mark a liability of between 10 per cent and 20 per cent of the amount of the forward contract in their books representing a 'lending' to the customer.

Benefits of forward contracts

Advantages	Disadvantages
• Firm contractual agreement by both parties.	• Somewhat inflexible
• Delivery on any working day.	
• Delivery can be on a fixed date or during an agreed option period.	• Delayed delivery might involve closing out/extension costs.
• Allows partial delivery under option forward contracts.	
• Usually customer does not pay until maturity.	
• Rate fixed now for future transaction.	

Obviously a UK trader invoicing or being invoiced in sterling will not incur an exchange risk. Life is not that easy, however, and your customer may have to deal in the currency of the overseas country to gain the business. Foreign currency invoicing does have advantages, e.g.

(a) *for the exporter:* who could make an exchange profit if the rate moves in their favour;

(b) *for the importer:* pricing could be fixed in their currency.

If a company has some control over the *timing* of payments and receipts, it can delay or speed up payments to its advantage, known as *leads* and *lags:*

Lead: if currency is expected from a weaker currency country, the company would want funds due to be received expedited to reduce the erosion of the domestic currency amount.

Lag: if currency is expected from a stronger currency country, the company may wish to delay receipt in order to take advantage of a possible increase in the amount of the domestic currency.

Major dealings in this manner may have an adverse influence on a country's balance of payments.

Export Credit Guarantee Department (ECGD)

ECGD is a Government department, with two principal functions:

1 To give guarantees, i.e. credit insurance, to banks to support finance to their customers.

2 To insure exporters against the risks of not being paid through buyer and country default.

Various risks are covered, for example, war, revolution, flood, earthquake, change of laws, restrictions on export/import, insolvency of the buyer, or default.

There are two types of cover: *specific,* which usually relates to export of capital goods sold on credit terms of, say, 2 to 5 years, and *comprehensive,* covering the total export turnover of the exporter for not less than 12 months.

The comprehensive insurance cover will usually be for normal trade on short-term credit up to 180 days. For a monthly premium and annual fee ECGD will cover 90–95% of the turnover depending on risk. Separate credit limits are approved for each overseas buyer. Cover takes effect on shipment.

If a customer has a foreign exchange borrowing or a forward contract then, for an additional premium, they may have a *forward currency contracts endorsement,* intended solely to cover loss either on repayment or on liquidation if funds are not received.

An ECGD policy may be assigned by the company customer to the bank to support borrowing. In such a case payments made under the policy will be forwarded direct to the bank.

Alternatively, ECGD may issue a direct *bank guarantee* in favour of the bank. In this latter case a preferential rate of interest would be available for the borrowing because of the value of the security. (*See* Chapter 4 on international trade for more information.)

Advances against bills for collection

A bank is usually prepared to grant an advance to an exporter pending receipt of the proceeds of a bill which it is collecting on the customer's behalf. There will be an exchange risk in the event of a currency bill being dishonoured when a bank exercises its right of recourse by debiting the customer. The exchange rate would have been fixed at the time of the original transaction and, since the customer will have to repurchase the currency at the current rate of exchange, the exchange risk occurs.

Elimination of exchange risk

Exchange risk can be virtually fully removed by:
1 forward contracts,
2 currency accounts,
3 currency options,
4 financial futures contracts.

Forward exchange contracts

Why do we need forward foreign exchange contracts? A number of different factors have established such a need. Customers wanting to establish the amount they will receive or must pay at the trade payment date in order to calculate their profit margins, will fix the price of the cost of the currency by entering into a forward exchange contract.

What are forward exchange contracts? They are:
• firm and binding contracts between bank and customer for the
• purchase or sale of a
• specified quantity of a
• stated currency at a
• rate fixed at the time the contract is made for
• performance at a future time
• agreed at the making of the contract.

The calculation of forward rates is based on the difference between the interest rates in the traders' own country and the foreign country. The forward rate is not a 'best guess' at what the spot rate will be at some future date.

Normally, rates are quoted for a fixed number of months ahead, e.g. 1, 2, 3, 6 and 12 months. Contracts up to one month are known as short (value dates) contracts, e.g.:

(a) Overnight (O/N),
(b) Tomorrow/next day (T/N),
(c) Spot/next day (S/N),
(d) Spot/week (S/W),
(e) Spot/fortnight (S/F).

Assuming that today is 1 February, *overnight* would be 2 February, *spot/next day* would be 4 February, i.e. 2 working days plus one day; *spot/fortnight* would be 17 February, i.e. 2 working days plus fourteen days.

Forward rates are issued at *premium* or *discount*.

When a currency is quoted at a premium it means that it is more expensive to buy it in the future rather than now at *spot*, given the existing differentials in interest rates in each country. It is referred to as a 'strong' currency. A currency quoted at a discount is cheaper to buy in the future as opposed to the spot rate now, and is known as a 'weak' currency.

In order to calculate the rate applicable for the transaction the bank operates on the following basis:

(a) *Premium:* The *premium* for the currency is *deducted* from spot to calculate the rate applicable.

(b) *Discount:* The *discount* is *added* to the spot rate to calculate the rate applicable.

Example

The financial press quotes a spread for the day in the US dollar at:

1.8410	–	1.8430	(spot)
0.0029	–	0.0026	(premium)
1.8381	–	1.8404	= one month forward rates

Thus, if the bank is selling US$10 000 at either spot or one month forward it will cost the customer:

US$10 000 @ 1.8410 (spot)   = £5431.83
US$10 000 @ 1.8381 (one month forward)   = £5440.40

        £   8.57

i.e. more expensive at one month forward

One way to remember which is which is by reference to that well-known brush manufacturer: ADDIS, *ADD* a *DIS*count.

Types of forward contracts

(a) fixed,
(b) option,
(c) close out,
(d) extension,
(e) liquidation,
(f) hedging.

So, what does each type of contract mean?

Fixed
It means performance on a specified date. The previous example highlights the way a rate is calculated for a trader to calculate the cost of the contract at a fixed future date.

Option
It means performance between two specified dates and certainly by the end date. The rate chosen is that most advantageous to the bank.

The rate quoted by the dealer for such a contract will be determined by the possibility of the customer selling the contract on the least favourable date *from the bank's point of view*.

Example

US$/£	spot rate	= 1.4565	–	1.4575
	1 month margin	= 0.0047	–	0.0042
	3 month margin	= 0.0079	–	0.0070

The currency is at a premium, therefore for a three-month option forward of US$1m, the calculation would be the best of:

Bank sells @ 1.4565
Less   0.0079
                       ‾‾‾‾‾‾‾
                       1.4486 = £690 322
                       (if spot or option forward up to 3 months, so the bank would receive more sterling than if it sold at spot)

or

The bank buys at:
   (a)   1.4575 = £686 106
                       (if spot or option to 3 months, so that the bank

would pay less sterling than if it bought at one
or three months forward)

or

(b)   1.4575

Less   0.0042
_____

1.4533 = £688 089

(if option is 1 to 3 months, so that the bank
would pay less sterling than if it bought at three
months forward)

To summarise:

	Premium	*Discount*
Bank selling	Premium charged to last date	If option from spot, no discount given. If option between dates, discount given to first date.
Bank buying	If option from spot, no premium given. If option between two dates, premium given to first date.	Discount charged to last date.

The shorter the option period, the narrower the difference
between the selling and buying prices.

Close out

When delivery is due but the customers cannot fulfil their part
of the forward contract because, say, the goods or payment have
not been received; the contract must be *closed out* to avoid breach
of contract.

If, for example, an exporter, Happy Boots Limited, has
contracted to sell US$5000 one month forward expecting to
receive payment from the US importer by then, but the importer
fails to remit the funds, the exporter will be forced to *buy* US$5000
at spot in order to fulfil the contract with the bank.

Extension

From the previous example, on the assumption that funds from
the US importer are merely delayed and are expected within a
specified period, the exporter may decide to *extend* or roll over

the contract, rather than just closing out; the resulting new forward exchange contract may be arranged by the bank at a slightly more favourable rate than spot (with less loss to the customer).

Example
Say an original contract was for the bank to buy US$1m at 1.4533, sterling equivalent £688 089, and the customer needs to extend the forward contract for 3 months. US$ are at a premium to sterling. Remember that you must *deduct* the forward rates. Today's rates are:

US$/£ spot rate	=	1.4390 –	1.4400
3 month margin	=	0.0032 –	0.0028
		1.4358	1.4372

(a) The original contract is *closed out* at spot:

$$1.4390 = £694\ 927$$

(b) The bank buys again US$1m, but at *sell* spot rate:

	1.4390
Less	0.0028 (3 months *buy* margin)
	1.4362 = £696 282

The customer has lost the difference between:

The *close out* price	=	£694 927
The original forward contract	=	£688 089
	£	6838

Liquidation
A forward contract may have to be liquidated before maturity. It is achieved by a 'swap' transaction. If the example above were to be liquidated after, say, 2 months and today's rates are:

US$/£ spot rate	=	1.4465 –	1.4475
1 month margin	=	0.0032 –	0.0027

(a) The original contract would be cancelled at the original rate:

$$1.4533 = £688\ 089$$

(b) A replacement forward deal would be struck at the *1 month* forward *selling rate*:

	1.4465	
Less	0.0032	
	1.4433	= £692 857
	£	4768 (cost to customer)

Hedging

Like the Stock Exchange 'stag' an investor may establish a forward exchange contract to sell in the belief that the currency may devalue in the meantime. In such event, the currency will be bought at spot for delivery against the forward contract.

Bank risk

A risk occurs when, at delivery, the bank either has to pay away funds or give irrevocable instructions to pay away funds before it has confirmation that funds have been received in settlement.

Currency swaps

These are simply traders simultaneously buying one currency at spot and selling forward, or selling at spot and buying forward.

Currency accounts

The Eurocurrency market

A Eurocurrency is any currency owned and traded *outside* its territorial borders. Such currency accounts are used for a variety of reasons:

- To avoid exchange risks for a future transaction.
- To collate a number of transactions in the same currency prior to conversion.
- To ease trade transactions.
- As a speculative hedge.
- To earn interest.

Eurocurrency transactions are so called because Europe was the centre where the trading of these currencies originated.

Transactions are deposits and loans in currencies other than the domestic currency of the country where they are held.

Interest rates on Eurocurrencies are normally quoted on a '360-day year' basis. There are exceptions and you need to be guided by your Head Office Foreign Exchange Department when calculating the benefits and drawbacks to a customer investing or borrowing on currency accounts.

Deposits or loans may be arranged by the correspondent banks. Sometimes, it may seem more attractive for a customer to borrow in a low interest rate currency or, conversely, to invest in a high interest rate currency.

Loans

You may be faced with requests from some customers for loans to be made available to them in currency. The usual principles of *canons of lending* will apply (*see* Chapter 6).

A company with expected dollar income in two months' time could *borrow* today US dollars and convert that to sterling to assist with working capital. When the dollars are received in two months' time, they are used to repay the dollar borrowing, thus eliminating any exchange risk during the two months. The cost to the customer is the interest on the US borrowing, less the cost of interest which would have been incurred by borrowing sterling for working capital. A significant reduction in borrowing costs could be achieved through this means when currency interest rates are lower than sterling – *providing there is going to be income in that currency.*

The cost of operating customers' foreign currency accounts depends on the type of transactions passed. For instance, if a customer tenders French franc *notes* for the credit of their French franc foreign currency account, a charge will be levied to offset the difference in the higher cost of handling notes and coins rather than passing bookkeeping entries. The same would apply if your customer wanted to exchange foreign currency bank notes for currency travellers cheques, or for a foreign currency draft where payment is tendered in bank notes of the same currency. Let us look at an example.

A UK company has US$1m available to place on deposit for 3 months pending settlement which must be made on a purchase for the same amount. The company could:

(a) deposit the funds in the UK for 3 months at, say, 9.5% per annum, or

(b) sell in exchange for, say, French francs at 7.54 and place those on deposit for 3 months at, say, 13% per annum.

On the face of it, the difference of 3½% seems worthwhile.

At maturity the results would be:

(a) US$1m   @ 9.5% p.a. × 3 months = US$1 023 750

(b) FF7 540 000   @ 13.0% p.a. × 3 months = FF7 785 050

However, the French francs now have to be converted back to dollars ready to meet the company's trade purchase.

The current spot rate   = FF8.0/$1

FF7 785 050 @ 8.0   = US$973 131.25

Loss in 3 months   = US$50 618.75

Instead of *gaining* 3½% per annum the customer has lost nearly 20% per annum. Of course, at the outset, the customer could have covered forward the French francs deposit, probably with little benefit or loss. The moral is that it is highly risky for a customer to borrow in any currency unless there is expected income in that currency. Losses due to exchange rate movements can far exceed any gains from interest rate savings.

Currency options

This service provides an alternative means of covering against exchange risk. Options are traded in London at the Stock Exchange, Over The Counter (OTC) and the London International Financial Futures Exchange (LIFFE – *see* Chapter 5).

Not to be confused with a *forward cover* option, where it is a matter of *when* not *if* the customer takes up the option, a *currency option* gives your customer the option *whether or not* they utilise the contract. The contract is a commitment from the bank, but is not binding on the customer.

A non-refundable up-front fee must be paid which represents the maximum loss which your customer can incur. The fee is based on:

- the length of the option period,
- the exchange rate requested in relation to the currency spot rate,
- the volatility of the exchange rate and the currency forward rate.

If rates move adversely, they are protected by the 'option'.

The right to buy or sell a given quantity of a foreign currency at a future date (usually after 3 months) can be exercised or lapsed or resold with cash settlement. There are two types:

(a) *call* option, which gives the customer the right to *buy* the underlying currency.

(b) *put* option, which gives the customer the right to *sell* the underlying currency. (*See* Chapter 5 for more information.)

What about an example? Say your customer, Harry's Wine Bars Limited, wants to import a large consignment of wine from West Germany at an invoiced price of DM360 000 at DM3.60 to the £, i.e. £100 000. In the normal way they could cover forward dependent on the rates applicable at the time. However, when currencies are at a premium, importers prefer to 'take a chance' that the rates will move in their favour.

The risk is that the Deutschmark has strengthened to, say, DM3.25 to the £ by the time payment is due, which would mean that Harry's Wine Bar would be faced with a bill of £110 769.23 – i.e., 10% more! Instead, they could pay a fee and take out a currency option at 3.60 to protect their pricing situation.

Whilst foreign currency options provide flexibility to a customer not available under a standard forward contract, the bank is taking all the risks, reflected by the amount of the premium; therefore, it will not normally recommend this method to your customer.

When to use options
- When there is exchange or interest rate exposure.
- Protecting investments.
- Tendering for contract in a foreign currency.
- For flexibility.
- International trading of price-sensitive goods.

Who should use options
- Corporate treasurers dealing in multi-currencies.
- Banks and financial institutions for trading and hedging.
- Any other company which needs to hedge.

So, foreign currency options are particularly useful during periods of high exchange rates and volatility. There is a non-refundable fee. Customers can choose the price, the period and whether to exercise the option contract. It gives them *flexibility* and *choice*.

Tender to contract

For a fee, an exporter can fix forward exchange rates to calculate their price for tendering for an overseas contract. If the tender contract is won, the forward exchange contract can be invoked; if the contract is lost, then the only penalty is the loss of the fee. (*See* Chapter 5 for more information.)

Summary

Whenever you are giving advice to a customer for dealing in any transaction which involves foreign currency you will need to remember the following:

1. A bank sells *low*, buys *high*.
2. *Spot* deals are settled in two working days' time.
3. Exchange risk can be eliminated by:
   - *forward contract*: fixed or option,
   - *currency accounts*: Eurocurrency deposit or loan,
   - *currency options*: call (i.e. buy), put (i.e. sell),
   - *tender to contract*: fixed forward contract for a specific fee,
   - *financial futures contracts*: (*see* Chapter 5).

Please do not be put off by the need for a pocket calculator when dealing with such transactions. Just identify what the customer needs and help them to complete the deal in the manner most satisfactory to all parties.

Self-assessment questions

1. If the one month forward rate for US dollars is at a premium of 0.0025 to the spot rate, which is 1.6454, how do you calculate the one month forward rate?
2. What represents the difference between a bank's buying and selling rate?
3. If a customer asks you to lend him the equivalent of £10 000 in Italian lire for three months, what specific question will you need to ask him about repayment before lending?
4. When is settlement made for spot deals?
5. Where is the market place for participants in the Foreign Exchange Market?
6. Which two categories of rates of exchange do banks offer?
7. A bank quotes the following rates for DM/£:
   (a) 3.8985
   (b) 3.8995
   Which is the selling rate?

8 State two methods of avoiding exchange risk.
9 When does a customer have to complete performance under a three-month forward option contract?
10 What does a *call* option give a customer the right to do?

4
International trade

Objectives

After studying this chapter you should be able to:
1   discuss the risks and problems inherent in international trade for both the exporter and the importer;
2   suggest how some of these might be managed or overcome;
3   describe the various methods of settlement available, together with the advantages and disadvantages of each method;
4   describe the documentation procedures and requirements of certain types of international settlements;
5   explain the terminology used in international trade;
6   describe the role and services of the ECGD;
7   explain the impact of exchange control restrictions;
8   describe the methods of finance available to exporters and importers;
9   list the services available from various advisory bodies;
10   describe the procedure for taking produce as security and explain its advantages and disadvantages.

Introduction

We discussed the simpler methods of payment and receipt for international transactions in Chapter 1 and here we will concentrate on the needs of importers and exporters, which are often more complex. As trade barriers break down and international trade increases, more and more businesses will want to buy and sell goods abroad. Bankers need to understand the additional risks this involves, how these risks may be diminished, and the procedures for financing and settling international payments. First-time exporters or importers, in particular, will be looking for advice and guidance as well as finance and you will need to be equipped to provide this information or to point them in the right direction. Experienced international businesses will require an efficient and effective means of dealing with the documentation and settlement, competitive finance, insurance against a variety of risks, introductions to new markets and status reports on new customers or suppliers. It is important, therefore, that you understand the procedures involved and can help your customers gain access to other services they might need.

'Are you sure that our ECGD will cover this type of exporting?'

Initial considerations

The two main problems, other than exchange risk, facing the importer and exporter which they will not encounter normally with domestic trade are *time* and *distance*. For UK importers or exporters there are particular problems with overseas trade in that it is literally 'overseas' and the same problems will apply to any business domiciled on an island rather than a continent. Bearing in mind these two major constraints of time and distance, perhaps businesses should consider the potential problems under four main headings:

(a) The market
(b) The buyer or supplier
(c) Transport
(d) Payment

The market

Exporters in particular need as much information as possible about overseas markets. They should consider the strength of local competition and be aware of both general and specific regulations which may affect their products. How big a barrier will be erected by language, technical specifications and local trading standards? Are there any import duties which will make their products more expensive or import restrictions to be overcome before they can sell?

The buyer or supplier

The exporter will wish to ascertain as far as possible whether the buyer is trustworthy and reliable and will abide by the terms of any contract. If the transaction is to be on credit terms, the creditworthiness of the buyer will need to be assessed. Importers need to be reassured as to the reliability of suppliers and the quality of their goods.

Transport

Both the importer and exporter will be concerned not only about the method of transport to be used and its cost, but also, and more importantly, as to who is going to pay the bill. They will want to consider the options available, their comparative cost and to ensure that responsibility for insurance has been clearly defined.

Payment

The method of payment will have to be agreed between the buyer and the seller, as will any period of credit to be allowed. The impact of any exchange control restrictions on the transaction must also be taken into account, because they may delay or prohibit payment.

Sources of information

You will understand from what we have said already that even experienced international companies have a constant need for information on markets, customers, rules and regulations in foreign countries. But they will have the advantage of knowing where to seek this information. The business or person new to international trade may well look to a bank for guidance and advice and you need to know what your own bank can provide and where to go for other information and assistance. Many of the larger banks will have their own Economic Information Departments, which produce reports on a wide variety of countries and industries. Banks will also be able to obtain *status reports* on prospective buyers or suppliers and provide *letters of introduction* to branches of their own or their correspondent banks abroad. A further service often provided is that of supplying names of potential customers or suppliers in industries or products related to those of the UK importer or exporter.

A further source of information and advice is *The Department of Trade and Industry* (DTI), which provides a wide range of services aimed particularly at UK exporters. The DTI can supply details of tariff and import regulations for specific countries, identify specific trading opportunities and help with trade missions. It will also provide support for trade fairs and exhibitions and supply statistical and other research-based information on specific overseas markets. The DTI sponsors the *British Overseas Trade Board* (BOTB), which will provide both advice and financial assistance, particularly to the smaller and medium-sized firms who wish to break into or expand overseas markets. The local *Chamber of Commerce* is always keen to assist companies considering trading overseas, particularly exporters, and will draw on the expertise and experience of members who have knowledge of the vagaries of particular overseas markets.

Contracts

When goods or services are being bought or sold on an international basis the transaction is subject to a contract agreed between the buyer and the seller. This contract will contain a description of the items being bought or sold, the method of payment agreed and where responsibility lies for arranging transport and insurance. The contract will also stipulate what documents should be delivered to the buyer and what detail these documents should contain. Customers unfamiliar with the documentary requirements of international trade will often need assistance in drawing up documentation and may well need some guidance on the meanings of the terms used in international trade, which often appear in shorthand form. It is important, therefore, that you understand and can explain the principal documents and terms used.

Documents

Errors in documents can delay both the transfer of goods and, perhaps more importantly, eventual payment. It is essential, therefore, that they comply with the terms of the contract. In some cases the documents represent the legal title to the goods to which they refer. This means that possession of the documents is a prerequisite for possession of the goods. Most of the documents you are likely to see in practice are listed and described briefly below, but to become properly familiar with them you should seek an opportunity to examine real documents as they pass through your bank's foreign department or through your own branch. The description of the documents given here is followed by details of the terms used and the relevant responsibilities of buyer and seller to provide you with a reasonably comprehensive picture, which should reduce the need for frequent reference elsewhere.

Bills of exchange

You will remember from your study of *Banking: The Legal Environment* that a bill of exchange is defined in the Bills of Exchange Act 1882 as:

- An unconditional order in writing
- addressed by one person to another
- signed by the person giving it
- requiring the person to whom it is addressed
- to pay on demand or at a fixed or determinable future time
- a sum certain in money
- to, or to the order of a specified person, or Bearer

The words 'on demand' mean 'at sight', requiring the drawee to honour the bill when it is presented to the drawee for payment. Alternatively, the bill could be payable on a fixed future date or a determinable future date. For instance, a bill payable at '90 days sight' means that it is payable 90 days after presentation. The payment date must be determinable and a phrase such as '90 days after arrival of the goods' would be insufficient because 'arrival' could mean the date the vessel docks, or the date the goods are cleared through customs. There is also the possibility that the goods will not arrive.

Commercial invoice

This is produced by the seller and addressed to the buyer. It will give details of the goods, including the price and packaging, measurements, the terms of shipment, together with details of freight. The invoice will be dated and will state the total amount payable including costs of insurance and freight if these are to be paid by the buyer. Several copies of the invoice may be prepared, as parties other than the buyer, such as customs authorities, may require them. There are alternative forms of invoice as follows:

Consular invoice
This may be demanded by particular countries and is obtained by the exporter from the embassy or consulate of the importer's country. Once completed, it must be returned to the embassy for stamping and may need to be accompanied by a *certificate of origin* of the goods. The production of this certificate can be undertaken by Chambers of Commerce authorised by the DTI. It consists of a signed and sealed statement describing the goods in detail, including the country of origin.

Legalised/visaed invoice
Some countries require the normal commercial invoice to be legalised by having it stamped by their embassy in the exporting country.

Bills of lading

A bill of lading is a document issued when goods are transported by sea. There are normally two or three originals which are signed by the shipping company. A bill of lading is:

- a *receipt* for the goods
- *evidence* of the contract of carriage
- most importantly, a *document of title* to the goods

Bills of lading are prepared by the exporter and presented to the shipping company for completion and signature. Where goods are received in good order the bills are said to be *clean* but if the goods are defective or damaged in any way the bills will be *claused* and will be known as *dirty* or *foul* bills of lading. When the goods reach their destination they will be released against surrender of a signed original of the bill of lading. There are some variations with bills of lading and a selection of these are as follows:

Short form bill of lading
While this operates like the *long form* bill of lading described above, the terms and conditions of the contract are not printed on the reverse of the form but are available for inspection at the shipping company's office.

Through bill of lading
This is a bill of lading which covers the shipment of goods on two separate vessels. It is used where there is no direct service available to the final destination and the goods have to be trans-shipped from one vessel to another.

Combined transport bill of lading
This replaces the traditional *port-to-port* bill of lading by covering the whole journey from the *place of acceptance* to the *place of delivery* and needs to allow for two or more modes of transport, for example, road-sea-road. The carrier is responsible for the goods on the whole journey from, say, the exporter's warehouse to the importer's factory.

Waybill
This is not a document of title but merely evidence of despatch of the goods. Used substantially for trade in Europe, it is comparable to an air or lorry waybill, since none of these will provide control for the exporter.

Air waybill/air consignment note

When goods are delivered to the airline the waybill is signed by them or their agents as a receipt for the goods. It may also provide evidence of despatch of the goods where it has been stamped indicating details of the relevant flight. But it is *not* a document of title to the goods.

Consignment note/lorry waybill

This is issued by a road haulier under CMR (*Convention de Merchandises par Route*) regulations, which are a set of rules agreed at an international convention covering international road haulage. It is a receipt and delivery document covering goods which are travelling by road between countries, the goods having to remain on the lorry at all times.

International trade terms

In international trade there is always the possibility of misunderstandings and disputes about interpretation of contract clauses, the respective responsibilities of the exporter and the importer, and the terminology used. To avoid this, international transactions are often made subject to *Incoterms* by agreement between buyer and seller. These are definitions of international terms of trade and responsibilities issued by the International Chamber of Commerce (ICC). The ICC also issues other publications which form the framework of rules and practice for much international trade. We have included a synopsis of the Incoterms in tabular form for you to refer to.

Incoterms – primary duties

Terms	Seller	Buyer
EXW (Ex Works)	Delivers the goods at seller's own premises.	Takes delivery of the goods at the seller's premises. Makes all arrangements at buyer's own cost and risk to bring the goods to the destination
FRC (Free Carrier)	Delivers the goods at the named point into the custody of the carrier named by the buyer. Provides export licence, and pays export taxes and fees if required. Provides evidence of delivery of the goods to the carrier.	Nominates carrier. Contracts for the carriage and pays the freight. Takes risk from delivery to carrier, therefore needs to take insurance.
FOR/FOT (Free on Rail/ Free on Truck)	Delivers the goods to the railway and, in the case of full loads, procures and loads the wagon(s).	Notifies the seller of the destination of the goods, and pays the freight. Accepts delivery of the

Terms	Seller	Buyer
	Furnishes the invoice and the usual transport document to the buyer.	goods and risk when they have been delivered to the railway and when the invoice and the transport document are given to the buyer. Needs to arrange insurance. Obtains export licence and pays export taxes and fees if required.
FOA (Free on Board Airport)	Delivers the goods to the air carrier at the airport of departure. Contracts for carriage unless contrary notice has been given. Notifies buyer if seller wishes buyer to contract for carriage. Provides export licence and pays export taxes and fees if required.	Accepts delivery of the goods to the carrier at the airport of departure. Buyer's risk once so delivered so must insure from this point. Pays freight. Notifies seller if buyer does not wish seller to contract for carriage.
FAS (Free Alongside Ship)	Delivers the goods alongside the ship. Provides an 'alongside' receipt.	Nominates carrier. Risk transferred to buyer once delivered alongside. Contracts for the carriage and pays the freight. Obtains export licence and pays export taxes and fees if required. Needs to arrange insurance.
DCP (Freight/Carriage Paid)	Contracts for carriage and pays the freight to the named destination. Delivers the goods into the custody of the first carrier. Obtains export licence and pays export taxes and fees if required.	Accepts delivery of the goods when they are delivered to the first carrier and when the invoice and, if customary, the usual transport document are tendered to the buyer. Risk passes to the

Terms	Seller	Buyer
	Furnishes to the buyer the invoice and the usual transport document.	buyer once goods are delivered into the custody of the first carrier, therefore needs to arrange insurance.
CIP (Freight/Carriage and Insurance Paid)	Contracts for the carriage and pays the freight to the named point of destination. Delivers the goods into the custody of the first carrier. Obtains export licence and pays export taxes and fees if required. Contracts for insurance of the goods during the carriage and pays the insurance premium. Furnishes to the buyer the invoice, the usual transport document and a transport insurance policy or other evidence of insurance cover.	Accepts delivery of the goods when they are delivered to the first carrier and when the invoice, the transport insurance policy or other evidence of insurance cover and, if customary, the usual transport document are tendered to the buyer. Risk passes to buyer once goods are delivered into the custody of the first carrier but seller has to insure.
EXS (Ex Ship)	Delivers the goods on board the ship at the port of destination at own risk and expense. Provides documents to enable buyer to take delivery from the ship, e.g. bill of lading or delivery order.	Takes delivery of the goods from the ship at the port of destination. Pays unloading costs. Obtains import licence and pays import duties, taxes and fees if required. Risk passes to buyer once goods placed at buyer's disposal at port of arrival.
EXQ (Ex Quay)	Delivers the goods on the quay at the port of destination at own risk and expense. Provides documents to enable the buyer to take delivery from the quay,	Takes delivery of the goods from the quay at the port of destination. Risk passes to buyer once goods are on the quay. Seller has to bear the full cost and risk

Terms	Seller	Buyer
	e.g. delivery order. Pays unloading costs. Obtains import licence and pays import duties, taxes and fees if required.	until then.
FOB (Free On Board)	Delivers the goods on board. Provides export licence and pays export taxes and fees if required. Provides a clean on-board receipt. Pays loading costs according to the customs of the port to the extent that they are not included in the freight.	Nominates carrier. Risk passes to buyer once goods over ship's rail at port of loading. Contracts for the carriage and pays the freight. Pays loading costs to the extent that they are included in the freight. Pays unloading costs. Needs to arrange insurance.
C & F (Cost & Freight)	Contracts for the carriage and pays the freight to the named destination. Delivers the goods on board. Obtains export licence and pays export taxes and fees if required. Furnishes to the buyer the invoice and a clean on board bill of lading. Pays for checking operations, if required. Pays loading costs. Pays unloading costs to the extent that they are included in the freight.	Accepts delivery of the goods upon shipment, when the invoice and the bill of lading are tendered to the buyer; the bill of lading is deemed to 'represent the goods'. Pays unloading costs to the extent that they are not included in the freight. Risk passes to buyer once goods over ship's rail at port of loading, therefore needs to arrange insurance.
CIF (Cost, Insurance and Freight)	Contracts for the carriage and pays the freight to the named port of destination. Delivers the goods on board.	Accepts delivery of the goods upon shipment, when the invoice, the cargo insurance policy (certificate) and the bill of lading are tendered to

Terms	Seller	Buyer
	Obtains export licence and pays export taxes and fees if required. Contracts for the insurance of the goods during the carriage and pays the insurance premium. Furnishes to the buyer the invoice, a clean bill of lading and a cargo insurance policy or certificate. Pays loading costs. Pays unloading costs to the extent that they are included in the freight.	the buyer; the bill of lading is deemed to 'represent the goods'. Pays unloading costs to the extent that they are not included in the freight. Risk passes to buyer once goods over ship's rail at port of loading, although seller covers the loss through insurance.
DAF (Delivered at Frontier)	Delivers the goods cleared for export at the named frontier (or the named place at that frontier). Provides documents to enable the buyer to take delivery at the frontier, e.g. document of transport or warehouse warrant.	Takes delivery of the goods at the named frontier (or the named place at that frontier) and risk from that point. Pays for on-carriage. Obtains import licence and pays import duties, taxes and fees, if required.
DDP (Delivered Duty Paid)	Delivers the goods at the named place of destination at own risk and expense. Obtains any import licence and pays import duties, taxes and fees, if required. Provides the documents to enable the buyer to take delivery at the named place, e.g. document of transport or warehouse warrant.	Takes delivery of the goods at the named place of destination.

Methods of payment or settlement

As we have already seen, one of the major concerns to any exporter is ensuring that the goods are paid for as agreed. To reduce the risk of non-payment, the exporter may obtain at the outset a status report on the buyer and, as we shall see later, can insure against certain risks which might give rise to non-payment. Similarly, an importer will want to ensure that possession of the goods is obtained and payment made as agreed so that the supply of goods in the future is not jeopardised. Some of the risks inherent in the settlement process can be reduced or eliminated depending upon the method of payment selected. There are three main *Terms of Settlement*:

    (a) Open account
    (b) Documentary collections
    (c) Documentary credits

We shall consider these individually, together with their respective advantages and disadvantages.

Open account

As you will see from Fig. 4.1, this is the simplest method of settlement. However, because the exporter is releasing the goods without payment or some absolute means of insuring that payment is received, this method presents the greatest risk. Despite this, the majority of international trade transactions continue to be settled in this way.

Open account settlements have some advantages for both the exporter and importer which make them attractive, but there are also disadvantages. The lists of advantages and disadvantages that

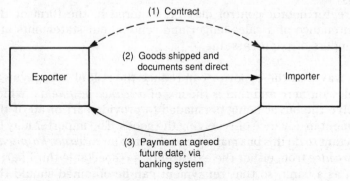

Fig. 4.1 Open account

follow, both for open account and the other means of settlement, are by no means exhaustive but should be seen in the context of the needs of the exporter and importer. The exporter requires payment, protection of the goods until paid and, perhaps, financial assistance in the intervening period. The importer wants the goods on time, at the right place and of the correct quality and, perhaps, with a period of credit.

Advantages to the exporter
1 Because this method of settlement tends to be used where there is a long-standing relationship between the seller and the buyer, the open account balance is settled on a monthly or quarterly basis and transactions can be dealt with in very much the same way as domestic trade.
2 Subject to any contract with the buyer, there are less constraints on documentation, the timing of shipments and on places of despatch – making this method more flexible.
3 As only the settlement payments pass through the banking system, no charges are incurred by the exporter.

Disadvantages to the exporter
1 There is no guarantee of payment and control of the goods is lost.
2 The exporter is exposed to political, economic and country risks unless other steps are taken to mitigate these.
3 Because there is often no specific constraint on the timing of the payments, it is difficult to control cash flow.
4 There is a possibility that delays in the banking system will delay the transfer of the funds.
5 Payment when received may be in the form of a foreign cheque which will have to be negotiated or collected, causing further delay.
6 Greater debtor control may be required in the form of the maintenance of a sales ledger and sending out statements and reminders of payments due.

One way that the exporter can reduce the risk of non-payment is relevant here and that is the use of *advance payments*, which involve the buyer being persuaded to provide part or all of the payment in advance of receiving the goods. The importer may be reluctant to do this but may agree subject to an *Advance Payments Guarantee* from either the exporter or a respectable third party, such as a bank, so that repayment can be obtained should the goods not be shipped.

Advantages to the importer
1 Few arrangements have to be made other than ensuring that funds are available to meet payments as and when they fall due.
2 The importer retains control over the timing of settlement and the method by which funds are remitted.
3 Inspection of the goods is usually possible before payment is made.

Disadvantages to the importer
1 The importer has little control over shipment details and the timing of the receipt of the goods.
2 There is no control over the quality of the goods and, if special documents such as certificates of origin are required, there is no guarantee that these will be received.

Documentary collections

This method of settlement provides some measure of comfort to the exporter, who will ship the goods and then arrange for the documents of title and collection instructions to be sent by the exporter's own bank (the remitting bank) to a correspondent bank (the collecting bank) in the importer's country (*see* Fig. 4.2). The documents may include a bill of exchange drawn by the exporter on the importer for the amount of the invoice and payable at sight or at a fixed or future determinable time. Where the bill of exchange is not accompanied by documents, these having been sent to the importer, the transaction is known as a *clean collection*.

The collecting bank will be instructed to release the documents, and, therefore, title to the goods, to the importer against payment (D/P) or acceptance (D/A) of the bill of exchange. Payment or the accepted bill will be sent to the remitting bank which will in the latter case, present it for payment on the maturity date.

There is a code of practice governing the terms used and procedures to be followed by all parties involved in documentary collections. It was drawn up by the International Chamber of Commerce and is known as *Uniform Rules for Collections*. The rules are set out in unambiguous terms and cover the liabilities and responsibilities of the parties, and such things as presentation, payment, acceptance, promissory notes, receipts and other instruments, protest, case of need and protection of goods, advice of fate, and interest charges and expenses. The full details can be studied by obtaining *ICC publication No. 322*, but there are

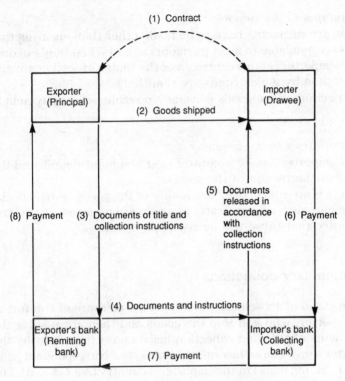

Fig. 4.2 Documentary collections

two items which require clarification here: *protest* and *case of need*.

Where a bill is dishonoured through non-payment or non-acceptance, the drawer (the exporter) may wish to take legal action against the drawee and other parties to the bill and to support this action needs to have the bill *protested*. This usually involves a notary public demanding of the drawee payment or acceptance and, if the bill remains dishonoured, recording the reasons, if any, given by the drawee. This information is then included in a deed of protest, a formal document which can be presented to the court as evidence of dishonour. *Case of need* is the term used to describe the exporter's representative or agent in the importer's country who may be contacted where problems arise in respect of goods which have been shipped but where there has been non-payment or non-acceptance by the importer.

Advantages to the exporter
1 The exporter has some measure of control over the documents

and the goods unless there is no document of title and/or the goods are consigned direct to the importer or the importer's agent.

2 If the exporter has to pay charges for the collection, allowance for these including interest can be made when the invoice price is calculated.

3 If the bill is dishonoured, protest can be arranged to support any legal action which may follow.

4 The collecting bank may act on behalf of the exporter by taking steps to protect the goods or pursue the importer for payment.

5 This method is less expensive than a documentary credit, which is discussed later.

Disadvantages to the exporter

1 If control is not retained through the documents of title, the exporter relies entirely on the ability and willingness of the importer to pay.

2 If documents against acceptance (D/A) terms are granted to the importer, control of the goods is lost once the bill of exchange has been accepted.

3 The cost of protesting and taking subsequent legal action may be excessive.

4 If difficulties do arise concerning payment or acceptance, finding an alternative buyer or reshipping may be necessary and expensive.

Advantages to the importer

1 A period of credit can be obtained by the use of a term bill or promissory note.

2 The exporter will normally be responsible for the charges.

3 Finance can be raised using the goods as security.

4 If the collection order specifically authorises it, payment can be deferred pending the arrival of the goods.

5 It is more convenient and less expensive than a documentary credit.

Disadvantages to the importer

1 Payment or acceptance is required on presentation when the commercial documents have arrived at the collecting bank and before the arrival of the goods, unless the collection order specifically authorises otherwise.

2 If the bill is accepted then the importer is legally liable despite, for example, any clauses in the contract relating to defective goods.

3 There is no guarantee that the goods will be received as ordered or on time.

Documentary credits

The safeguards inherent in the documentary collection process may be considered, particularly by the exporter, to be insufficient as there remains the problem of dishonoured bills of exchange. The exporter may attempt to overcome this by requiring the importer to establish a letter of credit in favour of the exporter by which a bank undertakes to make payment to the exporter on presentation of the stipulated documents completed as agreed. The requirement for the letter of credit will be contained in the contract between the exporter and the importer and when the letter of credit is issued it should describe the documentary requirements demanded of the exporter. As long as the exporter complies with these requirements and any other terms and conditions of the credit, then payment will be made as illustrated (*see* Fig. 4.3). As with documentary collections, there is an

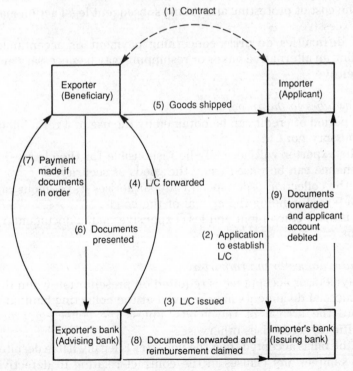

Fig. 4.3 Documentary credits

international code of practice governing the manner in which a documentary credit should be handled. This is issued by the International Chamber of Commerce (ICC) and is called *Uniform Customs and Practice for Documentary Credits (1983 Revision)*, contained in *ICC publication No. 400*. The articles cover such matters as the form and notification of credits, the liabilities and responsibilities of the parties involved with a credit, the documentary requirements and the definitions of the terms used. You should obtain a copy of these rules and become familiar with the general provisions because most banks include in their application forms for credits a clause stipulating that the rules will apply. You must particularly note that a credit is a separate transaction from the contract on which it is based and that the parties to the credit are dealing in documents and not in goods. There are a number of variations on the basic letter of credit and some of these are described briefly here.

Revocable and irrevocable credits

If a credit is issued in revocable form it means that it can be amended or revoked, although any amendment can be rejected by the beneficiary. An irrevocable credit, however, may not be amended or cancelled without the prior agreement of all the parties to the credit, a factor which makes this form of credit more attractive to the exporter.

Confirmed credits

Where a bank in the exporter's country, at the exporter's request, adds its undertaking to that of the issuing bank, it is said to be confirming the credit and becomes the confirming bank.

Transferable credits

These are credits whereby the beneficiary is entitled to instruct the bank to make the credit available in whole or in part to one or more third parties (second beneficiaries).

Back to back credits

These are explained most easily by way of an example. Exporter A agrees to supply an importer with goods against a letter of credit. Exporter A will not be manufacturing the goods but will be buying them from exporter B against a letter of credit in favour of exporter B. There are, therefore, two credits: one, the prime credit, in favour of A; the other, the second credit, in favour of B.

Your bank will be acting as issuing bank for those of its importing customers who require letters of credit for overseas exporters and you will need to examine the appropriate application form to understand fully the procedure involved in issuing a credit. Furthermore, the application will have to be assessed in just the same way as any other credit risk such as a loan or overdraft.

Advantages to the exporter

1 Dependence on the creditworthiness of an importer is replaced by dependence on a bank.

2 If the credit is confirmed by a bank in the exporter's country, the exporter is no longer subject to country risk.

3 If the credit is in irrevocable form it cannot be cancelled without the exporter's express agreement, but notice of revocation can be rejected if received after shipment.

4 The documents and therefore the goods will not be released until payment or a commitment to payment is made.

5 Where credit has been allowed the bill of exchange will have been accepted by a bank and can, therefore, be used to obtain finance by discounting.

Disadvantages to the exporter

1 The exporter has to produce the correct document, accurate in every detail. Even small discrepancies can cause delay.

2 If in revocable form the credit could be cancelled between shipment and payment.

3 The credit may be too complex or demanding to be workable.

4 Where the advising bank does not have immediate access to reimbursement by the issuing bank, payment may be delayed.

Advantages to the importer

1 The importer can provide for stringent documentary requirements.

2 Because the exporter is more assured of receiving payment, the importer may be able to negotiate better terms on the purchase of the goods.

3 The importer can control the timing of the shipment and destination.

4 There is reassurance that no funds will be paid unless documents of title are received and are correct.

5 Protection is provided by the Uniform Customs Practice for Documentary Credits.

6 The credit can be used as a means of finance either from the bank or to provide a period of credit from the exporter.

Disadvantages to the importer

1 Because the banks only deal in the documents and not the goods, they provide no protection against poor quality, or defective or incorrect goods.

2 If the credit is irrevocable it cannot be amended without the consent of the exporter.

3 The importer takes on the liability of the credit and remains liable regardless of any changes in circumstances.

4 Documentary credits can be expensive, although the importer can attempt to pass the charges on through increased prices.

Export Credits Guarantee Department

Being able to export its goods and services successfully is vital to any country's economic health but in most overseas markets there is intense competition either from the domestic producers or other exporters. To remain competitive UK exporters have to be prepared to offer credit to prospective importers and, as we have seen, this involves taking a risk because the exporter is releasing the goods before being paid. The longer the period of credit, the greater the chance of something going wrong and the greater the risk for the exporter. The exporter can insure in the normal way against the risk of loss or damage to the goods in transit and can also take some precautions, such as a letter of credit, to try to ensure that the importer pays. A variety of political and country risks also face the exporter, such as a change of government in the importer's country followed by a suspension of settlements of overseas debt which prevent the exporter being paid.

To persuade exporters to grant periods of credit and to take on these additional risks which cannot be covered by normal commercial insurance policies, the government set up a credit insurance scheme under the auspices of ECGD in 1919. In addition to providing insurance cover, ECGD also provides a range of guarantees to banks and other financial institutions to encourage them to provide finance to support exports. These guarantees extend to overseas buyers who are looking for credit to purchase UK exports. There is some confusion in terminology in that the insurance policies issued to the exporter have the word 'guarantee' in their title as do, of course, the direct guarantees given to banks. The risks covered by ECGD policies are listed below and the types of policy are described in Fig. 4.4.

ECGD – insurance for supplier credit

Policy	Risks covered	%	Cover for	Remarks
(a) Comprehensive short-term guarantee. (selling consumer goods)	(1) (2) (9) (4) (5) (6) (7) (8) (3)	90 95 72	Exporter must insure all export business or a portion acceptable to ECGD. Also available – sales from stock held abroad: sales to overseas subsidiaries/associates pre-credit cover (maximum 90% on all risks) foreign currency contracts	Accounts for the largest proportion of all ECGD business.
(b) Supplemental extended terms guarantee (selling production engineering goods)	As in (a) above	As in (a) above	As above but: sale to overseas subsidiaries/associates and pre-sales from overseas stock standard	Only available if comprehensive short-term guarantee held.
(c) Supplementary stocks guarantee (holding overseas stock)	As in (a) above plus: war requisition confiscation measures preventing re-export	As in (a) above	Stock held abroad prior to sale for up to 18 months from original shipment date.	Supplementary to the comprehensive short-term guarantee.
(d) External trade guarantee (dealing in foreign goods)	(1) (4) (5) (6) (7) (8)	90	Goods direct from overseas seller to overseas buyer but otherwise similar to (a) above. Maximum of six months credit.	Available to UK manufacturers, merchants, confirmers, but not if in direct competition with UK trade.
(e) Specific guarantees (selling semi/capital goods)	Can cover (1) (2) (4) (5) (6) (7) (8) (9)	90	Individual contracts – subject to negotiation between exporter and ECGD prior to finalising contract with buyer. pre-credit cover up to 2 years available foreign currency cover available	

Fig. 4.4 (see page 59 for definitions of numbers)

Principal risks for which ECGD will provide cover:

1 Insolvency of the buyer.
2 Buyer's failure to pay within six months of due date for goods which have been accepted.
3 Buyer's failure to take up goods despatched.
4 Moratorium on external debt, i.e. Government restrictions on settlement of overseas debt.
5 Government action preventing performance of contract in whole or in part.
6 Political events, economic difficulties, legislation or administrative measures outside UK preventing payment.
7 Legal discharge of a debt in a foreign currency resulting in a shortfall at date of transfer.
8 War and certain other events outside cover of commercial insurance.
9 Cancellation or non-renewal of export licence (only with pre-credit cover).

It is important to note that item 7 only covers an exporter who has tried to mitigate a possible foreign exchange risk by, for example, entering into a forward contract or by borrowing in the currency expected to be received from the importer. In item 9 there is reference to pre-credit cover and you should be aware that this is not available with the basic guarantee which runs from the date of shipment. Pre-credit cover, which can be arranged at extra cost, runs from the date of contract. Perhaps one of the more interesting aspects of ECGD policies as far as banks are concerned is the fact that the benefits are assignable to a third party. Consequently, where you are providing finance for exports you can arrange to have the policy assigned to your bank. In this way, any payment made by ECGD under the policy will go to the bank and not the customer.

ECGD direct bank guarantees for UK goods and services

These are detailed in Figure 4.5 and you will note that there is no bank guarantee for *short-term* export finance, i.e. up to two years. ECGD used to provide two types of guarantee but no longer does so and the gap has been filled by the clearing banks and other companies who provide a variety of products using either the customer's own ECGD policy or, where the customer has no policy, the bank's own policy or that of a third party specialist company. The bank normally will provide finance to the exporter to the extent of 90% of the invoice value of the transaction without recourse to the exporter should the buyer fail to pay. The maximum credit period is normally 180 days but occasionally some banks will consider financing longer periods up to two years. In certain circumstances, and depending upon who holds the ECGD insurance policy, some banks will finance up to 100% of the invoice value, but would retain a 10% recourse liability against the exporter.

Guarantee	Credit term	Policy	Operation
Specific guarantee (capital and semi-capital goods for contracts less than £1m)	2 to 5 years	Specific guarantee facility letter plus recourse agreement	Guarantee is for one transaction. Bank lends 100% of the principal values of the bills. Repayment is from the collection proceeds.
Buyer credit guarantee (capital goods and associated services – contracts in excess of £1m)	Over 2 years	Specific guarantee supporting the overseas buyer	Guarantee is for one transaction. Bank lends between 75% and 85% to the *overseas buyer* to purchase in UK.

Fig. 4.5

Methods of finance

Some of the ways in which banks can provide financial assistance both to exporters and importers have been covered elsewhere in this chapter but it is useful to summarise them here. You must recognise that an exporter may have to wait for payment from the importer and might need the bank to provide finance during this period. Additionally, where the exporter is a manufacturer, bank assistance may well be required in the form of working capital during the manufacturing process. On the other hand, the importer might be required to make an advance payment which needs funding and will often look to the bank for help where payment for the goods has to be made to the exporter before the importer has been able to sell them on and realise the proceeds.

The exporter

Overdraft or loan

The exporter can make use of straightforward overdraft or loan facilities on a secured or unsecured basis in exactly the same way as any other customer. Many exporters, as we have seen, trade on an *open account* basis and look to the overdraft to finance these overseas debtors alongside their domestic debtors. Where the exporter has established *ECGD cover* then your bank may be more inclined to provide finance because of the insurance against certain risks that this provides. Furthermore, if the exporter has decided that *documentary collections or credits* are preferable to open account transactions, these can also be financed through an overdraft or loan, particularly where the exporter has granted the importer a period of credit. Where the documentary collection or credit includes a bill of exchange, drawn either at sight or some future date, the exporter can approach the bank to *negotiate* the bill or provide an advance against the collection proceeds.

Bills negotiated

Banks will negotiate cheques, drafts, or bills drawn abroad and in so doing provide the customer with the full amount of the item and then collect the proceeds for itself, but with recourse to its own customer in the event of non-payment. By this means, an exporter can obtain cash for a bill of exchange immediately.

Advances against bills for collection

As the title implies, the bank will provide an advance against the face value of the bill and will then collect the proceeds on behalf of the customer. The amount advanced may be less than the face value of the bill, thereby limiting the risk for the bank and the interest charge for the customer. The balance of the value of the bill is paid over when the proceeds have been collected from the drawer.

Bills discounted

Where, for instance, a documentary credit requires documents to be released against acceptance of a bill of exchange drawn on the advising bank, the exporter could arrange for the bill to be discounted. For this facility to be made available the bill must be a term bill and must have been accepted by the advising bank. The exporter's bank will then purchase the bill at less than its face value, giving the proceeds to the exporter. The bank can then hold the bill until maturity, or rediscount it.

Other methods
These include *acceptance credits, forfaiting* and *factoring*, which are described in Chapter 5.

The importer

Overdraft, loan or produce loan
These will enable the importer to pay for goods on receipt or where no credit has been allowed by the exporter. As the goods are sold by the importer the borrowing is reduced or repaid. The bank may be prepared to provide facilities on an unsecured basis but equally may demand some security and this may take the form of the goods themselves. The bank initially will have control of the goods by possession of the documents of title. To effect the security, a *letter of pledge* or *hypothecation* must be taken from the importer and the goods warehoused to the order of the bank. Where the goods are released to the importer, a *trust letter* or *trust receipt* is signed by which the importer acknowledges acting as trustee for the bank, both in respect of the goods and the ultimate sale proceeds. (*See* 'pledge' in Chapter 9.)

Trade credit
The need for bank finance will be reduced or removed altogether if the importer can persuade the exporter to allow a period of credit before payment is made. As we have already seen, the exporter may be prepared to do this either on an *open account* basis or against a *documentary acceptance credit*.

Documentary credit
Where this allows for payment at some future date the importer has time to sell the goods before having to pay the exporter.

Summary

1 The three main problems facing the importer and exporter are time, distance and exchange risk. These give rise to considerations of the market, the buyer or supplier, transport and, most importantly, payment.
2 Information is very important to both the importer and exporter and there are several sources such as the banks, the Department of Trade and Industry, the British Overseas Trade Board and the Chambers of Commerce.

3   International transactions are normally subject to contracts between buyers and sellers and are often substantiated by a variety of documents such as bills of lading, invoices, certificates of origin and bills of exchange.
4   To avoid confusion and misunderstanding and to provide a framework for the procedures to be followed in international trade there are conventions such as *Incoterms*, *Uniform Rules for Collections*, and *Uniform Customs and Practice for Documentary Credits*.
5   Methods of settlement include:
   Open account
   Documentary collections
   Documentary credits
   Advance payments
6   Documentary credits can be revocable or irrevocable, confirmed or unconfirmed and can be transferable.
7   Each method of settlement will have advantages and disadvantages for both the exporter and the importer. The overriding factors are that the exporter wishes to ensure that the goods arrive on time, at the correct destination, are as agreed and that payment is received. The importer wishes to ensure that the goods are received as ordered, on time and at the right place.
8   The Export Credits Guarantee Department provides insurance policies which cover a range of political, country and non-payment risks and also provides bank guarantees in certain circumstances.
9   Methods of finance include overdraft, loan, negotiation of bills, advances against bills and discounting bills. Other methods are acceptance credits, forfaiting, factoring and produce loans.

Self-assessment questions

1   What information can a bank provide to a prospective exporter?
2   What is a bill of lading?
3   Describe an air waybill.
4   Where goods are FOB, who pays the freight?
5   Describe the open account method of settlement.
6   What is an advance payments guarantee?
7   List two advantages to the importer of a documentary collection.

8 Describe briefly a transferable credit.
9 List two advantages to the exporter of a documentary credit.
10 What percentage of cover does ECGD provide against the insolvency of the buyer?
11 Are bills negotiated with or without recourse?
12 What document does the importer sign when goods pledged to the bank are released?

5
Acceptance credits and other services

Objectives

Study of this chapter will:
1 help you to understand the purpose and method of operation of acceptance credits;
2 provide an awareness of the benefits and drawbacks of other services available to assist customers in international trade;
3 enable you to identify the most suitable service for a customer.

Acceptance credits

Merchant banks, some of which act as *accepting houses*, came into being by financing trade. Acceptance credits were introduced as the vehicle for providing the finance.

Banks lend their name to bills of exchange which make them 'first class' paper, i.e. bank acceptances in the eyes of the Bank of England. The bills can then be discounted on the money market at fine rates of interest because they have been accepted by a bank, thereby reducing the risk of dishonour. This type of revolving credit facility which operates in a similar way to overdraft in that funds can be drawn up to an agreed limit, is available to business customers. The facility is normally for working capital purposes, linked principally to the movement of goods and the sale or purchase of raw materials. The method of operation is for bills of exchange to be drawn in sterling for periods normally between 30 and 180 days. These are known as 'term' bills, as opposed to those payable on sight. They are often cheaper than overdrafts because the cost of discounting bills is lower than the margins charged for normal bank facilities, and provide a flexible method of obtaining funds. The service is available also

'Sorry, your overseas supplier's not very impressed with "Scout's honour"!'

for financing worldwide capital projects, e.g. hospitals, railways.

If there is a general shortage of funds, the Bank of England is prepared to lend to the discount houses in its role as 'lender of last resort'. The Bank of England will consider such bills as 'eligible' for discount at advantageous rates. Sometimes, however, the bank will charge penal rates, i.e. more than the rates available on the money markets to effect pressure to control the levels of funds.

Bearing in mind that the accepting bank is primarily responsible for the payment of the bill, it will accept bills only for customers of good standing. Consider the following example. Spend and Markhams plc want to import £500 000 worth of blouses from West Germany via a documentary inward collection, payable in 30 days. Pending sale of the goods at a profit they need to pay the overseas supplier and have sufficient working capital to operate the business.

Spend and Markhams could draw a bill of exchange on the bank for, say, £750 000 for 60 days. Once the bank has added its name, i.e. accepted it, the bill can be discounted on the money market, giving the company sufficient funds to pay the overseas supplier and provide working capital. When the goods are sold at the retail price within the 60 days, the retail price includes their profit and Spend and Markhams repay the acceptance credit bank borrowing.

Bank guarantees and bonds

There are a number of different types of guarantee which banks are prepared to issue to third parties for the benefit of their customers. A bank incurs a liability by becoming a party to bonds, guarantees and indemnities. Guarantees fall into two categories:

(a) *inland* – domiciled in the UK;

(b) *overseas* – domiciled abroad.

Most frequently banks issue guarantees to *overseas* beneficiaries which include:

- guarantees to overseas banks to cover borrowing facilities granted to their customers abroad.
- bail bonds to obtain the release of a ship in a foreign port which has been (or is about to be) 'arrested', e.g. in respect of legal action against the owners.
- contract guarantees.

The most frequent types of guarantees to *inland* beneficiaries include:

- indemnities for missing bills of lading, given to a shipping company in the UK on behalf of an importing customer.
- guarantees to Customs and Excise in respect of payment by customers of customs duty, excise duty, and VAT on imports.

In each case most banks will expect their customers to sign counter-indemnities to repay any payments made by the bank under the guarantee, including costs and expenses incurred.

The wording of a guarantee is very important. It needs to be: *clear, precise, simple.*

Important inclusions as far as the bank is concerned are:

(a) name and address of beneficiary,

(b) clear and unambiguous wording,

(c) definite expiry date,

(d) maximum bank liability stated,

(e) guarantees for *monetary* payment only, i.e. no goods involved,

(f) time period for submission of claims under guarantee,

(g) procedure for claims,

(h) drawn subject to English law, where possible.

Although, ideally, we would wish for the document to be subject to English law, this is not always possible and often overseas countries have different rules. For instance, there may be no limit on time or amount, which causes difficulties as far as a bank liability is concerned. We need to rely on our correspondents abroad to secure the cancellation and release of a bond to remove the bank's liability.

A guarantee must be non-assignable; obviously a bank would not wish to be caught up in a situation where its security is being transferred to unknown principals. Similarly, for its own protection, the bank will require the right under a guarantee to prove in a bankruptcy or liquidation. These guarantees are *real* rather than contingent (possible) liabilities for the bank because the bank will be called on to honour the amount outstanding if the supplier fails to complete the contract. It must then seek recourse separately from the supplier. Accordingly, the guarantees are viewed as lending facilities, with fees charged for the arrangement.

Contract guarantees

At some stage you are likely to encounter one or more of the following three usual types of guarantee to cover contracts for exporters:
  (a) tender (bid) bonds,
  (b) advance payment guarantees (bonds),
  (c) performance guarantees (bonds).

Tender bonds
When sellers tender for a contract they are often required to supply a guarantee or bond; usually the bond is for an amount between 1% and 5% of the contract price. The purpose of a tender bond, sometimes known as a *bid bond*, is to show to the buyer that the proposed seller will sign the contract if their tender is accepted. The buyer will be confident in the knowledge that the seller is financially able to enter into such an undertaking.

Whenever a bank issues this type of guarantee it must be alive to the probability that it will be called upon subsequently to issue a performance guarantee on behalf of the seller, i.e. the bank's customer, if the bid is successful. Should the bank refuse to issue a performance guarantee then the tender bond will be 'called' through the seller's failure to complete the contract, the issue of a performance guarantee being a term of the contract. That is why these types of guarantees are sometimes known as *penalty bonds.*

Advance payment guarantee

When a seller enters into a large contract which involves significant up-front costs the terms of the contract may contain the offer of advance payment. A bank may help by issuing an advance payment guarantee to enable the seller to receive such advance payments from the buyer, normally between 10% and 20% of the contract price. The bank will want its liability to be effective only upon receipt by the seller of the agreed advance payments, and for the liability to reduce as performance by the seller progresses under the terms of the contract.

Performance guarantees

The purpose of a performance guarantee is exactly what it states – to ensure performance by the seller (your customer) in accordance with their contractual obligations. A performance guarantee is usually issued on behalf of the customer to cover between 5% and 10% of the contract value.

These are the most commonly used types of guarantee or bonds and are sometimes required as a result of a successful tender by our customer; on occasion a performance guarantee will become effective on the expiry of a tender bond.

Types of contract guarantee

There are two main types of contract guarantee, only one of which a bank is usually prepared to be involved with:

(a) *Demand* – where the bank undertakes to pay away funds on claim.

(b) *Surety bonds* – where the surety is bound to make good any defaults of the contractor, e.g. remedial work.

Since a bank will not wish to have primary responsibility for the fulfilment of a customer's contractual obligations, the bank will issue only *demand* guarantees.

Demand can be:

- *simple* – when the beneficiary claims, bank pays, i.e. no conditions, or
- *conditional* – where the beneficiary must support the claim with specific documentation.

Any claim received where the guarantee is payable on *simple* demand must be honoured, whether or not the seller claims that they are not in default.

As the bank takes on a primary liability when issuing a foreign guarantee but is not involved in the underlying contract, the liability actually takes the legal form of an *indemnity* and not a guarantee.

Conclusion

There is a variety of guarantees which a customer could ask their bank to give, e.g. for retention monies under a contract. In any event, your prime concern will be to limit the bank's guarantee as to: *time* and *amount*.

Factoring

Some of the bank's smaller but reputable customers may be moving into export markets for the first time and are concerned about dealing on open account. The risk is that the overseas buyer may refuse to pay on the due date leaving your customer with the problem of how to collect across the miles. However, there is a service available to help them – factoring – which basically is the purchase of a book debt at a discount.

A factor purchases book debts of a client company, usually buying those payable within a maximum period of 180 days. Up to 80% of the invoice value is paid to the client company immediately, the remainder, net of fees and expenses, is paid after the debts have been cleared.

One of the main benefits to the client company is that all the bookkeeping and administration of invoicing debtors is removed and handled by the factoring company, thereby releasing staff for more-effective work. Alternatively, it may mean that less staff need to be employed. On the other hand, the cost of borrowing can be expensive, up to 3% above the standard bank lending rate, but the cost is offset by improved cash flow and a reduced bank overdraft. The factoring service is available both for home and export debts, and falls into two categories:

(a) *with recourse*: in the event of non-payment by the debtor the client company stands the credit risk.
(b) *without recourse*: in the event of non-payment by the debtor the client is covered by debt insurance from the factor.

Invoice discounting

There is a 'half-way house' service called *invoice discounting*, where the client company continues to administer the bookkeeping, and the factor underwrites debts and advances funds against invoiced values. The benefit of this option is that the buyer is unaware of the factor's existence.

Conclusion

While factoring can be expensive, the service can provide finance and the cost can be offset by savings in staff time (maintaining sales ledgers, credit control, etc). So what does the service provide for your customer?

Benefits
- Advances against exported proceeds up to 80%.
- Credit cover – 100% of approved sales.
- Improved cash flow.
- Avoidance of debt collecting on *approved* sales.

Drawbacks
- It can be costly.
- Factoring companies are very selective about the business they approve.

Forfaiting

The forfaiting service was born in Europe to provide supplier and buyer credit facilities for the continental banks' customers who did not have the benefit of our ECGD service. (*See* Chapter 4.)

As an alternative to ECGD cover for exporters in the UK, forfaiting is primarily a method of providing fixed rate finance in support of the sale of capital and semi-capital goods over credit periods of up to seven years. Repayment is made in instalments. It can be used also to provide short-term credit for non-capital goods.

The service is based on first-class commitments only, which means that the drawee must be of undoubted standing, and a bank guarantee is required. The forfaiter purchases trade receiveables, i.e. invoices, acceptances, bills of exchange, promissory notes, at a discount and without recourse to the exporter.

The forfaiter bears all political and currency risks. Thus, the exporter will not need to enter into forward foreign exchange contracts, nor will they need to worry about the problems of bookkeeping and debt collection. On the other hand, apart from the relatively high cost, the exporter may receive only 80–90% of the value of the debt. The forfaiter may require the difference to be paid immediately in cash.

How it works

Stage 1: Exporter and importer agree credit terms and interest rates applicable.
Stage 2: Bank assesses risk of buyer, buyer's guarantor (bank in own country) and country concerned. Appropriate discount rate quoted.
Stage 3: Bills or notes *avalised* (see below) by importer's bank.
Stage 4: Bills or notes presented to exporter's bank for discounting. Providing all documentation is satisfactory, bank buys the bills or notes without recourse to exporter.

Avalising is the term used when a bank adds its name to a bill of exchange or promissory note, thereby standing as surety for the obligation of the drawee of the bill or the maker of the promissory note. *Pour aval* means that payment is guaranteed.

As a guide, fees charged for a bank's commitment will be about 0.1% per month from the date of commitment until the date the bills are presented.

When it works

Forfaiting may be more appropriate than other official export credit arrangements when, for example:

(a) The buyer insists on 100% finance, but official arrangements only permit a maximum of 85% finance.

(b) The buyer wants a different repayment programme from that officially laid down.

(c) The equipment being exported does not qualify under the export credit arrangements for the period of credit the buyer wants, or does not qualify at all.

(d) The finance has to be arranged very quickly, and the various steps under the official arrangements will be slower.

(e) The exporter does not want any rights of recourse retained against them.

(f) The overall cost of the credit provided may be lower by forfaiting.

(g) The official agency, e.g. ECGD, is not prepared to provide cover for the particular country risk.

Conclusion

As an alternative means of finance, forfaiting is easy, flexible and fast. Benefits to your customer, the exporter, are:

(a) It is without recourse.

(b) No exchange risks or interest rate risks (eliminated from the day of discounting).

(c) 100% finance to the buyer can be offered.

(d) Cash flow is improved.

(e) Normal banking facilities are not affected by forfaiting.

(f) No debt collecting problems.

(g) Certain types of finance may be available for longer periods than, for example, the ECGD can offer.

(h) The importer need not know that the exporter is discounting bills; competitors will not know that forfaiting is being used as a method of export finance.

Financial Futures (LIFFE)

Following an upsurge in the rate of inflation in the USA in the late 1960s, coupled with a relaxation of interest rate regulations, the Financial Futures Market emerged out of economic necessity in the light of higher, and more volatile, interest rates. It became risky to hold stock or borrow or lend money, and commodity prices became more volatile. Consequently, there came about a greater demand for dealing in 'safe' commodities. The first Future Exchange in the world was established in Chicago in 1972 (called the *International Monetary Market* – IMM), designed to trade financial futures contracts.

In the early 1980s several other financial centres opened up their own futures exchanges. The *London International Financial Futures Exchange* (LIFFE) started trading in September 1982 and deals in futures contracts in currencies, interest rates and the value of quoted ordinary shares. Only members of the Exchange are allowed to conduct trading and before dealing a prospective buyer or seller must first open an account with a member firm. The Exchange's Clearing House acts as a guarantor to both parties, taking a security deposit ('margin') from buyer and seller. Settlements are made daily, when the Clearing House credits members' accounts with net gains and receives immediate payments from members with net losses. So, who are the participants in this market place?

The participants

Floor traders/brokers
Every member on the floor is his/her own auctioneer and receives a small fee for each transaction achieved. Essentially they are speculators, trading for themselves.

Futures commission merchants
Intermediaries for the brokers and the customers provide a fast and efficient communication system, linking the customer quickly with the auctioneering situation.

Speculators
Their sole motive is profit by dealing with changes in the expected price levels over time. Normally they do not personally own the commodity in which they deal. They provide fluidity to the market and by their activities they help to set the price, allowing hedgers to buy or sell in volume without difficulty.

Hedgers
They use the Financial Futures Market as an insurance against possible adverse price movements, thereby reducing their exposure to the risk of losses. Hedging is of particular benefit to corporate customers, pension funds, brokers and dealers, banks and other financial institutions. The service also provides a means of hedging for those who want to lock-in current exchange rates on future currency transactions.

How does it work?

A financial futures contract is an agreement to buy or sell a standard quantity of a specified currency or financial instrument at a specified future date and at a price agreed between the parties through open outcry, i.e. continuous auction, on the floor of an organised exchange. The instruments can be anything from three-month time deposits, twenty-year gilt-edged stock, foreign currency to a 100 share index.

Let us look at an example. It is 1 February. A borrower has a £500 000 three-month rollover loan from the money market at a rate of 10% which is due to be rolled over on 1 April. The borrower is worried that rates will have risen by then. The borrower decides to use LIFFE's Three-Month Sterling Interest Rate Contract to cover the risk of higher interest rates. This contract is for a three-month deposit facility of £500 000 commencing in March or June or September or December. At any time contracts for all these different months are being dealt in on the Exchange. The borrower selects the June contract because the March contract will have already matured before his rollover is due.

The contract is priced by deducting the interest rate to be paid on the deposit from 100. On 1 February the interest rate is 10.00% and the price of the contract is accordingly 90.00. The price of the contract changes up or down in minimum movements of 0.01 known as 'ticks'. The value of each tick is therefore:

0.01% p.a. of interest	×	the face value of the contract, i.e. £500 000	×	one quarter = £12.50 of a year

Being worried that the interest rate will rise and hence that the price of the contract will fall, the borrower sells one June contract at a price of 90.00.

By 1 April when the borrowing is rolled over the interest has risen to 12%. The result of the hedge is shown in the table below.

Money market	*Futures market*
1 February He plans to rollover the £500 000 three-months borrowing in April. Current rate on loan is 10%.	Sells one futures contract, June (£500 000) Three-Month Sterling Interest Rate at a price of 90.00 (rate = 10%).
1 April He rolls over the borrowing at the new rate of 12%.	Buys back June futures contract at the new price of 88.00 (rate = 12%).
Extra cost: 2% on £500 000 for one quarter = £2500.	Gain: 200 ticks at £12.50 = £2500.

This hedge worked out perfectly – the gain on futures was exactly equal to the extra interest paid. Thus, the hedger achieved a net borrowing cost of 10% per annum. In practice such perfect matching will usually not be achieved. Futures prices may not move exactly in line with money market rates. If interest rates had fallen the hedger's loss on his futures position would have been matched by lower interest payments so that his net borrowing cost would still be 10% per annum.

Conclusion

This service provides major corporate customers with a method of hedging and speculating on future trends in a variety of exchange and interest rates through the London International Financial Futures Exchange.

Summary

1 Acceptance credits: revolving credit facility for business customers, normally for working capital purposes.
2 Bank guarantees and bonds are given to (a) overseas beneficiaries on behalf of exporting customers to cover contractual liabilities; or (b) to inland beneficiaries to cover payment of duties, etc., for importing customers. In both cases the bank will take a counter-indemnity.
3 Factoring: the purchase of book debts at a discount, payable within 180 days, plus a bookkeeping and administration service where appropriate.
4 Forfaiting: the purchase of longer-term overseas trade receivables at a discount and without recourse, subject to a bank guarantee.
5 LIFFE: a centre for the trading of futures contracts.

Self-assessment questions

1 What does a factor do to the book debts of a client company?
2 In the UK, which institution is the lender of last resort?
3 Which service was introduced initially on the continent to provide buyer and credit facilities?
4 How regularly are settlements made on the Financial Futures Exchange?
5 Which type of bank contract guarantee is the bank prepared to issue – surety or demand?
6 What is the sole motive of speculators?
7 Which two limitations will a bank wish to place on a guarantee it gives in favour of a third party?

6
Canons of lending

Objectives

After studying this chapter you should be able to:
1   briefly understand how a bank's lending policy affects a branch's ability to lend to certain types of customers;
2   explain the principles of lending by reference to a mnemonic;
3   identify the additional information required from commercial customers when financing trading or lending for the purchase of fixed assets.

Introduction

'Will you lend me some money?' There are occasions when we are asked this question by members of our family, or friends, perhaps even only acquaintances. The decision you make depends on the answers to the questions raised in your mind:
• How much do they want?
• How long do they want it for?
• What is it for anyway?
• When will I be repaid?
• How will it be repaid?
• What assurance do I have that it will be repaid?
If you are satisfied with the answers – with or without the need to ask depending on your knowledge of the individual – then you may lend (providing, of course, that you can afford to!).

Sometimes we make a mistake in lending, with disappointing results to our cost. What lessons can be learned from such an experience? Let us explore the principles known as the *canons* of good lending.

'So this is your idea of a source of repayment for the brewery loan!'

Lending policy

Banking is all about borrowing money from one source and lending it to another. From time to time bankers will have to repay the money they borrow and so they will wish to ensure that the money they themselves lend (which belongs to other people) is safe, profitable and relatively easy to get back (liquid).

A bank will have a declared lending policy which it will change from time to time in the face of market conditions or Government regulations. For instance, comment has been made that some banks have adopted 'stop-go' policies concerning mortgage lending for house purchase. This may lead to customers looking elsewhere for funds because they do not realise that money is available. In any event, a bank would not wish to place all its eggs in one basket – just imagine the problems if a major portion of bank lending at the time of Black Monday on the Stock Exchange in October 1987 was to finance the purchase of shares on the Stock Market!

So, having established the amount of credit to be made available to certain countries, certain sectors of industry, certain types of customer, the senior management of the bank will delegate authority for taking decisions on borrowing propositions. That authority is represented by discretionary limits given to lending officers (sometimes known as MDL – Manager's Discretionary Limits).

Depending on the experience of the lending officer and the size of the branch portfolio, the lending may be authorised at branch level. For larger advances, application for sanction must be made to the area or regional office which has a greater discretion. For exceptionally large advances sanction will be given by a committee of head office general managers or board of directors. Figure 6.1 gives an example of the process for sanctioning.

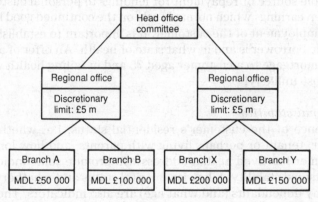

Fig. 6.1

There may be an occasion when the lending officer will not wish to recommend a customer's borrowing application which falls outside MDL. Nevertheless, it is the practice of many banks that the officer must submit the application to the regional office, adding remarks as appropriate. Thereby, if the borrowing request is declined the customer is seen to have received a fair deal from the second look. Should the regional office overturn the branch manager's decision, however, there might be some embarrassing moments for all concerned.

Principles of lending

Quite often bank officers will tell you that they make their lending decisions based on 'gut feeling', which is all very well when you have had experience already but not much use to you when you are trying to assess your first proposition. Before you have had the opportunity to develop judgement and experience there are some basic considerations which can help you to reach your decision. One easy way to help you to remember is by using a mnemonic like CAMPARI, which stands for *c*haracter, *a*bility, *m*argin, *p*urpose, *a*mount, *r*epayment and *i*nsurance, to determine whether the risk is acceptable. The first two principles, character and ability, concern the prospective borrower.

Character

Age/health
The sole source of repayment for lendings to personal customers is often earnings which normally rely on the continued good health and employment of the customer. It is important to establish how old the borrower is and in what state of health. An offer of a long-term mortgage to a customer aged 75 and in failing health would be most unlikely!

Personal stability
Evidence of the customer's residential status, i.e. whether an owner, tenant or perhaps living with parents, and how long the customer has lived at that address will provide some indication of personal stability. Likewise, marital status and whether there are any dependants (and what age) are also indicators. The type of occupation could be important to your decision. How long has the customer been in that employment and what position do they hold? How secure is the job?

Integrity and honesty
Whether we feel that we can trust the borrower depends upon our own subjective view, but previous dealings can help to identify how honest and trustworthy the customer has been in the past. You could check branch records to find out how well previous borrowings have been repaid and how long the customer has been known to the bank. For new propositions you may find that the prospective customer is known by members of staff who have personal knowledge of them which can be of great help in assessing their integrity.

Personal resources
Establishing the extent of an individual's wealth is not always

easy, although reasonable indicators can be found by a visit to the customer's home or place of business, and also during conversation. For instance, you can find out whether the customer owns their own home and how much equity there is in it. What funds have they invested and are there any additional sources of income apart from salary? You would need to take care that you do not make assumptions when visiting a customer's home and seeing opulent surroundings – it might all be on hire purchase!

Outgoings
What type of life style does a customer enjoy and how much does it cost in regular expenditure? A check of the bank records for standing order payments may reveal evidence of hire purchase commitments, payments to in-store companies (e.g. Marks & Spencer), finance payments, etc. The account should also reveal whether the existing regular commitments can be met from income.

If the customer has growing children then commitments might increase for education, clothing, travel.

Connections
There may be influential connections which we would wish to take into account like, for instance, that the borrower is a director of a company which maintains high credit balances with the bank. The individual might be a key business influencer, introducing several new accounts. There might be strong family connections. Having said that, we must only bear these connections in mind and never lend if repayment is doubtful no matter how good the connection.

Ability

Providing that the individual has the legal capacity to borrow funds then we need to check that they have the ability to manage their financial affairs effectively and will succeed in their aims. Can they really afford to involve themselves in the proposition?

The remaining five principles of lending: margin, purpose, amount, repayment, insurance, concern the proposition itself. The bank needs to examine these to establish *safety, liquidity* and *profitability*.

Margin

You must decide what remuneration or return you can expect for the type of borrowing requested. The greater the risk, the higher the interest rate to be charged. If the borrowing is taken on overdraft or on some types of loans, the interest rate is expressed as a margin over the bank's base lending rate, 3% over base for example. Fixed rates of interest are applied for certain types of loans. Depending on the standing of the customer a finer rate may be offered if security is to be held. Similarly, you may be able to cross-sell some other services to help the customer which might affect the rate you will agree to charge depending on the worth of the whole package from the bank's point of view.

Purpose

We need first of all to ensure that the purpose for which the money will be used is legal and that there are no government restrictions on lending. Furthermore, it may be bank policy from time to time to reduce the availability of funds for certain types of lending; speculative property development may be one. We need to satisfy ourselves also that we believe the reasons given for the loan are valid – sometimes a customer might ask for a loan to purchase a car and we discover later tht he really needed it for paying off his gambling debts. There will be the occasion when you will decline a proposition because you feel it is not in the customer's best interest. Your experience will tell you that the customer is much too optimistic about the prospects of a particular proposition.

Although a customer is not best pleased at the time of the decline, it really does give a banker a warm feeling to be thanked at a later date for saying 'no' because the customer has found out that it was the right thing to say with the benefit of hindsight.

Amount

With regard to personal loans for consumer durables, guidelines are laid down to help you determine minimum and maximum amounts for certain types of lending, and also the size of the stake you should expect from the customer. We would always expect some contribution from the borrower to show evidence of commitment to the proposition; the bank cannot be expected to take all the risk. Besides it provides a good incentive for achievement of the proposed outcome. Relating the amount requested to the purpose of the advance you will need to establish whether the amount required is correct and that all other considerations have been taken into account (e.g. fees and expenses for, say, house moves). If a customer has underestimated the amount they will need to complete the purchase of a property then you might be faced with the dilemma either of having to lend more money than you had originally agreed or of knowing that the money you have already lent is in danger because of the customer's position.

Due account must be taken of the discretionary limit afforded to your branch or section.

Repayment

Technically, most bank lending on overdraft and loan is repayable on demand. It would be unrealistic to expect such immediate response from a customer and usually agreement is reached on the timescale for repayment. Having said that, you might question a customer requesting a five-year loan for a holiday in Australia – you may never see them again!

An assessment needs to be made of the commitments on the customer's income to identify whether the repayments can be serviced without strain. Salary being paid direct into a customer's account is to the bank's advantage. There may be other sources of income, however, like dividends, trust income, a spouse's salary.

In the case of a bridging transaction, the source of repayment tends to be from the sale of an asset (e.g. life policy proceeds, Stock Exchange securities, house). The individual may be asked to complete a budget planner so that you can ascertain their income and expenditure. You can also check the bank records to see whether there have been signs of saving or budgeting in the past.

In the case of consumer durables repayment should always be obtained within the lifespan of the item purchased.

Insurance

All advances should be granted or declined on the basis of the satisfactory answers to the previous six areas for consideration. If the proposition does not seem appropriate without taking security which would have to be realised on the failure of the debtor, then you should not be lending in the first place. Security should be considered only as a safety net, not as the prime point of consideration in whether to lend – that is *pawnbroking*. Security is insurance against unforeseen events which affect adversely what otherwise would have been a good proposition.

If security is required then it must be perfected before lending. In addition you might need to consider whether life, accident and sickness insurance might be helpful both for the customer's and the bank's benefit. Any security taken should be:

- easy to value,
- easy to charge (for the bank to obtain a good title),
- easy to realise.

(*See* Chapter 9 – General Principles of Security.)

Case studies 1 and 2 show you examples of a proposition.

Case study 1

James Hale is a Chartered Surveyor, aged 39. He has banked with you for several years and maintained a well-run account with occasional overdrafts being repaid in accordance with arrangements. His present income is £23 500 and he has written to you asking for the bank to lend him £2500 towards the purchase of a new car costing £10 000. He has found a buyer for his existing model at £7500 and proposes to repay the borrowing over three years.

Even if we did not know whether Mr Hale was married or owned his own home we could still apply the principles of CAMPARI to the proposition before speaking to him to decide whether or not we might lend:

Character: respected in the local community and maintained a satisfactory bank account for several years. His occupation and present age would indicate stability.

Ability: previous borrowings have been repaid in accordance with arrangements and the amounts involved would appear to be within Mr Hale's resources.

Margin: this type of borrowing would normally attract a standard fixed interest rate and fees for personal loans.

Purpose: a loan granted for car exchange is a common form of bank lending.

Amount: the bank is asked to lend 25% towards the purchase cost, with the sale proceeds of the previous car providing the balance. Usually, the bank is asked to lend 75% – or more – for this type of borrowing which normally would be still acceptable.

Repayment: Mr Hale's salary of £23 500 should be adequate to service the repayment programme over three years and the previous run of his account shows him to be unlikely to enter into a commitment he could not fulfil.

Insurance: It would be a good idea for Mr Hale to take the optional health insurance as part of the monthly repayments to cover the eventuality of his being ill and to avoid any problems or unnecessary strain in trying to meet repayments during such a period. It would be unlikely for the bank to want security. If a customer of Mr Hale's integrity fails to repay through outside factors, then the car could be sold to obtain repayment and there is a good margin of safety in its value.

Case study 2
Maurice Landon moved into the area six weeks ago and opened a current account at your branch. Previously he had not had a bank account. He is aged 31 and is living in a rented flat above the local newsagent. Currently, he is working as a storekeeper in the supermarket. He has discovered that further down the terrace one of the flats is up for sale at £19 000 but it needs a lot of work doing to it. Mr Landon sees this as a perfect opportunity to make some capital so that he can buy his own home eventually. He is good at DIY and feels that it will cost about £6000 to refurbish the property in his spare time over the next few weeks, after which he can sell it for £31 000. He asks you to bridge him the £25 000 so that he can complete the work pending sale.
 Applying the principles of CAMPARI:

Character: apparently this customer has no track record with any previous banker which, at age 31 is somewhat surprising. He lives in rented accommodation and seems to move from job to job.

Ability: nothing is known about him, his honesty or integrity and whether he has any personal assets.

Margin: this type of proposition is highly risky from a bank's point of view and lending margins would reflect that risk.

Purpose: although banks sometimes do lend for speculative conversions, a loan of 100% would not be entertained; indeed, 50% lending for this type of proposition might be more than current bank policy dictates.

Amount: the bank has no idea whether £6000 is going to be appropriate for the refurbishment costs.

Repayment: the local estate agents will be able to indicate the proposed sale value, providing that the work is satisfactorily completed. However, we do not know what is involved and whether planning permission may be required for the refurbishment. Is there an alternative source of repayment if all goes wrong? How long is a 'few weeks' in terms of finishing the work and obtaining sale of the property?

Insurance: the bank could obtain a legal charge over the property but should not use that as an excuse to lend. In fact, the refurbishment might make the property more difficult to sell than in its present state if the bank was having to force the sale before all renovation work had been completed.

There is a high and, probably, an unacceptable risk to this proposition. It should be declined.

Commercial customers

The canons of lending apply both to personal and commercial customers. The principles under the mnemonic CAMPARI lead us to ask further questions of commercial customers. For the smaller business you may be dealing with just one person and you will want to assess whether the management has the skills necessary to run a business in terms of expertise, experience, drive and energy. Obviously the longer the business has been trading and has an established reputation the more chance of its survival. There are many areas that a bank needs to examine when dealing with commercial customers and the following are some examples. The bank would need to know the state of the order book, whether increasing or decreasing, and which products made the most profit for the customer. If we were to lend with all of the business eggs in one basket, i.e. that sales are dominated by a few customers, then there is the obvious risk that those few customers would cease trading with our borrower. It depends on the competition and whether the customer's business can deliver on time. Similarly, where does the business get its own materials from? Again, if there are a few suppliers, there could be risks involved in non-delivery.

The bank will want to identify what management information exists, for instance, cash flow forecasts, profit projections and balance sheets, and how well they are monitored by the company, together with the assumptions upon which they are based. Prior to lending, a bank would want to analyse the latest audited accounts to review the track record of the business (*see* Chapter 12 on interpretation of financial statements).

By its nature, a business is likely to have quite a few entries passed over the account and the bank will negotiate with a customer a commission tariff for operating the account in addition to management fees for the day-to-day review of the account and negotiation fees charged for the preparatory work and agreement of lendings. During interviews the bank officer will be able to identify cross-selling opportunities to satisfy the customer's business needs which could have an effect on the cost of the remuneration package for the bank. Furthermore, where we are asked to finance trading there may be ways other than the traditional overdraft which are more beneficial from the customer's point of view. Government policy may dictate that restrictions are placed on the type of lending proposed. On the other hand, there may be lending incentives like the Small Firms Loan Guarantee Scheme, which is designed to encourage banks and other financial institutions to lend money against a Government guarantee to small and growing businesses. On 22 June 1988 the Government launched an amendment to this scheme for businesses based in the Inner City Task Force Areas (ICTFA). The guarantee was increased from 70% to 85% as one of the Government's initiatives designed to encourage economic success in the inner cities.

We are normally asked to lend for two principal purposes, i.e. to finance trading or to purchase fixed assets.

Finance for trading

Facilities provided to cover timing differences between payments made and invoices settled should be of a short-term nature only and we would wish to establish what exactly we were financing, i.e. stock, debtors, etc. A cash flow forecast should be produced evidencing the need for the borrowing. The customer's previous track record might confirm whether the assumptions are realistic.

Purchase of fixed assets

This type of borrowing is normally made by loan account with repayment to be made within the life of the asset purchased. The bank will need to satisfy itself that sufficient profits will be made to generate cash flow to finance the repayment programme. Depending on the purpose of the borrowing we should seek competitive estimates for the asset being purchased and, for a building proposal, for example, establish whether planning permission is necessary. Sometimes the need to finance a fixed asset purchase like an extension of the business premises might have a knock-on effect on cash flow: the business may need to close for a few days or, alternatively, stock up prior to the event if manufacturing has to cease for a short while. Additional working capital finance is likely to be requested.

One point to remember when assessing whether the business proposals are realistic is that repayments come from *cash flow* not *profits*. A company may be making all the profits in the world but, unless there is cash available to meet debts as they fall due, then the company could be liquidated. In terms of insurance, apart from taking a charge on assets, one important consideration is whether the proprietor is a key person in the business. What would happen to the worth of the business if that individual became ill or died? There are special insurance policies available to cover such contingencies. In addition, the assets of the business should be covered for the same risks as for your own home, e.g. fire, theft. One additional risk that a business might need to consider that does not usually affect the individual is insuring against bad debts.

Before lending to any limited company you must check the Memorandum and Articles of Association to confirm that the company is legally entitled to borrow and that the borrowing powers of both the company and the directors fall within the parameters of the proposition.

Case study 3
Cuddly Toys Limited was incorporated twenty years ago and has banked with you since that date. The company has a good track record for repaying previous borrowings and has a good reputation from its profitable trading in the market place. The directors ask

for an overdraft facility of £6500 to assist in the manufacture of a large order for delivery within the next three weeks. Repayment will be achieved from the sale order totalling £10 000.

(a) Would you lend in this case? The answer should be yes!

(b) Would you need security? No, apart from the consideration of taking guarantees from the directors because the company is a separate legal entity. However, if the total assets in the balance sheet are worth £½ million, then you might consider it unwise to seek guarantees for a mere £6500.

Summary

Lending to customers is fundamental to a bank's business. Until you have had sufficient opportunity to develop a sound judgement and, through experience of lending to customers, a *gut feel,* you should apply the principles of CAMPARI to every type of lending proposition presented to you. Providing you are satisfied with the answers, through objective not subjective appraisal of the background to the case, then you should not suffer greatly from the incidence of bad and doubtful debts. Anyone can say 'yes' to a lending proposition; obtaining repayment can be more difficult.

Character	• Integrity and honesty?
	• Personal stability/resources/liabilities?
	• Age/health?
	• Connections/introductions?
Ability	• Management ability?
	• Can customer manage their financial affairs?
Margin	• Interest margin?
	• Commission and fees?
	• Cross-selling?
	• Business development opportunities?
Purpose	• Why is loan needed?
	• In customer's best interest?
	• Against bank/Government policy?
	• Trading finance?
	• Purchase of fixed assets?
Amount	• Customer's stake?

- Is the amount correct: have all associated costs been included?
- Manager's discretionary limit.
- Ensure stake is injected before lending.

Repayment	• Source: sale of assets – cash generation – profits?
	• Proposals realistic: question customer's statements? test assumptions?
	• Income?
	• Expenditure?
	• Can repayments be met without strain?
	• Repayment amount and period within guidelines?

Insurance	• Is security necessary?
	• Ensure perfected before lending.
	• Valuation correct in present climate?
	• Life accident and sickness insurance necessary?

Self-assessment questions

1 Which one of the following lending considerations is the least important?
   (a) customer's ability to repay
   (b) purpose of loan
   (c) security available
   (d) amount required.

2 Repayment of a borrowing for working capital purposes usually comes from:
   (a) profits
   (b) sale of fixed assets
   (c) cash flow
   (d) capital introduced

3 At what stage should security be perfected for a borrowing?

4 What is a stake and why do we ask for one?

5 How do we find out about a personal customer's resources and liabilities?

6 What is the purpose of an interest margin?

7
Personal borrowers

Objectives

After studying this chapter you should be able to:
1 recognise which loans are subject to the conditions of the Consumer Credit Act;
2 explain briefly the benefits of credit scoring;
3 identify which type of lending service is most appropriate for your personal customer's need;
4 take account of particular risk when lending to minors.

Introduction

The Consumer Credit Act 1974 was introduced to protect individual borrowers by regulating credit agreements within a prescribed limit, currently £15 000. The Act does not apply to corporate borrowers. All lenders must be licensed to trade in credit by the Office of Fair Trading. One condition of the Act is that all agreements to lend money to individuals (as well as to sole traders and business partnerships) by way of personal loan or hire purchase must be in writing. Overdrafts, budget accounts and revolving credit accounts are regulated agreements but they are exempt from the requirements of the Act. It is an offence to solicit minors, i.e. persons aged under 18, to borrow money or obtain credit. You may find it helpful to look at the literature concerning the range of facilities offered by your own bank to see how the principles of the Act are explained to customers. The summary of alternatives shown at the end of this chapter will identify the different types of lending offered.

To enable a customer to make comparisons between borrowing costs from various potential lenders the legislation requires that the *true* cost of borrowing is declared by the proposed lenders

'You mean to tell me that my hat-trick against United doesn't count as credit scoring?'

known as the *annual percentage rate* (APR). For instance, a loan quoted at a flat rate of 18% may attract a true cost of 19.6% because the amount of interest is based on the capital sum originally borrowed plus other costs, unlike overdrafts where interest is charged only on the amount outstanding on a daily basis. The Consumer Credit Act also imposed equal liability on credit card companies in the event that a customer cannot obtain reimbursement for faulty goods or poor service from a supplier. So, if you purchased a pair of shoes from a High Street retailer using your credit card in payment, and the sole falls off a shoe, you can turn to the credit card company if the retailer fails to compensate you properly. They can then argue amongst themselves!

If facilities are granted other than to individuals, then joint account mandates will be required in which each party undertakes to be jointly *and* severally liable for any indebtedness. For example, you have the following accounts in your books:

Mike and Sheila Noble   Current Account   £549 Dr (limit £600)

| Mike Noble | Current Account | £351 Cr |
| Sheila Noble | Current Account | £ 39 Cr |

If the borrowing on the joint account is in default, the bank has *three* rights of action because legal action could be taken against both of them jointly and as individuals to recover the full debt against the parties concerned.

Hence, the bank can sue:

Mr and Mrs Noble jointly	for £549
Mr Noble individually	for £549
Mrs Noble individually	for £549

but cannot recover more than 100p in the £!

Furthermore, the mandate gives the bank the *right of set-off* which means that the funds in the individual accounts can be taken in reduction of the joint borrowing.

Finance can be made available to consumers in a variety of forms for the purchase of cars and consumer durables such as televisions, videos, washing machines. Finance is also available for home improvements and for the purchase of the home itself. Where consumer durables are concerned, frequently the finance is offered at the point of sale. The benefit to the customer is that all the formalities can be completed on the spot; the drawback is that the customer could have shopped around for a cheaper deal if they had obtained the finance through their bank. So, what options are available? Before we explore the alternative ways in which we can offer financial help to our customers let us consider the increasingly popular use of credit scoring of propositions.

Credit scoring

From past experience banks have been able to define which types of customers are most likely to repay their borrowings. The characteristics of such customers can be defined and measured in terms of 'points'. Thus, the assessment of the credit risk of a potential lending can be made quickly and objectively by scoring the points given under certain headings:
- age
- occupation
- length of current employment
- number of years at present address

- type of accommodation
- marital status
- number of dependents
- previous track record.

A lending official will quickly vet the application form to check that the correct repayment term is quoted for the purpose stated in line with government and current bank policy, that the purpose is acceptable to the bank, the repayment amount is correct, and the proposed borrowing falls within the minimum and maximum criteria for the type of lending. The application is then processed via the computer. Suppose that the maximum score achievable is 500 and the bank decides that a score of about 350 qualifies, the computer files can be programmed accordingly. When the lending clerk feeds in the information on age, occupation, etc., the computer will produce an immediate response. The response could be one of three alternatives:

(a) give loan
(b) decline loan
(c) make further enquiries.

The first answer means that the score was above 350; the second answer, obviously below that score. The third answer is on the borderline, say 340 to 360, and the bank needs to make additional CAMPARI checks (*see* Chapter 6) before reaching a decision. It is always possible for the lending officer to override the computer response, e.g. the score may be below 350, but there is evidence of an existing well-run account. Alternatively, repayment of previous loans might have been unsatisfactory and, despite the 'give loan' response, the lending should be declined. Overrides should be strictly limited, however, to ensure that speed and objectivity are maintained. Credit scoring takes the hassle out of this type of personal loan lending and the job can be performed by relatively inexperienced lending officers.

Overdraft

This type of facility is for short-term purposes only, generally on an 'in case of need' basis. The account should fluctuate between debit and credit within an agreed overdraft limit, anticipating salary or other funds. The margin of interest charged is linked to base rate and depends upon the background history of the customer, the amount required and the purpose and term of the borrowing; it will usually be between 3 and 7% above base rate.

Interest is calculated daily and usually charged quarterly. The customer pays interest only on the fluctuating outstanding daily balance. In some cases a fee may be charged to cover the commitment of the funds by the bank even though the facility is never taken up. If Mary Smith wants to borrow £500 for 3 months to pay for her holiday pending the maturity proceeds of a life policy, then it would be likely that you would lend on overdraft. If Jack Jones wants to borrow £1000 for furniture, repayable over two years, then we are talking about a loan.

Loans

Ordinary loans are provided on a structured basis for longer-term borrowing. Interest rates are usually expressed as a margin over base, although sometimes a fixed rate is agreed. While technically the borrowing is repayable on demand only if we say so in the facility letter, a repayment programme is established over an agreed term. Interest is charged quarterly to current account except for specific types of loans where it is charged to the loan account itself, thus increasing the outstanding balance temporarily pending repayments which are inclusive of interest.

Loans to professionals

Recognising the importance of good introductions from professionals like solicitors, accountants and surveyors, banks now provide loans for their businesses at preferential rates. These tend to be long-term, mortgage-type loans linked to the professional's own private pension fund and are, for example, used to provide finance for the purchase of a partnership or expansion of the business premises. Quite often the loan, mostly secured, and usually by the assets purchased, will be granted on an endowment basis. Thus, interest and pension premiums are paid monthly with capital repaid at the end of the term when the policy matures. In such cases there is invariably a surplus available for the customer's own benefit.

Bridging loans for house moves/purchase for first-time buyers

If you or your family have ever been involved in buying or selling a property you will know how expensive it can be. Surveys need to be carried out, solicitors appointed to prepare the legal contracts, and there are estate agents' fees to pay. It can all be very stressful and difficult for a customer. A bank is often asked to lend at various stages of the transaction so that a purchaser can pay for the new home pending receipt of sale proceeds from the previous property and the new mortgage proceeds. This type of finance is usually provided through bridging loans to identify interest available for tax relief purposes. Arrangement fees are charged to cover the cost of administration in setting up the facility. One of the most important facts to establish is the true amount required for the bridge.

Case study
Mr and Mrs Neil Smith are selling their existing home for £55 000 with an outstanding mortgage of £30 000. They are buying a new house for £75 000 and have obtained a new mortgage of £55 000. How much can you, should you, lend? First of all, look at the available margins between the transactions and establish the source of payment of fees and expenses:

Selling old property for	£55 000	Purchasing new property for	£75 000
Less outstanding mortgage	£30 000	Mortgage obtained	£55 000
Net amount available	£25 000	Amount required	£20 000

In this case, if all goes according to plan, Mr and Mrs Smith will have £5000 to cover removal expenses, not much of a safety net for all the costs involved, so you would want to establish that they have personal resources available to meet those costs. The bridging loan could be provided in three ways:

Ten per cent deposit only
Providing contracts are exchanged for the sale, then the bank will be required only to assist the customer in meeting the required deposit on exchange of contracts for the purchase, unless there is a time difference on completions.

Repayment of existing mortgage
If contracts for the sale of the old property have not been exchanged, then you may be faced with having to lend for the repayment of the old mortgage to allow the mortgage company to provide the new finance, assuming it will be available at the date of purchase completion. Mortgage companies will not lend

simultaneously against two properties and will provide replacement mortgages only if greater than the existing one. In the Smith's case the bank will consider lifting the old mortgage to obtain a first legal charge on the existing property as security to cover the bridge for the new home. Hence, you would lend:

To clear the old mortgage		£30 000
Purchase price of new property	£75 000	
Less new mortgage	£55 000	
		£20 000
		£50 000

Repayment will come from the sale of the existing property at £55 000.

Lending total purchase cost
Sometimes it is not possible for a solicitor to arrange the simultaneous sale and purchase of your customers' property. Say that the Smiths have to complete the purchase on 1 June but will not complete the sale until 10 June. If the new mortgage is not available on that date the bank will be asked to lend the purchase price of £75 000 and repayment will come from the sale of the existing property, net £25 000 after repayment of the old mortgage, plus the new mortgage of £55 000. Some banks use a standard form of questionnaire to cover the details required to decide whether the proposition is realistic and the availability of a mortgage. Such an aide memoire would cover:

(a) That the properties have been realistically valued by the bank and are both worth their asking price. This is particularly important in the case of open-ended bridges (i.e. where contracts for the sale have not been exchanged) since interest charges will accrue and any available equity can be wiped out before repayment; indeed, there could be a residual loan outstanding.

(b) Confirmation of availability of the new mortgage and the customer's authority to forward the funds to the bank.

(c) Whether the bank will require the security of the deeds.

(d) The details of the solicitors acting who will be giving the bank their undertaking to hold the deeds to its order pending completion of the transactions and to forward necessary funds to repay the bank's borrowing. If the solicitors are not known to the bank then a status enquiry will be made.

It is necessary to obtain insurance cover on the purchased property at exchange of contracts, as the purchaser must still pay for it even if it is destroyed by a freak whirlwind before completion! For properties being built the bank would need to check the reliability of the builders in the event that stage payments will be required for the building programme.

Depending where you live there may be a buyer's or a seller's market for domestic properties. Customers very often overestimate the worth of the home they are selling and this may result in the property being overpriced and difficult to sell. This is particularly so in times of high interest rates when people are reluctant to move into more expensive properties. For this reason banks are reluctant to lend on an open-ended basis because payment could be protracted; a residual loan might be the consequence when the customer is forced to reduce the sale price in order to sell, especially after incurring bridging loan interest charges for a period.

Arrangement fees and other commission costs will be charged as soon as the transaction is completed. In the Smith case study, from the bank's point of view, the best option would have been to advance the 10% deposit only, which gives a reduced liability for the bank, an identifiable source of repayment, i.e. the sales/mortgage proceeds, and the likely timescale, since contracts for both properties will have been exchanged with completion probably within the month. The customers benefit also by paying less interest, although they will be committed to paying the new mortgage immediately. Another advantage to customers could be the eligibility of interest for tax relief if the new home is to be their main residence.

Bridge-overs for other purposes

Your customer might have an immediate problem if their washing machine has broken and they need to purchase a new one pending repayment from another source, the receipt of the sale proceeds of shares for example. In bridging for this consumer durable the customer has the advantage of purchasing the asset immediately and can shop around and bargain for a cash discount.

Personal loans

This type of borrowing is becoming more and more popular because, quite often, the customer does not even need to see the bank manager. Completion of a basic application form is all that is required for the loan to be credit scored. Hence, the borrowing is quick to arrange, simple to operate and can be profitable for the bank, which can 'fine-tune' its personal loan allocations more easily because the arrangement time is less. Funds can be used for all consumer durables and home improvements, a new fitted kitchen or central heating for instance. The borrowing is taken over a fixed period at a fixed rate of interest which does not change despite base rate changes during the life of the loan. Usually there are minimum and maximum age limits between 18 and 70, and the normal loan duration tends to be between 12 and 36 months. For home improvements it may be possible to borrow up to 5 years. Interest is calculated for the term and included as part of the monthly repayments of capital borrowed.

For example:

Capital borrowed	£1000
Interest payable	£ 198.83
	£1198.83 = 24 payments at £49.95

APR = 19.6%

This type of facility can be cheaper to the customer than point of sale finance and it gives them also the ability to shop around for cash discounts. The difference between this type of lending and hire purchase is that the goods purchased through a personal loan become the immediate property of the borrower. Goods bought via hire purchase belong to the finance company until the final payment has been made. Subject to satisfactory evidence of identification and a search at a credit reference agency which includes a confirmation of the address through the Voters Roll, these loans can also be made available to non-customers.

Because no security is required the rates charged reflect the higher risk; nevertheless customers find personal loans easy to operate because they know that all they have to do is to make a regular payment of an agreed amount over an agreed period with no hidden extras to pay.

Revolving credit accounts

By paying fixed monthly payments into a special account a customer has the option to withdraw by cheque up to 30 times the monthly payments. For instance, with effect from 1 January John Smith transfers £50 per month from his ordinary cheque account to his revolving credit account. In late March he issues a cheque for £1500 to pay for his holiday, leaving the account £1350 overdrawn. Regular payments continue and in July he withdraws another £350 to pay for his travel facilities, leaving the account £1500 overdrawn. Mr Smith enjoys the flexibility of spending any funds available whenever he chooses without having to ask the bank for a loan. Usually interest on the borrowing and charges for operating the account are debited to the revolving credit account unless the customer makes arrangements for them to be charged to his ordinary cheque account.

Budget accounts

Bills, like buses, have a habit of arriving three at a time. Budget accounts are separate nominated cheque accounts which spread the cost of household expenses over twelve months. The customer determines their annual bills like telephone, gas, electricity, car, rent, insurance, etc., then divides the total cost by twelve. A monthly standing order from the ordinary cheque account services the budget account. Then as bills arrive they can be paid immediately by drawing a cheque on the special account. If the account is in credit then some banks pay interest on the credit balance. Bank charges for interest on overdrafts and commission for operating the account are charged direct and the facility is reviewed annually with monthly transfers increased as appropriate.

Hire purchase

Hire purchase is an agreement to hire an item for a given period plus an option to purchase after the last instalment has been paid. Until the balance is paid the hire company owns the title to the goods. The Consumer Credit Act protects the customer from the unscrupulous dealer by preventing repossession of the goods once a certain percentage, currently one-third of the debt, has been repaid. These agreements must be in writing and certain information must be disclosed to the prospective borrower to provide them with certain legal rights, like the rules for calculating the amount payable if the individual wishes to make early repayment. Most banks now operate either their own finance house or have links with established firms which provide a range of hire purchase and other financial services for instalment credit.

Conditional sale

Although very similar to Hire Purchase, a conditional sale legally binds a customer to complete the payment and purchase of the goods involved in the underlying contract.

Credit sale

This is similar again to Hire Purchase, but in this instance a customer pays by instalments and has immediate title to the goods.

Credit cards

These pieces of plastic overcome most of the need for customers to carry cash or cheque books and can be used for the purchase of virtually all goods and services. Depending on the time in the month when the purchases are made the customer may have up to six weeks of free credit until repayment is required. The payment date and amount are shown on a monthly statement. Even then the whole balance need not be repaid but the amount left outstanding will be charged at a published interest rate. Advances of cash for various reasons may be taken up to an agreed credit limit. This type of revolving credit facility is usually more expensive than a personal loan. Some customers find themselves in difficulties by adopting a 'live now, pay later' approach to using their credit card. They keep no proper tally of the costs of their purchases and receive a nasty shock when the monthly statement arrives. Not only does a bank receive interest on the amounts advanced to the customer, they also receive a commission from the merchants accepting the credit card in payment for goods and services. So, from a bank's point of view, the service can be a most profitable one.

Mortgage schemes

Many banks are now in direct competition with building societies in the provision of long-term finance for the purchase of homes. A banker's philosophy is to 'borrow long term, lend short term'. Consequently, unlike the usual type of bank borrowing repayable on demand, bankers find it difficult to cover long-term money up to 25 years when credit balances belonging to their other customers are repayable on demand – hence 'borrowing short, lending long'. Economically, borrowing at money market rates to cover that gap is expensive and for that reason the banks limit their exposure to this type of lending. There are many opportunities for cross-selling, however; e.g. personal loans for carpets, furniture, review of wills and trusts, extra accounts, all of which provide an incentive for banks to lend to this sector. Generally, a bank will lend up to three times an individual's salary up to a maximum of 80% of the valuation of the property concerned. First-time buyers may be offered a mortgage of the purchase price up to 100% under certain circumstances. Mortgages can be granted either on a monthly repayment basis inclusive of interest and principal over an agreed term, or linked to an endowment assurance policy where the monthly payments cover the assurance premium and interest only; the capital is repaid from the maturity funds of the assurance policy after the agreed term. Given the long-term nature of this type of lending, security is normally taken in the form of the property being charged and the assurance policy being assigned to the bank. Apart from the disadvantage of the long-term nature of the borrowing, it is profitable and safe for a banker.

Probate lending

When a customer dies and there is inheritance tax to be paid on the estate, the Inland Revenue will not allow probate – the legal authority to deal with the assets of the estate – to be granted until the tax has been paid. Consequently, the executors, or administrators if there is no will, are unable to perform their duty in collecting and distributing the net assets of the deceased in the meantime.

Bank help is normally provided to meet the tax liability by way of a special probate advance on loan account. A copy of the death certificate would need to be obtained from the representative of the deceased and status enquiries made on them if they are not known. Personal representatives are personally liable for any borrowing in this connection. An executors' or administrators' account should be opened for all the entries to be passed which specifically relate to the collection and distribution of the estate. Generally this type of lending is safe, profitable and liquid providing that the assets in the estate are not all represented by property which will take time to sell. As soon as funds flow from collecting the sale proceeds of the assets, the borrowing can be repaid.

Student accounts

Looking to the future, banks will want to be as helpful as possible to students to encourage them still to maintain their account when they progress into their professional careers. Incentive packages of free gifts are provided to attract accounts which will be given special services:

- Free banking up to an overdraft limit.
- Standard overdraft limit at preferential rates.
- Credit card with a small credit limit.
- Bankers cheque guarantee card.

Students will have little or no track record of dealings with the bank and you may not even have any family connections to provide you with much information about their background. Do not develop prejudices by hearing stories from colleagues about bad experiences with one or two students, however. It does not mean that all such accounts are troublesome and, indeed, these customers could become very profitable to the bank in the future. Student business officers based at branches on or near college, polytechnic or university campus offer financial assistance to students.

Minors

The Infants' Relief Act 1874 rendered absolutely void all contracts entered into by minors for the repayment of money lent. This Act was repealed by the Minors' Contracts Act 1987. Such contracts are now merely unenforceable, i.e. court action cannot be taken to recover the debt. More importantly, Section 2 of the Act provides that if the minor's debt is guaranteed 'the guarantee shall not for that reason alone be unenforceable against the guarantor'. Most banks' forms of guarantee incorporate an 'indemnity' clause which means that the guarantor will promise to pay whether or not the principal debtor is liable. Such a clause is no longer necessary as far as a minor is concerned. Since the wording in the guarantee form is likely to remain, however, the bank will have the benefit of a 'belt and braces' cover. In the event that a bank is asked to lend money to a person aged under 18, then the lending officer might wish to take a guarantee from a parent who could be asked for repayment in the event of default by the minor.

Summary

Alternatives for personal borrowers

Type	Interest rate link	Repayment programme	Description/purpose
Overdraft	Usually margin 3–7% above base rate, charged quarterly on outstanding daily balance.	Fully fluctuating within agreed limit.	In case of need facility taken on normal cheque account.
Ordinary loan	Usually linked to fixed or fluctuating base rate as above. Margin depends on risk which can be diminished by security. Interest charged quarterly to current account.	Regular agreed reductions within agreed term up to 3 years (or 5 years for home improvements).	Short to medium-term finance for customers where security is available and/or personal loan product deemed inappropriate.
Budget	Fixed rate, reviewed annually. Debit interest charged quarterly direct to account.	Fixed monthly payment at 1/12th of annual amount borrowed.	Payment of annual household bills through regular monthly payments on a special cheque account (NB interest may be given on credit balances).
Revolving credit	As above	Fixed monthly payment.	Revolving credit facility on a special cheque account.

Type	Interest rate link	Repayment programme	Description/purpose
Credit card	Fixed published monthly rate paid on outstanding balance after period of grace for repayment.	Minimum amount payable monthly by date stipulated on statement.	Plastic card-based transactions facility with extended credit option.
Personal loan	Fixed rate, charged monthly.	Monthly, inclusive of interest and capital within agreed term (6 months–5 years).	Fixed term, fixed rate, unsecured loan for consumer purchases and other term borrowing needs.
HP	Fixed rate, charged monthly.	As above	Fixed term, fixed rate, unsecured loan for consumer purchases.
Bridging loan	Standard margin above base normally 3–4%. Payable in lump sum at end of borrowing.	Usually one capital repayment from an agreed source.	Temporary finance to cover purchase of assets pending income from another source. Sometimes secured.
Mortgage scheme	Fixed rate, reviewed following base rate changes. Debited quarterly.	Monthly inclusive of interest and capital or if endowment linked inclusive of interest and assurance premium with capital paid at maturity of policy.	Term loan for purchase, construction or improvement of UK residential property – can be linked to personal pension or endowment.

Self-assessment questions

1 A customer asks the bank to lend towards the cost of a hi-fi unit costing £1200. The customer has £200 of his own money and the bank agrees to the proposition which will be made available most probably through:
  (a) Budget account
  (b) Overdraft
  (c) Personal loan
  (d) Revolving credit account.

2 Customers use budget accounts for:
  (a) Making regular monthly payments to meet mortgage, instore card accounts, etc.
  (b) Regular savings
  (c) Consumer durable purchases
  (d) Spreading the cost of household bills over 12 months.

3 Funds lent to pay inheritance tax are granted through:
  (a) Bridge-over account
  (b) Probate advance
  (c) Personal loan
  (d) Medium-term loan.

4 An open-ended property bridging advance is where:
  (a) Contracts for the sale have not been exchanged
  (b) Contracts for the sale have been exchanged
  (c) Completion of the sale is effected before the purchase
  (d) The customer decides whether to take the borrowing.

5 Balances on credit card accounts must be paid for:
  (a) At the time of purchase of the underlying goods
  (b) Within 14 days of purchase
  (c) At a fixed monthly repayment rate
  (d) Within the date specified on the monthly statement.

8
Other borrowers

Objectives

After studying this chapter you should be able to:

1 explain the particular application of the canons of lending to appropriate types of borrowing customers;
2 identify the special considerations applicable for non-personal customers when lending for:
- buying a business
- borrowing for trading purposes
- borrowing for capital expenditure;
3 decide whether lending should be by overdraft or loan;
4 discuss the most important clauses and articles contained in a company's memorandum and articles of association as far as they affect a lending banker.

Introduction

The relationship between a bank and its customer is one of debtor and creditor. When the customer has a credit balance on their account they are the creditor. The relationship is reversed when the bank lends money to its customer by overdraft or loan. Apart from personal borrowers there are certain special considerations which need to be applied to different types of borrowers – clubs, associations, trustees, sole traders, partnerships. and companies. We do not intend you to become a legal expert in the workings of the various Companies Acts. All that you need to know is which section of the current Companies Act affects the lending banker and what effect it has on the proposition. You must know also the difference between a sole trader, a partnership and a company as far as it affects you, the lending banker.

'Look, if you're sure that all club members have to be liable for this loan, Mr Mote, it will probably be about three weeks before we can let you have the money.'

Clubs, associations, societies

With the exception of incorporated bodies, these types of clubs, associations and societies are run by committees which normally abide by a set of rules. However, the 'business' itself is not a legal entity. For the banker this means that the club, etc., has no contractual powers and cannot be sued for its debts. Accordingly, if you are approached to lend money to such a body you will find that the club itself owns no property and its members cannot be held personally liable for debts. So, should you lend? First, you will need to check the rules to establish that the club or society is allowed such borrowings. If you can be assured that the lending is to be of very short duration only, then you may decide – subject to the usual canons of lending – that there is no undue risk involved in repayment. However, if the borrowing was to be of a longer-term nature, say, to purchase a capital asset, then you will need the personal guarantees of officers of the club, people capable of repaying the borrowing and who will assume the responsibility of the debt if the club does not repay. In addition, you must seek legal advice to check the extent of the officers' powers for such an agreement. Any property purchased would need to be held by trustees. In the event that you do agree to lend,

then a separate account must be opened to identify the extent
of the liability, with set arrangements made for repayment.

Trustees

In your personal capacity, if you should be lucky enough to benefit
under the terms of a trust drawn up in your favour, the property
held for you as beneficiary will be managed by trustees. Such
trustees cannot delegate their powers and they have limited
borrowing powers conferred upon them under the Trustee Act
1925. Before a bank lends to trustees it will need to be assured
that the trust deed empowers them to borrow and, if necessary,
to give security. Trustees have *no* implied powers to charge trust
property unless:

(a) The trust deed gives permission.
(b) The charge over security is so that the trustees may exercise
their power (under the Trustee Act 1925, s. 16) to pay or apply
capital money for a specific purpose.
(c) The loan is for a specific reason, e.g. to make improvements
to the trust property: (Settled Land Act 1925, s. 71).
(d) The beneficiaries give permission.

All the trustees will need to enter into the agreement for facilities
with the bank. A separate account must always be used for the
operation of the trust fund borrowing and a mandate obtained
for *joint and several liability*. Trustees are *personally* liable for
any borrowing. Lendings should be made by way of a loan
account.

Sole traders

Sole traders are in business for their own personal benefit. They
are personally liable for any business debts and, if they cannot
pay, could be made bankrupt by their creditors. They may be
shopkeepers, like newsagents or grocery stores; they may
manufacture items on a small scale – a 'cottage industry'; or they
may provide a service, like cleaning windows or being one of the
growing number of management consultants. When we lend to
this type of customer its purpose usually falls into one of three
categories:

(a) Help in buying the business.

(b) Support for working capital for trading.

(c) Provision of finance towards the capital cost of repairs, refurbishments, or purchase of new fixed assets.

Buying the business

It is unusual for a bank to finance the total cost of the purchase of a business; if it did so, the bank could be construed as owning it! The customer should, in theory, invest more than 50% of the cost from their own sources. One question which must be asked right away: 'Why is the vendor selling the business?' Do they know something your customer does not know which will have an adverse effect on trade, or is it a genuine move? Before discussing the proposition in detail, you will want to satisfy yourself that your customer has the necessary ability and drive, and sufficient knowledge of the business to be able to make it a success.

What is the customer actually buying? If it involves freehold or leasehold property you would want a representative of the bank to see and value it. If it involves a lease of short term, then it may not be worth much as bank security. However, there are some special cases, for instance a fish shop which attracts a very large 'goodwill' element because permission from local councils to operate such businesses are hard to come by. A lease could be worth very little if the business failed and the customer is forced to go elsewhere. Stock may be included as part of the purchase price, in which case your customer will need to identify how saleable it will be, or whether more borrowing may be necessary to purchase more stock. The condition of the fixtures and fittings will need also to be taken into account – how long will they last before needing replacement?

Whenever you appraise a lending proposition, the first considerations are always the basic canons of good lending, as highlighted in Chapters 6 and 7. In the case of a business, there are further enquiries you need to make to assess the safety, liquidity and profitability of the proposition. Often your ability to make that assessment realistically is hampered by the lack of background information provided by the customer. You may have heard other bankers use the expression 'back of a fag packet', which means that the information they received could all have been written on a cigarette carton! For this reason, many banks now provide business customers with a Business Plan check list to help them to formulate the information on which a reasoned decision can be made by the bank. A sample of such a plan is shown at Fig. 8.1. The completed Business Plan document can then form the basis of a discussion between you and the customer, when you can satisfy yourself that, for example, the premises, plant and equipment are adequate and necessary for the business. You can test the assumptions on which sales turnover, pricing and profitability have been projected in the light of your own knowledge of the area.

If the customer is buying an existing business there will be recent VAT returns from which you can check the present position. The bank statements and trading accounts of the previous owner should highlight the level of turnover and profit being earned, and your customer can explain to you their strategy for improving the level of income to help service the requested loan. In projecting future income your customer must identify who are the business's competitors, and whether or not the customer is likely to settle down and be accepted by the local community. The area in which the business is situated may also be an important factor. Furthermore, the seasonality of income must be considered. If your customer is selling greengrocery then the income will be regular and mostly for cash. On the other hand, a business manufacturing swimwear will have a quite different cash flow base.

Is your customer going to be running the business personally, or will they need to employ staff, another cost to consider? Having established what the customer is getting for their money, you can then help them to calculate whether the funds requested from the bank, plus their own stake, will be sufficient to launch the business. The information contained in the Business Plan can help you to carry out a simple break-even analysis, using the formula:

$$\text{Break-even} = \frac{\text{Fixed cost} \times \text{Sales}}{\text{Contribution (i.e. Sales less variable costs)}}$$

$$\text{say} = \pounds \frac{15\,000 \times 40\,000}{40\,000 - 20\,000}$$

$$= \pounds 30\,000$$

Determining which are fixed and which are variable costs depends on the type of business. Usually, materials consumed are variable and most overhead costs (like rent, heat) are fixed. In some businesses, like banking, the labour force is considered a *fixed*

YOUR BUSINESS PLAN

Your bank manager is unlikely to lend you much money if you don't have sensible plans.

Once you've drawn up a business plan, you'll realise why it's so useful and how valuable it is in helping you make decisions. That's your most important task of all.

Believe it or not you already have a business plan. It's just a question of writing it down and being as specific as you can.

Here are the ingredients of a typical plan:

A business plan check list

Objectives:
What are your personal objectives?
What are your business objectives?
Are they specific?
Have you thought of the consequences?

The business:
History if already established.
Accounts for previous years trading.
Present financial position.

Management:
Experience of proprietors/managers.
Responsibilities of managers.
Is the team complete or is further recruitment necessary?

Market:
How large is it?
Is market research possible/available?
What is the competition?
What advantages do competitors have?
What advantages does your product/service have?
What are the distribution channels?
What advertising or marketing will you need?

Products:
Do they meet customers needs?
Have they been tested including production methods?
How have costs been calculated?

Pricing:
How have prices been arrived at?
Are they competitive?

Suppliers:
Are adequate supplies available?
Is quality known to be acceptable?
What credit is available?

Physical resources:
What premises are available?
Are they adequate?
What is the cost?
What machinery/vehicles are required?
What is the cost?
How are they to be financed?

Personnel:
How many will be needed?
What training will be required?

Profit and cash forecasts:
Are they available?
Are the assumptions valid and clearly stated?
What are the risks?
Can the business survive if it sells 20/40% less than planned?

Outside finance required:
What does the business need:
for fixed assets?
for working capital?
How long is it required for?
What is the programme for repayment?
Have you produced a monthly cash plan for the first year?
What cash projections are there after the first year?

Fig. 8.1

cost because staff is retained even though turnover falls (if in doubt, treat staff as a fixed cost). So, if this customer needs sales of £30 000 to break even, how does this match up with their Business Plan?

Armed with all this information you can then check that the amount requested by your customer appears reasonable and realistic for the purpose required. You can also ask some 'What if . . .?' questions to test for flexibility if there is a potential of future strain against the limit. Examples might be 'What if . . . your new suppliers won't give you 30 days' credit?' or 'What if . . . your competitors start undercutting your prices?'. As the lending banker you can then help your customer to assess what action they would need to take in such an event and how it might affect the bank account.

If you decide that the proposition is worthy of bank assistance, you may feel happier if some form of security is obtained as 'insurance' for the lending. The form it takes depends on the assets being purchased and their value. During your discussion you may be able to help satisfy some of your customer's other business needs, like property and stock insurance, loss of earnings insurance, and life cover. If the business will be providing credit it may need to be registered under the Consumer Credit Act 1974.

Working capital for trading purposes

If the business is likely to keep high stocks, like a furniture company, or a large volume of debtors in monetary terms, like a builder, then the bank may be asked to finance those assets until they turn into cash, i.e. when an item is sold and the debtor pays. You must be careful, however, that you are not being asked to finance losses. You may be able to highlight these through a change in the run of the bank account, pending receipt of up-to-date trading accounts. Lending in order to finance working capital should, by its nature, be for short term only and, in the customer's best interest as well as the bank's, it will be wise to monitor such borrowings to ensure that they are repaid within the agreed timescale.

Capital expenditure

Whilst lending to finance working capital is expected to be short term only, advancing sums for capital expenditure can sometimes be very protracted. Say, for instance, that your customer, Mr

Graham, trading as Graham's Newsagents, wants to borrow to help him to extend his shop and buy new shelving and display stands. It is quite likely that trade will be adversely affected while the work is being undertaken, if the shop has to be closed for any length of time. The newly furbished shop will not necessarily attract new or increased business immediately, if at all. So, where is the money to come from to repay the loan for all this work that has been carried out? The business may not make sufficient profits to service such a repayment programme. Ensure that the usual canons of lending are applied in every case.

Business lending

Quite often these days a bank can offer simple, packaged 'off-the-shelf' loans of up to £15 000 over five years which operate rather like personal loans. The business customer completes an application form, agrees with the bank whether the life insurance cover option should be taken and, if sanctioned, receives the funds immediately. Repayment is made at regular monthly intervals inclusive of interest over the life of the loan. In the case of a new business, in particular, there is sometimes an opportunity of a capital repayment holiday for up to, say, six months. This means that the customer pays only the regular interest payments on the loan during that initial period, easing their cash flow.

Packages for large amounts are also available for periods up to 25 years. The main point to consider is that these types of loans for the purchase of capital items – fixed assets – will, by their nature, take time to repay from the profits generated by the business.

Business loans

Although most banks reserve the right to obtain repayment of loans 'on demand', in practice there is an agreement to repay over a period of time – a term. Depending on the expected life of the asset being purchased, some customers may wish to borrow over a medium term, say 1 to 7 years, or long term, say 8 to 25 years. One of the criteria for you as the banker to consider is whether sufficient profits can be generated by the newly purchased asset so that it pays for itself during the term of the lending. Fixed rates are sometimes negotiated for longer-term lending, with agreed reviews – known as *roll overs*. These are related to the London Inter-Bank Offered Rate (LIBOR) which can be more cost effective, both for the banker and customer, than an agreed margin over base rate.

Business overdraft

Overdrafts are a banker's 'bread and butter' in terms of lending. They are of short-term duration, with reviews agreed for periods up to 12 months. The account is expected to swing regularly between the agreed overdraft limit and a credit balance, to finance normal trading, and delays between paying creditors and receiving income from debtors. The borrowing is effectively repaid time after time, on each occasion that the account reverts to credit. However, you will want to keep an eye on such lendings to check that they are fluctuating as expected, and that there is no undue pressure against the limit.

Overall, you would expect the sole trader's objectives to be set at a *high* but *achievable* level, *appropriate* for the business and *flexible* to meet the changing needs of the market place.

Partnerships

The professionals – dentists, medical practitioners, solicitors, accountants, architects, etc. – are usually borrowers of the highest integrity and can be relied upon to honour their commitments. Furthermore, they provide a ready source of introductions to other potential and profitable customers within the local business community. Lending to partnerships is normally either for financing a new partner to purchase a share in the business; or for the business itself to purchase capital items, like computers and cars; or for short-term overdrafts in anticipation of fee income, etc.

Rarely are there *partnership* assets available as security but, providing that the bank has obtained the usual joint and several liability signature mandates by the partners themselves, it may decide to obtain charges over the partners' personal assets. You might decide, however, that the financial standing of one or more partners is so undoubted that you would not consider seeking security.

Nowadays, one of the most tax-efficient ways that professionals seek to borrow is via a personal pension plan linked scheme. The individual contracts to cover interest and pension premiums during the life of the loan, with repayment of the capital made upon maturity of the pension plan at retirement. Pension premiums attract tax relief at the individual's highest rate of tax and contributions grow in a fund exempt of tax. After repayment of the loan on retirement, the balance can be used to purchase an annuity for future pension payments. Although of a long-term nature, this type of borrowing sometimes *may* be granted on an unsecured basis. However, the bank will no doubt want life cover on the borrower and would prefer some sort of security if available.

In a professional business the audited accounts may not justify the amount of the borrowing requested, particularly when the main asset is goodwill. So you will have to satisfy yourself that the earning capacity of the business is sufficient to repay the borrowing within an agreed period of time.

Companies

A company is a body incorporated under one of the Companies Acts. On incorporation a company becomes an entirely separate legal entity from the individuals who set it up. Therefore, in its own name, a company can sue or be sued, make contracts through its agents, own and dispose of property in the same manner as an ordinary individual, and trade within its powers like an ordinary individual. So, if an individual must make a certain contract by deed, i.e. a sealed document, then so must the company. If the contract is to be in writing, then the same is the case for the company *unless* the memorandum and articles of association state that the document must be sealed. If an individual can contract orally, then so can a company, again *unless* the memorandum and articles of association state otherwise (see below).

Opening the account

It may be considered necessary to take up references if the directors are not known to the bank. A resolution appointing the bank as banker to the company should be passed by the directors and a company mandate stating the signing authorities of the parties involved must be completed. A certificate of incorporation – the company's birth certificate confirming its legal entity – must be shown to the bank. You will want to obtain for perusal and retention a copy of the company's memorandum and articles of association. So, what are these?

Memorandum of association
This document represents a permanent record of the objects and powers of the company and must contain a certain limited amount of information:

- full name of the company
- in which country the company is registered
- the objects of the company
- the limit of liability of its members
- details of capital and the shares breakdown

Articles of association
These contain the rules and regulations, formulated by the shareholders, which govern the *internal* procedures of the company and the powers of its directors and officers. There is one rule of 'ostensible authority', which means that persons dealing with a company are not bound to be concerned with the regular observance of internal company formalities and are protected, providing that:

(a) the person seeking to rely on the rule does not know that matters relating to internal management have not been complied with;
(b) the document on which the person relies is not a forgery;
(c) representatives of the company do not exceed their apparent authority.

This rule was stated in *Royal British Bank* v *Turquand* (1856) where the company's articles of association authorised the company's directors to borrow money and to issue debentures as security, providing the company in general meeting passed an appropriate resolution. No such resolution was passed, but the directors nevertheless borrowed from their bankers, giving a debenture as security. In the resulting action brought by the bank, the lack of the company's resolution was set up as a reason for holding the debenture invalid, but it was held that the debenture was binding on the company and that the bank was entitled to assume that the required resolution had in fact been passed.

As far as the bank is concerned you will be protected, providing that you can show that you relied upon your knowledge that a particular transaction was *not* outside the actual or ostensible authority of a director or officer of the company who authorised or carried out the transaction – so ensure that you have *carefully perused* the memorandum and articles of association.

Statutory restrictions

A company is registered under whichever of the Companies Acts – 1862, 1929, 1948 or 1985 – immediately preceded its incorporation. For *disciplinary control* purposes, however, companies are governed by the Companies Act 1985, administered by the Department of Trade.

Certain transactions between a company and its shareholders are subject to statutory restrictions, designed to protect the remaining shareholders and creditors. Such transactions fall under three headings:

1 Purchase by a company of its own shares: 1985 Act, s. 143 and ss. 159–177.
2 Assistance given by a company for the purchase of its own shares by a third party: ss. 151–8.
3 Loans to directors: ss. 330–44.

By their very nature the statutory restrictions are complex. If you were approached by a customer in one of these circumstances, then you would wish to seek the guidance of your legal department before proceeding.

Objects clause

If you propose lending money to a company, you must first check the objects clause of the memorandum of association to ensure that the purpose for which the money is required is covered in that clause. If you lend for any transaction not covered, then the loan will be null and void against a liquidator or creditor of the company and you may not be able to recover the funds; this type of borrowing is called *ultra vires*. A well-known case in point was *Introductions Limited* v *National Provincial Bank* (1968), where the facts were:

A company formed to provide information and facilities for visitors to the Festival of Britain 1951, later engaged, as a sole activity, in pig breeding, for which purpose it borrowed money from a bank under a debenture. Reliance was placed on the power to borrow by the issue of debentures which was expressly given in the company's objects clause. The company was compulsorily wound up in 1965 with assets of £100 000 and liabilities of £2 million. The court held that borrowing was not a separate object of the company and borrowing was only authorised for the legitimate purposes of the company within the objects stated. It could not be used for pig breeding purposes since this was ultra vires.

Had the National Provincial Bank insisted that the company regularised its position by amending the objects clause, then it would not have lost the case – and £50 000! We understand, however, that the *ultra vires* rule is likely to be abolished over the next year or so. This may result in a company being bound by any contract it can legally and physically perform.

Borrowing powers

When a company customer requests financial help from its bank there are certain procedures and checks you must carry out in addition to the normal principles of CAMPARI before advancing any funds. First, what is the purpose of the advance? You must examine the *objects clause* of the memorandum to check that the borrowing will be *intra vires* – that is that the purpose is contained therein. The objects clause may include details of the power of the company to borrow money. If no such information is found there is an implied power to borrow in the case of a *trading* company for any monies reasonable and necessary for carrying out the company's objects. Unless stated to the contrary, the power to borrow incorporates an implied power to give security. A non-trading company has no such implied powers. Second, you will need to scrutinise the articles of association to check the borrowing powers of the directors. Usually such articles include the adoption of a model set of articles known as 'Table A', relevant to most companies. The clause in Table A will state the extent to which, and the methods by which, the directors may exercise the company's powers. Alternatively, there may be a specific borrowing clause. If there is neither set of information, then the directors' powers will be the same as the company's powers.

Sad to say, there are occasions when the bank lends to a company *intra vires*, but the company then uses the money for a purpose *outside* its objects. As a banker, you have a right to expect that the directors will work within their implied warranty of authority on behalf of the company. If you should see cheques drawn on the company's overdrawn account which seem to be for a purpose other than the reasons lent, then you would be put on enquiry. There is case law which gives protection to a banker, *Re David Payne and Co Ltd* (1904), which held that 'there is no duty on the lender to check the use of the monies and that the bank can, therefore, rely on the original information as to the purpose of the borrowing'. It just shows, though, how careful you must be.

Extracts from the relevant Table A of the Companies Acts 1929, 1948 and 1985 are shown in Fig. 8.2. You will need to remember that the directors' powers can never exceed that of the company.

Interested directors

Whenever first or third party security, or a guarantee (*see* Chapter 9) is taken from a company, you must decide whether such an action is likely to place one or more of the directors in a more favourable personal financial position. For example, say that John Jones personally guarantees the £15 000 overdraft limit of Cane Makers Ltd, and the bank subsequently obtains a legal charge on the company's own leasehold premises, worth £25 000. If the bank seeks repayment it will look first to Cane Makers Ltd and have recourse to the leasehold security before looking to John Jones as a third party to honour his guarantee liability. In such a case, Mr Jones is an 'interested director' in the transaction. Before lending in such circumstances, you must check the articles of association to establish the company's rules and to overcome the problems experienced in *Victors Ltd* v *Linguard* (1927). In this case, one of the articles stated that no director should vote on a matter in which he had a personal interest. Despite the fact that the directors had previously given guarantees to secure the company's overdraft, the bank accepted without enquiry their resolution to create a debenture and affix the company seal to the form of charge. It was held that the bank knew too much of the circumstances of the issue for it to argue that it assumed that the seal had been properly affixed under appropriate authority, and the courts held that the debenture was a nullity. So always check the appropriate article to find out the requirements for declaring interest by the directors. If the articles do not give authority for such a transaction, then the shareholders will need to give prior approval in general meeting. One important point to remember is that, if guarantees are given by the directors *at the same time* as security is given by the company itself, then the

Borrowing by a company

Extract from Table 'A' of the Companies Act 1929

Article 69. The amount for the time being remaining undischarged of moneys borrowed or raised by the directors for the purpose of the company (otherwise than by the issue of share capital) *shall not at any time exceed the issued share capital* of the company *without the sanction of the company in general meeting.*

Extract from Table 'A' of the Companies Act 1948

Article 79. The directors may exercise all the powers of the company to borrow money, and to mortgage or charge its undertaking, property and uncalled capital, or any part thereof and, 'subject to Section 14 of the Companies Act 1980', to issue debentures, debenture stock, and other securities, whether outright or as security for any debt, liability or obligation of the company or of any third party:

Provided that the amount for the time being remaining undischarged of moneys borrowed or secured by the directors as aforesaid (apart from temporary loans obtained from the company's bankers in the ordinary course of business) *shall not* at any time, without the previous sanction of the company in general meeting, *exceed* the nominal amount of the *share capital* of the company for the time being *issued*, but nevertheless no lender or other person dealing with the company shall be concerned to see or inquire whether this limit is observed. No debt incurred or security given in excess of such limit shall be invalid or ineffectual except in the case of *express notice* to the lender or the recipient of the security at the time when the debt was incurred or security given that the limit hereby imposed had been or was thereby exceeded.

Extract from Table 'A' of the Companies Act 1985

Article 70. Subject to the provisions of the Act, the memorandum and the articles, and to any directions given by special resolution, *the business of the company shall be managed by the directors who may exercise all the powers of the company.*

Date of incorporation	Limitations
For companies incorporated:	
prior to 1.10.1906, Table 'A' of the Companies Act 1862 applies	no limit
from 1.10.1906 and prior to 1.4.1909, the 1906 Table 'A' issued under an order of the Board of Trade applies (Article 73)	
from 1.4.1909 and prior to 1.11.1929, Table 'A' of the 1908 Consolidation Act applies (Article 73)	limited to issued share capital
from 1.11.1929 and prior to 1.7.1948, Table 'A' of the 1929 Companies Act applies (Article 69)	
from 1.7.1948 and prior to 1.7.1985, Table 'A' (Article 79) of the 1948 Act applies	limited to issued share capital but with additional restrictions re third party liabilities
from 1.7.1985, Table 'A' (Article 70) of the 1985 Act applies	same powers as the company

Fig. 8.2

'interested directors' situation does not apply because both transactions are part of the same agreement.

Guarantee given by a company

The power to give a guarantee must be expressly provided in the company's memorandum of association. Any charge on security to secure the liability of a third party is equivalent to a guarantee. Such guarantees must be signed on behalf of the company, and a certified copy of the resolution authorising the signing must be kept with the charge form. The memorandum or articles of association may require that the guarantee is to be given by deed. There must *always* be *consideration* for giving a guarantee; that is, the guaranteeing company must receive benefit in some way by its action. You may be safe in assuming that, when a parent company guarantees a subsidiary, that special relationship proves some benefit to the parent in pursuance of its own objects. However, if it were the subsidiary guaranteeing the parent, then you cannot assume that such benefit exists and you are put on enquiry.

Searching at the Companies Registry

Having established that the purpose of the advance is within the authorised objects of the company and the company has the power to borrow, you will need to make a search at the Companies Registry to find out the extent to which the company's assets are already subject to any registered charges. The decision to search may be made whether or not you are taking security to support a lending.

Registration of a charge

Most types of charges over security require registration within 21 days of their creation. Failure to do so would render the charge void. Under the Companies Act 1985 s. 395, a liquidator or any other creditor of the company may turn aside such a voidable charge. It does not, however, preclude repayment by the company itself, although the debt is deemed to be unsecured.

Certain types of charges do not have to be registered, for example, stocks and shares, and life policies. (*See* Chapter 9 for more detailed information.) The table (Fig. 8.3) highlights the main points.

Companies: borrowing and the giving of security

	Presently authorised	*Proposed*
Purpose		Consider in terms of length of time, source of repayment, security offered, amount required, to determine loan or overdraft.
Objects	Per **memorandum of association.** Must give *specific* cover.	Special resolution to change objects if different.
Powers of company	Per **memorandum of association.** If silent and trading company – implied power to borrow and give security. Care re guarantees (objects, power, benefit and amount).	Include all existing borrowing. If ultra vires company, special resolution required to amend memorandum. Cannot be ratified.
Powers of directors	Refer to **Articles:** Relevant Table A applies unless deleted or amended. If deleted and no further mention then same as company.	Include all existing borrowing. If ultra vires directors, (a) Special resolution required to amend articles or (b) Ordinary resolution to authorise specific borrowing.
Interested directors	Check **Articles:** Three options: (a) Quorum may include interested directors. (b) Quorum may have to be made up of disinterested directors. (c) Shareholders resolution required if articles silent or there are insufficient disinterested directors.	Consider re existing/proposed security. Care re Substantial Property Transaction.

	Presently authorised	*Proposed*
Loans to directors	**Companies Act 1985** Section 330 prohibition (possible relief of s. 332–344).	Must be strictly in accordance with provisions laid down by statute.
Purchase of own shares	**Companies Act 1985** Section 143 prohibition (possible relief of s. 143 and s. 159–177).	
Assistance for purchase of own shares by a third party	**Companies Act 1985** Section 151 prohibition (possible relief of s. 153–158).	
Consumer Credit Act	Strictly per **Consumer Credit Act.**	Check requirement for Consumer Credit Act licence.

Fig. 8.3

Summary

1   When lending to a small business or to a company you can decide whether to lend by overdraft or loan if you determine the purpose for which the borrowing is required:

- buying a business
- trading
- working capital purposes
- captial expenditure

2   When lending to a company you must read the important clauses covering the purpose and borrowing powers of the company and its officers – which depend on the particular Companies Act preceding the date of incorporation.

The final Figure 8.4 outlines the options for overdraft or loan, the mandate requirements and liability of the officers concerned.

Type of account	Overdraft	Loan	Mandate	Liability
Clubs, Associations	Not recommended	Yes, subject to rules	Officers to sign in accordance with set of rules	Club has no contractual powers Personal guarantees of officers required for long-term lendings
Trustees	No	Yes, subject to provision of Trust	Joint and several	Trustees personally liable
Sole traders	Yes	Yes	Single signature of proprietor or joint and several signatures if more than one (NB Some traders may want *both* to sign)	Personally liable
Partnerships	Yes	Yes	As for sole traders (NB Sometimes partners may want a minimum number to sign for items above a certain amount)	As above
Companies	Yes	Yes	Resolution passed by directors stating signing authorities of the officers	Company is a separate legal entity Directors can be sued when in breach of personal powers under Companies Act

Fig. 8.4

Self-assessment questions

1 An unincorporated club:
 (a) Has a separate legal identity
 (b) Has contractual powers
 (c) Is subject to a set of rules
 (d) Can be sued for its debts.

2 Trustees:
 (a) Have unlimited borrowing powers
 (b) Are personally liable for any borrowings
 (c) Are governed by a set of rules
 (d) Have implied powers to charge trust property.

3 A sole trader needs to borrow for working capital purposes to:
 (a) Finance high stocks
 (b) Purchase capital assets
 (c) Finance creditors
 (d) Sell for cash.

4 Lendings to partnerships are normally secured by assets belonging to:
 (a) The partnership
 (b) Individual partners
 (c) All partners jointly
 (d) The senior partner.

5 A company's birth certificate is the:
 (a) Memorandum of association
 (b) Articles of association
 (c) Trading certificate
 (d) Certificate of incorporation.

6 Before a bank lends money to a company it needs to check that the purpose for which the money is required is covered in the:
 (a) Articles of association
 (b) Table A
 (c) Objects clause
 (d) Borrowing powers clause.

7 When a company gives security to the bank to cover its borrowing a director is said to be 'interested' in the transaction when he:
 (a) Increases his personal guarantee at the same time
 (b) Has not previously given, and does not intend to give a personal guarantee

(c) Agrees to give his personal guarantee some time in the future

(d) Leaves his personal guarantee in place.

8 A legal charge of a company's assets needs registering within:

(a) 7 days

(b) 21 days

(c) 14 days

(d) 28 days.

9 Break-even can be calculated by the equation:

(a) $\dfrac{\text{fixed costs} \times \text{sales}}{\text{contribution}}$

(b) $\dfrac{\text{fixed costs} \times \text{sales}}{\text{variable costs}}$

(c) $\dfrac{\text{variable costs} \times \text{sales}}{\text{fixed costs}}$

(d) $\dfrac{\text{variable costs} \times \text{sales}}{\text{sales} - \text{fixed costs}}$

10 The seasonality of a business has a major effect on:

(a) Profitability

(b) Safety

(c) Cash flow

(d) Liquidity

9
General principles of security

Objectives

After studying this chapter you should be able to:
1 identify the features of ideal security;
2 apply the features to various types of security;
3 understand the different means of obtaining a charge over security and explain which type of charge relates to a particular security;
4 understand the difference between first and third party security and select the correct category according to the circumstances;
5 describe the process for taking, realising and releasing as security, stocks and shares, life policies, land, and guarantees;
6 identify the relative advantages and disadvantages of each type of security;
7 understand the rights and duties of the debtor, chargor, and creditor, particularly in relation to realisation or release of security.

Introduction

While it is true to say that banks still lend substantial amounts to customers on an unsecured basis, there remain many instances where security is taken. A bank takes security so that, if things go wrong, and the customer will not or cannot repay, the bank has an alternative means of getting its money back.

A banker should not, however, be looking at security as some substitute for the proper assessment of a lending proposition. Security will not turn a poor or very marginal proposal into a sound banking proposition and it is in no one's interest, least of all the customer's, that security be taken in circumstances where there is a distinct likelihood of its having to be realised.

Many textbooks, including this one, and most theoreticians will tell you that security should be the last consideration in assessing a lending proposition. In practice, it often comes much higher up the list because it is a form of insurance that sometimes allows a lending banker to sleep at night!

'Your wife may well be a "little treasure", but you still can't offer her as security for a loan!'

The features of ideal security

If security is to perform its true function as insurance against the borrower's failure to repay it should, ideally, satisfy certain conditions as follows:

- It should be *easy to value* and have a *stable* or *increasing value.*
- It should be *easy to take,* and the bank should be able to obtain an *indisputable title.*
- It should *not impose any liability* on the bank.
- It should be *easy to realise* should the bank wish to do so.

We will consider these characteristics later in relation to different types of security but some examples here are appropriate.

Easy to value

Obviously the bank will need to know the value of the security when it commits itself to the loan or overdraft to ascertain to what extent it is covered. In some cases the bank will be entirely happy only if there is *a margin in the security* over and above the maximum borrowing requirement. This will apply particularly where the value of the security is likely to fluctuate as in the case of stocks and shares. For instance, a bank may be considering a loan of £10 000 against stocks and shares as security. It may insist that a margin of, say, 10% be maintained between the amount of the loan and the value of the shares. Initially, shares to the value of £11 000 would be required and further shares would have to be deposited or the borrowing reduced to maintain this margin.

Similarly, a bank will only rarely lend the full amount of the value of a property. If it limits its exposure to, say, 80% of the property's value, then it has a margin of safety of 20%.

If there is a likelihood that the security will increase in value during the life of the loan or overdraft, then this will have considerable appeal as far as the bank is concerned because as the borrowing reduces and the value increases the margin of safety improves.

It also helps if the process of valuation is fairly straightforward and can be completed quickly. For instance, shares in a publicly quoted company can be valued very quickly by reference to current prices as listed in the financial press. Conversely, the valuation of complex factory premises may take a considerable time and, in any event, will be beyond the competence of the average bank manager. A professional valuation will be required which will, of course, entail additional expense for the customer and take time.

Finally, security will need to be revalued on a regular basis during the currency of the borrowing and the quicker and less complicated this process the better for the bank.

Easy to take

The title that a bank acquires to security will vary depending upon the type of security, the charging documentation and, to some extent, the procedure adopted. The simpler the procedure the less the likelihood of mistakes being made and the bank's title being successfully challenged. The nature of the security and the type of title to it also may have an effect upon the bank's ability to realise the security. If the bank has a full *legal* title then on default by the customer it should be able to sell the security without further reference to the customer. If, however, the bank has an *equitable* title then it will require the co-operation of the chargor before being able to realise the security; if this is not forthcoming the help of the courts must be sought.

A fuller explanation of the differences between legal and equitable mortgages is provided later.

If at any time the bank's title to security is open to question or dispute, then less reliance should be placed upon it. A bank needs to have confidence that, if correct procedures are followed, indisputable title can be obtained and decisions can be made relying on that security.

No imposition of liability on the bank

Circumstances in which a bank incurs a liability when it takes security should be rare but need to be considered. There are possibilities which are likely to be infrequent in practice if only because banks are careful to avoid them. These would include a bank incurring liability for *repairs to leased premises* where a charge has been taken over the lease. A further example is a *charge over partly paid shares* where a bank might incur a liability for further calls on the shares.

While bank charge forms normally will contain an indemnity making the chargor liable for any payment or liability that the bank may incur, this is often little consolation. When the banker is trying to recover a bad or doubtful debt caused by the customers refusal or patent inability to repay, enforcing the indemnity may be difficult if not impossible. If the customer has insufficient funds to meet the borrowing commitment, a further liability under the indemnity could present an insurmountable problem.

Easy to realise

When a lending goes wrong the option to sell an item of security at little expense for cash is a great boon to a banker. It keeps the recovery period as short as possible, the costs down, and the accumulation of often irrecoverable accruing interest to a minimum.

This means, therefore, that the *nearer to cash* that the security is, the better. Publicly quoted shares are conspicuously better in this respect than factory premises, for instance.

The simpler and less problematic the realisation process the more a banker likes it. Obtaining the realisation proceeds of a life policy will be straightforward compared to the often difficult process of realising the value in a residential property. This sometimes can be very drawn out with the resultant bad publicity should the bank have to resort to having occupants evicted.

The general point regarding the essential, practical difference between a *legal* charge and an *equitable* charge has already been made but bears repeating here: realisation of security charged legally should be easier than that charged equitably because there is no need to obtain the co-operation of the chargor.

Types of charge

The type of charge or title that a bank acquires will depend in varying degrees on one or more of the following:

(a) the nature of the item being charged;
(b) the contents of the charging document;
(c) the statutory criteria.

Over many years banks have seen fit to add clauses to charging documents which specifically exclude some of the statutory protection available to debtors and chargors to limit the number of loopholes through which either or both may escape. We shall see some examples of these as we cover particular types of security.

Lien

A lien is the right of a creditor to *retain possession* of the debtor's property until such time as the debt is repaid. This right to retain possession arises automatically by operation of law, there being no requirement for a specific agreement between the debtor and creditor. When you hand over a suit or coat to a dry cleaners it is on the basis that the dry cleaners can retain possession of those articles after they have been cleaned and until such time as the cost of cleaning has been paid. Other examples under this heading would be items of jewellery left for repair with a jeweller, cars at a garage for servicing, and films left for processing. Apart from some exceptional cases, the right to retain possession of the item cannot be translated into a right of sale without the permission of the court.

There are two types of lien: *particular* and *general*. A particular lien relates to a specific item and its associated debt, whereas a general lien gives the right to retain possession until such time as all debts, related to the goods or not, have been settled.

Bankers have a general lien on all items deposited with them by customers unless there is an express or implied contract which is inconsistent with lien. As a consequence, safe custody items cannot be subject to a lien in favour of the bank because their deposit creates a contract of bailment. Similarly, items charged as security to the bank will be subject to the terms and conditions of the relevant charge forms and not the law relating to lien.

There are in practice a limited number of occasions or examples where a bank can claim legitimately to have a lien. Two of the more common items which may fall into this category are:

(a) Cheques or bills paid in for collection;

(b) Life policies handed in to the bank for collection of the maturity proceeds.

While lien does not usually give the creditor a power of sale without the consent of the Court, a banker's lien is exceptional in that in certain circumstances it does give that power. It should be noted, however, that a lien depends upon possession and control. If the item in question, say, a cheque, is released to the customer, or to anyone who is not accountable to the bank, the bank's lien is lost.

Pledge

A contract of pledge may be defined as one in which the owner of a chattel deposits it with another person as security for the payment of a debt. A *chattel* is any tangible, movable article of property. The owner or depositor is known as the *pledgor* and the recipient as the *pledgee*. The pledgee must have actual or constructive possession of the property but the legal ownership remains with the pledgor. The most easily recognisable pledge transaction is the deposit of goods with a pawnbroker in return for a loan. If the loan is repaid the goods are redeemed; if not, the goods are sold.

As with a banker's lien there are limited practical applications of pledge, by far the most common being produce advances. A bank will advance funds to a business customer who wishes to import goods. The goods will form the security for the advance and the bank will take constructive possession of the goods initially by holding the title documents – usually bills of lading.

Actual possession by the bank will normally be impracticable. When the goods are released so that they can be sold the bank will ensure that the customer completes a *trust letter*. This stipulates that the customer only has possession of the goods as trustee for the bank and, as such, must account to the bank for the sale proceeds. This procedure ensures that the pledge is not lost when actual possession is transferred to the customer.

Mortgage

A mortgage is a conveyance of a legal or equitable interest in property as security for the payment of a debt or for the discharge of some other obligation. In this context the word 'property' should be used in its widest sense and not confined to land. The person owning the property and transferring the interest is the *mortgagor* and the lender taking the security is called the *mortgagee*. The *mortgagee* does not need to have possession of the property to make the charge effective. There is occasionally some confusion in terminology here because many people use the words mortgage and charge as if they were synonymous, but in practice banks always take charges, as strictly defined, over land and not mortgages. To add further confusion, the word mortgage is often used to describe the loan raised against a property.

There is a technical difference between mortgage and charge. As we have already stated, a mortgage involves the actual transfer of an interest in a property, i.e. some or all of the rights of ownership. A charge, on the other hand, does not constitute such a transfer but merely gives certain rights over a property. For example, the right to sell the property – this arises by virtue of the charge and not by virtue of ownership.

There are two types of mortgage: equitable and legal. An *equitable* mortgage gives the right to reimbursement from the sale proceeds when the security is sold. Such a mortgage can only be enforced by a Court Order if the co-operation of the chargor is not forthcoming, the mortgagee having no automatic power of sale. It is important to note that an equitable mortgage can be obtained without a formal charging document. If a customer deposits the title deeds to a property stating that they can be held as security for a borrowing, then an equitable mortgage by deposit is created. Most banks would wish in these circumstances to take a charge form as it provides clear evidence of the intent of the customer and there is benefit to be gained from the various clauses in the charge form.

A *legal* mortgage is one which is specially recognised and protected at law in that it gives the mortgagee rights against the property itself without recourse to the Courts or to the mortgagor. The most important of these rights or remedies is the power of sale.

There is a further important difference between legal and equitable mortgages which it is appropriate to mention here. The rights of a legal mortgagee are subject only to those prior interests in a property of which the mortgagee is aware. This is in contrast to the equitable mortgage where the rights are subject to all prior interests whether or not the mortgagee is aware of them. This can have serious consequences where there are competing interests in a property, the earlier interests taking priority, perhaps leaving subsequent interests unsecured.

Debenture

This is the only one of the types of charge covered here which relates solely to company customers. A debenture is simply a written acknowledgement by a company of a debt. It is usually sealed by the company and states the terms and conditions of the borrowing. When a company issues a debenture to a bank it will usually be in a form devised by the bank and it will incorporate a *fixed and floating charge* on the assets of the company. It will state that the debenture is taken to secure *all monies* owing at any time by the company and will also seek to charge assets acquired by the company in the future.

The *fixed charge* usually covers the freehold and leasehold property of the company and the fixed plant and machinery. The bank obtains a legal mortgage over these assets once the debenture is sealed and thereafter the company is prevented from selling or disposing of these assets without the consent of the bank.

A fixed charge over other assets is also created but not by way of a legal mortgage. The most important of the assets so charged are the debtors which traditionally were covered by the floating charge. As banks realised the importance of debtors as a means of reducing or repaying the company's debts many changed their debenture forms to incorporate debtors under the fixed charge which improves the claim on them, as we shall see later.

The *floating charge* is an equitable charge on all the assets not covered by the fixed charge. These will tend to be those assets which change frequently because they are directly affected by the activity of the business. The best example of the impact of the floating charge relates to stock. A manufacturing company's stock typically will consist of raw materials, work-in-progress and finished goods. The composition of each will change as the company works through its production/selling cycle. It is important for the efficient running of the business that the company controls and has access to the stock on a day-to-day basis. This ability to deal freely with the stock will cease and the floating charge 'crystallise' or become fixed either when the company goes into liquidation or the bank takes steps to realise its security on default by the customer. Crystalisation will also occur if the company ceases to trade without going into liquidation or an administrative receiver is appointed.

First and third party security

When security is offered or requested, it will usually be charged by the person who is borrowing the money. However, there will be numerous occasions where somebody else, a third party, will give security for a customer's debt. The most common form of third party security is the guarantee, under the terms of which the guarantor promises to meet the commitments of the debtor should the debtor fail so to do.

When the security is jointly owned but only one of the owners is borrowing, the security is third party.

It is important in practice to decide correctly whether a security should be first party or third party. The charge form required will be different as will be the charging process and it is vital that the correct choice be made if the security is to remain fully valid and effective.

The simple rule to remember is that where any party to the security is not a party to the borrowing or liability then the security is third party. All other situations will be first party. The examples on page 138 will illustrate this. These illustrations are not exhaustive and it is important to mention here an option which is often used in practice but is not included overleaf.

Suppose you wish to lend Mr Shepherd £30 000 and you have been offered as security a guarantee by a colleague of his, a Mr Finch. You are keen to take the guarantee but feel that it is not sufficient

Account/liability in the name of	Security in the name of	First or third party	Who signs
A	A	First	A
A & B	A	First	A
A	A & B	Third	A & B
A	B	Third	A & B*
A & B	A & B	First	A & B
A & B & C	A & B	First	A & B

* If the security in this example was a guarantee this would be signed only by 'B' the guarantor and not by 'A' the debtor. As a general rule, however, third party charge forms will be signed by both the chargor and the debtor. NB: Some banks only obtain the third party's signature to third party security and there are complications with regulated borrowers under the Consumer Credit Act.

in itself. Mr Shepherd has no security but Mr Finch has stocks and shares valued at £20 000. You agree that these will strengthen the security position sufficiently and proceed to take a charge. Do you take a first or third party charge?

If you take the stocks and shares in support of the guarantee then the immediate liability, the guarantee, is in the name of Mr Finch and a first party charge must be used. If, however, you dispense with the guarantee then the stocks and shares will be in direct support of the loan to Mr Shepherd and therefore third party security.

First party
Finch   supporting Finch   supporting Shepherd
Stocks and shares ──────▶ Guarantee ──────▶ Loan

Third party
Finch   supporting   Shepherd
Stocks and shares ──────▶ Loan

For regulated borrowings under the Consumer Credit Act, special guarantee forms, not third party charge forms, should be used.

When a decision has been taken to lend money against third party security, it is necessary to consider whether or not the chargor is being unduly influenced by the principal debtor. If, for instance, a solicitor is the principal debtor and the security being provided is the personal guarantee of one of his clients, then there is a danger that the client has been persuaded unfairly by the solicitor to take this action. The law recognises this danger of *undue influence* and seeks to protect certain classes of relationship where it presumes that the possibility of undue influence exists unless the contrary is proved. The relationships protected in this way are:

(a) parent and child;
(b) guardian and ward;
(c) trustee and beneficiary;
(d) solicitor and client;
(e) doctor and patient;
(f) religious leader and follower;
(g) fiancé and fiancée.

The practical consequences of this for the bank are that the security can be invalidated where the chargor claims undue influence. Whilst undue influence is not presumed as between husband and wife or vice versa such a claim by one party or the other nevertheless could be made. Fortunately, however, it is now established that a contract will not be avoided for undue influence unless there is clear evidence that the party influenced was exploited by the other and that the contract made was distinctly to their disadvantage and the other's advantage.

To avoid claims of undue influence the banker, when taking third party security, should examine the relationship between the chargor and the principal debtor. If it is a protected class of relationship, or unprotected but open to undue influence, then the banker should ensure that the subservient party be *independently advised* as to the nature and consequence of the transaction. In practical terms this means sending the person to an independent solicitor who will go through the charge form explaining the contents and their implications. If the person still wishes to sign the charge form the solicitor will attest in writing on the form that the contents have been fully explained and apparently understood before signing and will then witness the signature.

Finally, on the subject of third party security it is necessary to mention that the Statute of Frauds (1677) demands that third party security be evidenced in writing and signed by the chargor or an appointed agent acting on the chargor's behalf. This, of course, will invariably be the case with a bank guarantee.

Further mention will be made of first and third party security in the section entitled 'Types of Security', but before considering these it is necessary to consider the main constituent parts of charge forms used by banks. These will give an insight into some of the rights and duties of the debtor, the chargor if different, and the bank.

Charge form clauses

Although it is easy to complete a charge form correctly without any knowledge of its contents, an understanding of the main provisions of the form is advantageous to the banker.

The charge forms of various banks will differ in detail but the main clauses will be similar. The charge forms themselves will have been amended and expanded as law and practice have changed and will reflect particularly the decisions of relevant cases.

The main functions of a charge form can be summarised as:

(a) to provide evidence of the intention or purpose of the chargor;

(b) to set out precisely the terms and conditions of the contract between the chargor and the bank;

(c) to enable the bank to acquire whatever right or interest in the security it is seeking.

In seeking to ensure that there is no doubt about the nature of its security or the rights of the respective parties, most banks are likely to have in their charge forms the following clauses:

'All liabilities' clause

This states that the security is taken to cover all liabilities owing to the bank on any account, whether alone or jointly, actually or contingently, as principal debtor or as guarantor.

'On demand' clause

This is to ensure that the chargor is legally obliged to pay all moneys due on demand by the bank. There are two other reasons why this needs to be stated. First, any power of sale the bank might have only arises when the moneys become due, following demand and non-payment. Second, the time available for the bank to take legal action against a chargor is limited by law (Limitation Act 1980) but the time allowed will not begin to elapse until demand has been made.

'Power of consolidation' clause

If a banker has made different advances against different securities charged by the same person, this clause allows *all* the security to be retained until *all* the debts have been repaid. A simple table will illustrate the benefit of this to the bank.

	Loan	Security	Chargor
A	£1000	Land	X
B	£2000	Life Policy	X

Even though Loan A might be repaid, the bank can retain the land as security for Loan B; it does not have to release it.

'Continuing security' clause

This is a good example of a clause being inserted to overcome a problem created by case law. The case in question was *Devaynes* v *Noble (1816)*, more popularly known as *Clayton's Case*. The 'rule' stated in this case was that 'in a running account the first item on the debit side is discharged or reduced by the first item on the credit side and so on, in date order.' The possible adverse impact of this in relation to security can be illustrated as follows:

Account of R Stevenson

	Debits	Credits	Balance	
Balance forward			1000 Dr	Security taken
Subsequent entries	500	1000	500 Dr	

Applying the rule in *Clayton's Case*, the credit for £1000 has discharged the overdrawn balance outstanding when the security was taken. The debit for £500 is new borrowing and not, therefore, covered by the security unless the charge form contains the 'Continuing security' clause, i.e. the security continues for future debts.

'Joint and several liability' clause

Whenever security is charged by more than one person then the chargors assume liability both in their joint names and individually because of this clause. In law, joint parties incur only joint liability. This clause is an example of a constriction of the common law rights of chargors by banks so as to strengthen their position at the expense of the chargors. There are even more stringent examples whereby banks actually seek to eliminate by means of clauses in the charge form some of the legal rights chargors might otherwise have, and some of these will be described later.

'Recovery of costs' clause

This, as the name implies, gives the bank the right to recover all the costs it might incur in perfecting, maintaining, and realising the security.

These clauses are amongst the main provisions of most bank charge forms. There are others but there will also be specific clauses relating to the type of security being taken.

Types of security

Banks have taken some strange items as security over the years but we shall concentrate on those that you are likely to see more commonly in practice.

Stocks and shares

When an enterprise, be it a company or other organisation, is owned by several people, they are often called *shareholders*, sometimes *stockholders*. As such they are entitled to participate in the success of the enterprise but may also suffer from its demise. If the company is successful then the value of their stake should increase enabling them to realise a profit should they wish to sell their shares. It is this *sale or market value* which provides the bank with the security it may be seeking.

Stocks and shares are otherwise known as *securities* and there are two main categories, *registered* securities and *bearer* securities.

Registered securities
These are given this title because a register of shareholders will be maintained by the company or other organisation which issued the shares and each of the shareholders will receive a certificate as evidence of their title to the shares. The certificate will contain details of the shareholder's name and address, the number, nominal value, and type of share and a certificate number. The certificate has to be relinquished when the shares are sold and the vendor has to transfer title to the purchaser by signing a transfer form. The certificate and completed transfer are lodged with the registrar who will delete the details of the previous owner from the register and enter the details of the purchaser who will

then be issued with a new certificate. Most British companies and the British Government when issuing stock use this registered securities system.

Bearer securities

These are again issued by various companies and organisations but no record is kept of the owners and this detail is not recorded on the certificate. As the name implies the bearer or holder of the certificate or bond is deemed to be the owner as all bearer securities are negotiable instruments. The lack of a register makes it impossible for the company to know to whom to send dividend or interest payments so the certificate usually has coupons attached to it for the holder to submit in sequence when dividend or interest payments are due.

Taking a charge

A simple *equitable* charge can be created by the mere deposit of the share certificates with an intent to charge, but this presents two problems:

    (a) proving such a charge exists, and
    (b) realising the charge.

In practice, banks will normally taken an appropriate *Memorandum of Deposit* to ensure that there is no dispute concerning the existence of a charge and the terms and conditions under which it was taken. If the bank takes the process no further, then realisation still may be difficult as the chargor's signature would be required to the stock transfer form and this may be difficult to obtain when the bank is trying to enforce this security. It is common practice, therefore, to obtain a signed stock transfer form at the same time as the Memorandum of Deposit so that if the bank should wish to realise the security it merely has to transfer the shares into its name using the stock transfer form and it can then sell the shares on the open market.

While an equitable charge strengthened by a signed stock transfer form is the norm, it is possible to obtain a full *legal* charge over stocks or shares. The initial procedure is exactly the same as for an equitable charge, but to obtain a full legal charge the bank must transfer the title of the shares into its name, and for this purpose it normally uses the name of a separate nominee company. This means that the share certificate and the completed stock transfer form have to be sent to the company which issued the shares so that the name of the bank's nominee company can be entered in the share register as the new owner of the shares and an appropriate certificate can be issued.

As already stated, bearer securities are negotiable instruments, legal ownership passing by mere delivery. As long as the bank receives the certificates without notice of any defect in the chargor's title, in good faith, and for value, then its position is virtually unassailable. The mere deposit of bearer securities with the intention of creating a charge is sufficient to create a legal charge in favour of the bank. However, a completed Memorandum of Deposit should be signed by the chargor as evidence of the terms and conditions upon which the security has been given to the bank.

Unit trusts

These are a form of investment whereby the investor is allocated a number of units in a fund which is spread across a wide variety of shares. There is an ever increasing number of trusts managed by professional investment management companies.

A certificate is issued to the investor as evidence of the number of units held and the prices at which the fund managers are prepared to *buy (bid) and sell (offer)* are quoted daily in the financial press.

The charging procedure is similar to that for registered securities except that there is often a form of renunciation on the reverse of the unit trust certificate. If an equitable charge is being taken then this can be signed by the chargor to be used later if the bank needs to realise the security. Alternatively, a stock transfer form can be signed and this is the option usually chosen.

If you wish to take a legal charge then the *form of renunciation* will be completed to transfer the units into the name of the bank's nominee company (e.g. Barclays Bank (Nominees) Ltd).

American and Canadian type securities

These are often described as 'quasi-negotiable' in that they are registered in the name of the owner and this information appears on the front of the certificate. There is a form of transfer on the reverse which when signed in blank makes the certificate transferable by mere delivery. To improve transferability and acceptability the certificates are often registered in 'marking names', usually stockbrokers or finance houses. The Stock Exchange recognises among these certain *'good marking names'* and you should ensure that any certificates offered as security are registered in one of these. You must also be sure that the endorsement has been completed correctly and must agree in every detail with the name on the face of the certificate. Having taken deposit of the certificates it is necessary to obtain a completed Memorandum of Deposit just as with bearer securities.

Advantages and disadvantages of stocks and shares as security
Advantages
The procedure for obtaining a charge on stocks and shares is simple, the only tedious aspect being the need to revalue regularly during the currency of the loan or overdraft.

The valuation process for shares in *quoted companies* should not present any difficulties as the prices are published daily, and assuming a signed transfer form has been taken, realising the sale of the shares in quoted companies should be straightforward. As has been seen, the procedure for dealing with bearer securities is simplified by their negotiability and this characteristic also facilitates their sale.

Disadvantages
The value of stocks and shares can fluctuate often dramatically and they do not, therefore, provide a banker with the stability normally required. In an attempt to alleviate this problem, there is usually a clause in the Memorandum of Deposit which demands that the customer maintains a margin between the value of the shares and the amount being borrowed. If the margin erodes because share values are falling then either further shares have to be deposited or the borrowing reduced.

While valuing shares in quoted companies presents few problems, this cannot be said for unquoted companies. By definition, there is no open market for the shares and no quoted prices. Valuation may be possible by analysing the latest balance sheet, although this is long-winded and the balance sheet is likely to be out of date. Alternatively, the issue price could be used or the price at which shares last changed hands. None of these methods is entirely satisfactory and consequently unquoted shares are less attractive as security.

Unquoted shares will usually be in private companies and this also causes problems. Despite some relaxation in the law concerning the ownership and transfer of shares in private companies, many will still be subject to such restrictions. This may mean that even if the bank succeeds in obtaining a charge there may be a very limited market for the shares on realisation. The company's Articles may demand that the shares must be offered to existing shareholders or directors first or that prospective purchasers have to be approved by the company. A further drawback can occur where it is a director who is charging his shares in his company and he is obliged to hold a certain number of shares to remain eligible to be a director, known as *qualifying shares*. Should this be the case then the taking of a legal charge transferring the shares into the name of the bank is not possible as it will have the effect of disqualifying the director.

Sometimes shares are not fully paid up when they are issued and the company has the right to call for further payments at some future date. For example, a company issuing £1 shares at their nominal value may initially ask only for 50p per share. These shares are described as *partly paid*. Where you have taken an equitable charge then any further calls will be directed to the chargor who has remained the registered proprietor. This may be little consolation if you have to lend further monies to enable the calls to be met and thus avoid forfeiting the shares which form your security. The liability for further calls is the reason why banks are reluctant to obtain full legal charges over partly-paid shares. The demand would be sent to the bank as the registered owners which would be liable to meet the call, although under the terms of the charge form any payment could be passed on to the customer.

With an equitable charge, as we have seen, the shares remain in the name of the chargor and it is possible, therefore, for the chargor to write to the company claiming to have lost the certificate and request a duplicate which could then be used to support a sale of the shares without the bank's knowledge. There are two rarely used options available which may provide some protection against this eventuality. The first is a *stop notice* which is served on the company which issued the shares. Application has to be made to the Supreme Court before such a notice can be served, making this an expensive and long-winded process which is only used in exceptional circumstances. The effect on the company is that it has an obligation to give the bank eight days' notice of any attempt to transfer the shares.

The second option is for the bank to notify the company of its charge, but this will only apply to unquoted shares. The company is not obliged to acknowledge this notice or to record it and it will normally reply stating this. Despite the official reply, the company may mark its records accordingly and contact the bank should there be an attempt to transfer the shares or obtain a duplicate certificate.

A further disadvantage of an equitable charge is that all correspondence concerning bonus or rights issues will be sent to the registered owner, the chargor, who is normally obliged by the charge form to hand this to the bank but may fail to do so.

In these circumstances, the value of the bank's security could diminish. For instance, if a company has a bonus or scrip issue of one new share for each existing share held, then Mr Toad who owns 1000 shares will receive an additional 1000 free shares. Because the number of issued shares will double, the market value will halve. If you have taken a charge over the original holding and do not receive the bonus shares then the value of the security will reduce by 50%.

If the example used involved a rights issue then Mr Toad would be required to pay for the new shares if he wished to acquire them. If he did not then he could sell the rights in the open market, thereby depriving the bank of the proceeds. Furthermore, the rights issue will have an adverse effect on the existing holding, reducing the value of the security. If the market value of the original holding was £1600, i.e. 160p per share, and the rights issue was at 100p per share, the share price will reduce to 130p and the value of the security to £1300. This is because there are now twice as many shares issued at a combined value of 260p making each share worth 130p.

Conversely, if you have taken a legal charge and your bank's nominee company is now the registered proprietor then all correspondence concerning bonus and rights issues will be sent to the bank which must then ensure that the interests of the customer, who is expecting to have the shares released when the borrowing is repaid, are protected. This imposes an additional administrative burden on the bank but also ensures that dividends are directed to the customer's account, possibly in reduction of the indebtedness.

The list of disadvantages of taking stocks and shares as security is conspicuously much longer than that of the advantages but, in practical terms, this type of security remains very attractive where the shares are quoted because of the simplicity of the procedure and the ease of valuation and realisation. Furthermore, the only monitoring required once the security has been taken is regular revaluation of the shares.

Releasing the security
With registered stocks and shares the release of an equitable

charge is simple in that the Memorandum of Deposit and signed stock transfer form can be cancelled and placed to lapsed or old papers and the certificate returned to the customer against a suitable receipt. This same procedure can be adopted for unit trust certificates.

With registered securities the shareholding under a legal charge will need to be transferred back into the name of the chargor and the new certificate returned against a receipt. With bearer securities the release is effected by the return of the bearer certificate and this procedure also applies to American and Canadian type certificates. In all cases the charge can be cancelled and placed to old papers.

Realising the security

You must ensure when realising any security that the terms of the charge form governing the method of making demand upon the customer are properly observed.

As long as the stock transfer form was obtained in addition to the equitable charge form then the shares can be sold and effectively transferred to the purchaser. If no stock transfer form has been signed by the chargor then this must be obtained; if this proves impossible, the assistance of the court must be sought.

Under a legal charge, as the shares are in the bank's name a sale can be effected without recourse to the chargor. The same facility is available with both bearer securities and American and Canadian type certificates.

Life policies

Life assurance is a contract whereby the insurer undertakes to pay the beneficiary a sum of money upon the death of the life assured or on a fixed future date. The contract is evidenced by a policy document and the insurer is paid a premium or premiums by the policy holder.

There are three parties to a life policy in addition to the issuing company:

(a) The person taking out the policy, known as the *proposer* or *member*.

(b) The person whose life is assured or covered, known as the *life assured*.

(c) The person entitled to receive the proceeds of the policy, known as the *beneficiary*.

Where Mrs Arbuthnot takes out a policy on her own life for her own benefit then the proposer, life assured and beneficiary are one and the same person. If Mr Arbuthnot takes out a policy on his life for the benefit of Mrs Arbuthnot then he is both the proposer and the life assured, and Mrs Arbuthnot is the beneficiary.

It is possible to take out a life assurance policy on somebody else's life but there must be what is known as an *insurable interest*. This requirement, which is contained in Section 1 of the Life Assurance Act (1774), demands that at the date of the contract the proposer must have an insurable interest of a pecuniary nature in the life assured. This means that the relationship is such that the proposer would suffer financial loss in the event of the death of the person whose life is to be covered by the policy, e.g.

- husband/wife
- wife/husband
- creditor/debtor
- company/managing director.

If there was no insurable interest present originally then the insurer could seek to have the contract avoided.

An insurable interest is assumed where people take life assurance on their own lives or where the relationship is that of husband and wife. But parents do not have an insurable interest in the lives of their children or vice versa unless some independent pecuniary interest can be proved. Parents may, however, arrange life assurance in the child's name and for the child's benefit. With a reputable assurance company the fact that a particular policy has been issued is sufficient proof that there is an insurable interest.

The words *assurance* and *insurance* tend to be used synonymously in everyday language but there is a technical difference. Insurance relates to protection against events that might happen whereas assurance should be used to describe cover against something that is bound to happen. For example, we *insure* our cars against accidents that might happen, but we take out life *assurance* against death which is an inevitability for us all.

When negotiating an ordinary contract no party must mislead the other party, otherwise the contract may be avoided. A life policy being a contract of assurance is a contract of utmost good faith (*uberrimae fidei*), which means that both parties to the contract are obliged *to disclose all material facts*, a more stringent requirement than for ordinary contracts. The failure of either party to adhere to this rule makes the contract voidable at the option of the other party. In practical terms a proposer wishing to take out life assurance must not hide or suppress any relevant information when completing a proposal form.

Types of life policy
There are several types of life policy but the two main ones are *whole life* and *endowment*, either of which may or may not participate in the profits of the issuing assurance company. As a bank principally is interested in the present cash value, known as the surrender value, rather than the benefits on death, 'with profits' policies are more attractive because their surrender value should increase more quickly than those policies 'without profits'.

(a) **Whole life.** As the name implies, this type of policy covers the life assured for their whole life and is, therefore, only payable on death. However, these policies do acquire a surrender value even if they are 'without profits', when the surrender value will be a proportion of the premiums paid.

(b) **Endowment.** Under an endowment policy the policy monies are payable at a fixed future date or on previous death. The practical difference between this type and the whole life policy is that, if you take out an endowment policy on your own life for your own benefit and you survive to the maturity date, you rather than your heirs will receive the proceeds. Endowment policies are often used in connection with mortgages for house purchase. The borrower pays only the interest on the mortgage and the endowment premium, the principal being repaid when the policy matures.

(c) **Equity linked.** This is a form of policy where a proportion of the premium is invested in unit trust units and the maturity or surrender value of the policy will depend upon the performance of those investments. This is in contrast to a 'with profits' policy where the value is dependent upon the profit performance of the assurance company. Most equity linked policies will have a guaranteed minimum value on the death of the life assured.

(d) **Mortgage protection.** These policies assure repayment of mortgage commitments should the mortgagor die. The face value decreases as the mortgage is repaid and the policy will form part of the security where the bank is providing the mortgage. They do not acquire a surrender value and are therefore unsuitable as security where the bank is trying to guard against the failure of the customer to repay the borrowing.

(e) **Term assurance.** These policies are payable only if the assured dies within a stipulated period. They are useful where the bank requires life assurance cover on a customer as part of a security package and the customer may also benefit because next of kin will not have to carry the burden of the debt, which will be cleared by the policy monies. Again, however, these policies do not acquire a surrender value.

Taking a charge
It is possible to take either an equitable or legal charge on a life policy. An equitable charge can be achieved by mere deposit but it would be normal to support it with a memorandum of deposit. However, it is rare for banks to take equitable charges and so only the procedure for a legal charge will be detailed here.

The form of legal charge used by banks is an *assignment under seal* and there are several well-defined steps in the assignment process as follows:

(a) read the policy carefully

(b) obtain the surrender value

(c) complete the form of assignment and have it signed by the chargor(s)

(d) give notice of the assignment to the assurance company

(e) confirm that the premiums are paid to date.

Perhaps the most important of these steps is a thorough examination of the policy document. The banker needs to establish that the policy will be acceptable as security and in so doing will be asking the following questions:

(a) what is the status of the assurance company? Is it reputable?

(b) what is the sum assured? Is the policy with or without profits?

(c) where and when are the maturity monies payable and in what currency?

(d) what type of policy is it?

(e) who are the parties to the policy, i.e. the proposer, life assured, and beneficiary?

(f) can the policy be assigned and, if so, who needs to sign the form of assignment?

(g) are there any restrictions within the policy on such things as the occupation of the life assured? High risk occupations such as 'racing car driver' are unlikely to be covered.

(h) has the age of the life assured been admitted?

An explanation of the last question might be needed. As the level of life assurance premium depends upon the age of the life assured, the assurance company will at some stage require evidence of the date of birth. The birth certificate can be produced at the time of taking out the policy but, if not, will be demanded by the company on maturity or surrender. A bank may wish, therefore, to submit this evidence at the time of taking the charge so that the policy can be amended to show that age has now been admitted. In practical terms, if the age of the life assured is incorrectly quoted the assurance company normally will adjust the amount payable on surrender or maturity and this may leave the bank insufficiently secured.

The surrender value can be obtained by writing to the assurance company and this is usually done at the same time as the giving of notice of the assignment. With some policies the surrender value can be ascertained from a schedule in the policy.

The bank will also ask the assurance company to confirm that premiums are paid to date and to advise the bank should premiums not be paid in future. This will give the bank an opportunity to pay the premiums itself to ensure that the policy does not lapse. A further way to overcome this problem is to arrange for premiums to be paid by standing order or direct debit through the customer's bank account. The bank then will know immediately should payments not be made or cancelled.

When deciding who has to complete the charge form the impact of the *Married Women's Property Act 1882* (MWPA) may have to be considered. *Policies* issued under the provisions of Section 11 of this Act are known as *settlement policies* and give rise to special problems. An MWPA policy is one in which:

- a husband insures his own life for the benefit of his *named* wife and/or children

or

- a wife insures her own life for the benefit of her *named* husband and/or children

Note that the policy must always be on the life of the proposer and that the wife/husband/children beneficiaries should be named to avoid confusion where people may have remarried. Most such policies will state that they are issued in accordance with the provisions of the Act.

The problem created by these policies for the banker is that they create a trust in favour of the beneficiaries who must join in any assignment to the bank. For example, if Mr Green took out a policy on his own life for the benefit of Mrs Green and then wanted to charge that policy, Mrs Green would have to sign the form of assignment as well as Mr Green. Furthermore, in addition to the relationship of husband and wife, there would also be a relationship of trustee (Mr Green) and beneficiary (Mrs Green) under the terms of the policy. This would demand that the bank consider the question of undue influence before Mrs Green signed and that independent legal advice be obtained if necessary.

Where children are beneficiaries then the policy may not be suitable as security because if they are under the age of eighteen they have limited legal capacity and will not be able effectively to complete the assignment forms.

Advantages and disadvantages of life policies as security
Advantages
As we have seen, obtaining the value of a policy is a simple matter. The surrender value can be obtained by writing to the assurance company and the sum assured from the policy itself. Under normal circumstances, the surrender value of the policy should increase as premiums are paid, giving the banker additional security. This will apply particularly to 'with profits' policies.

The procedure for taking a charge is straightforward and enables the bank to obtain an indisputable title to the policy by way of legal assignment. The charging of a life policy will not impose any liability on the bank other than the possible need to pay premiums if the customer fails to do so, in which case the bank will debit these to the customer's account as they are usually empowered to under the terms of the charge form.

If the life assured dies before the borrowing is repaid then the full amount of the sum assured becomes payable and can be used to repay or reduce the borrowing.

Disadvantages
While surrender values should increase over time, it has been known for assurance companies to reduce surrender values where there have been serious investment difficulties such as a collapse of stock market prices. These occasions are rare thankfully and there is a possibility that the assurance companies may honour the original surrender value in favour of a legal assignee such as a bank. Assurance companies will also do this where a policy is voidable due to the proposer not disclosing all material facts at the outset. This serves to highlight a possible disadvantage with a life policy because the life assured may fail to abide by conditions laid down in the policy, making it voidable at the option of the assurance company. There may, for example, be a prohibition against participation in dangerous sports, and there could well be a clause stipulating that proceeds will not be payable on the suicide of the life assured. It is likely that if death occurred in

either of these circumstances the assurance company would still acknowledge the position of the bank as an innocent third party and pay over the sum assured to the bank or the legal assignee for value.

Releasing the security

The release procedure is straightforward, requiring the reassignment of the policy to the chargor, the return of the policy together with the form of assignment, and the withdrawal of notice from the assurance company. The reassignment is effected by the completion by the bank of a form of reassignment which is usually pre-printed on the charge form. The reassigned charge form then becomes part of the permanent title to the policy and must be handed over to the assurance company on surrender or maturity. When the policy and charge form are handed to the chargor a suitable receipt must be obtained.

Realising the security

Having observed the terms of the charge form concerning demand you have to complete a surrender application form provided by the insurance company and submit this, together with the policy, the charge form, any previous assignments which should have been discharged, and evidence of age, if necessary, to the insurance company. If the policy is being realised on death then a copy of the death certificate must be submitted to the insurance company.

Land

This is probably the most complex security that you will encounter and its complexity is one of its drawbacks. Because land or property is often the most valuable asset an individual or company owns it is frequently offered as security and banks are very willing to accept it despite what can be a long-winded charging procedure. There are some basic steps in the procedure for charging land which you will have covered in your studies of *Banking: the legal environment* and which will apply no matter which type of land or title the chargor has. We shall look at these later. It is in the detail for each type that problems can occur and to cope with these certain concepts relating to land or property need to be understood.

Legal estates in land
Under Section 1 of the Law of Property Act 1925 the number of
ways in which land could be held was reduced to two –*freehold
and leasehold.*

(a) **Freehold.** It is defined as an estate in fee simple absolute
in possession. *Estate* means an interest in land protected by law
and *in fee simple* means that this interest can be passed on to
whomsoever the holder chooses. *Absolute* confirms that the
interest in the land is not dependent upon anything and is not
liable to be diminished or removed in the future. For practical
purposes freehold is absolute ownership and the best legal estate
which can be held.

(b) **Leasehold.** This is technically defined as a term of years
absolute, which means that a leaseholder or lessee only has an
estate or interest in the land for a specific period of time. This
interest is granted by the freeholder and at the end of the
stipulated period the interest ceases and the land reverts to the
freeholder.

Sole or joint ownership
If there is a single absolute owner then there should be few
problems or difficulties where the land is offered as security.
However, if the property concerned is a matrimonial home, as it
so often is for personal loans and mortgages, then there are
dangers where the legal estate is in the sole name of either the
husband or the wife. They are able to give an effective legal
mortgage to the bank, but the law and the courts have recognised
the equitable interest of the partner whose name does not appear
in the title documents.

This principle was enforced in two well-known cases, *Williams
& Glyn's Bank Ltd* v *Brown* (1980) and *Williams & Glyn's Bank
Ltd* v *Boland* (1980). In both cases the matrimonial homes, which
were in the sole names of the husbands, were mortgaged as
security in support of personal guarantees for companies of which
they were directors. The bank sought to realise the security on
default in respect of each property and both Mrs Brown and Mrs
Boland sought to establish and protect their respective interests
in their properties. The Court of Appeal upheld their claim
confirming that as occupiers who had contributed money or
money's worth to the matrimonial home they had an equitable
interest in the property. This decision was upheld in the House
of Lords. The consequence of these decisions was that the bank
was unable to enforce its security as it could not effect a sale with

vacant possession. However, in a subsequent case, *City of London Building Society* v *Flegg* (1987), where the property held on trust was vested in *joint names*, the House of Lords ruled that payment of loan or purchase moneys to at least two trustees overreaches the interest of the beneficiaries under the trust even though they contributed towards the purchase price and are in actual occupation. The net result of these cases is that when you propose taking a charge over land from a *sole owner* you must establish whether there are any occupiers with a financial stake in the property and, if so, obtain their agreement to the mortgage. This agreement normally will take the form of a deed of postponement allowing the bank's interest in the property to supersede the interest of the occupier(s).

When dealing with land owned by more than one person, there are additional points to consider. The title to jointly-owned land has two component parts:

(a) the legal estate
(b) the beneficial interest, which is equitable.

A trust is created automatically whereby trustees own the legal estate on behalf of the beneficiaries who have the beneficial interest. This is not as complicated as it sounds because in most cases of co-ownership the trustees and beneficiaries are one and the same as with a matrimonial home owned jointly by the husband and wife.

The Law of Property Act (1925) defines two different forms of co-ownership, joint tenancy and tenancy-in-common. The main distinction between the two lies in the right of survivorship, where with a joint tenancy it is not possible for the co-owners to bequeath their interest in the land. On the death of a co-owner under a joint tenancy the interest vests in the survivor(s). In the case of tenancy-in-common, a co-owner's interest does not pass to the surviving co-owners but to the executors or administrators of the estate who must deal with it as directed in the will. The following examples will help to illustrate the difference between the two types:

(a) joint tenancy: A, B and C are joint tenants – C dies – the whole of the property is now vested in A and B as joint tenants.

(b) tenancy-in-common: A, B and C are tenants-in-common – C dies – the interest is bequeathed to D and E – the property is now vested in A, B, D and E as tenants-in-common.

The co-ownership of the *legal estate* must always be a joint tenancy and a maximum of four joint tenants is allowed by law.

The *beneficial interest* can be co-owned either as a joint tenancy or as a tenancy-in-common.

Practical difficulties arising from this will be rare because most property charged will either be in a sole name or, where it is jointly owned, the trustees of the legal estate and the beneficiaries will be one and the same. Where this is not the case, beneficiaries who are not trustees must also join in the charge form.

Unregistered and registered land

These are two further distinctions or definitions which can make even more difficult the study of land as security. Prior to 1925 much land in the UK was unregistered as there was no country-wide registration system. The system introduced with the Land Registration Act 1925 was set up to simplify and streamline what had become a very cumbersome and inefficient process. Registration was modelled on the system applicable to stocks and shares:

- title is evidenced by a certificate
- transfer is by means of a simple form
- a central register is maintained.

The registration process has been going on ever since but it is not yet complete. One of the reasons for this is that registration of a title to land is only compulsory where the land is in a designated registration area and one of the following applies:

- the freehold title is being transferred on sale
- a lease of 21 years or more is being created
- an existing lease with 21 or more years to run is being assigned.

When one of these things happens the title documents are examined, a registered title is given, and a Land Certificate is issued. Where a freehold or leasehold title has already been registered and a new lease of 21 years or more is being created then this must also be registered. Despite its name implying the contrary there is a register relating to unregistered land and this is called the *Land Charges Register* which is maintained at the Land Charges Department in Plymouth. With registered land there are several district Land Registries and it is important that you remember the relevant register for the type of land:

(a) unregistered: Land Charges Register, Land Charges Department

(b) registered: HM Land Registry.

Taking a charge

Your bank will have its own procedures and possibly an aide-memoire to which you should refer but, as stated previously, there is a basic procedure to be followed no matter what type of charge over land you are taking, it is only in the detail that the various types of charge differ. It will help to clarify matters if this basic procedure is stated here and the relevant details applied to it as each process is examined.

- examination of title
- valuation
- search
- completion of the charge form
- registration (with one exception)
- insurance.

To further clarify and simplify the various procedures they are dealt with in the following order:

1 unregistered: (a) freehold – first mortgage, (b) leasehold – first mortgage, (c) second or subsequent mortgage.

2 registered: (a) freehold – first mortgage, (b) leasehold – first mortgage, (c) second or subsequent mortgage.

3 sub mortgages.

1 Unregistered land

It is possible to obtain an equitable charge or mortgage by way of deposit of the title deeds, with or without a charge form. While most banks have this option and appropriate equitable charge forms for completion under hand or under seal, it is infrequently exercised mainly because of the weaknesses of equitable mortgages, which bears repetition. They are subject to all prior equitable interests, whether known or otherwise, whereas legal mortgages are only subject to those about which the mortgagees knew or should have known. Furthermore, the assistance of the court may well be required to enforce the security where the co-operation of the chargor is not forthcoming. This is in contrast to a legal mortgage granting the mortgagee a power of sale.

(a) Freehold – first mortgage
- Examination of title

The title documents need to be examined to ensure that the prospective chargor is the legal owner and that there is a *root of title* at least fifteen years old. Some banks appoint solicitors to do this work and produce a *report on title*. The documents of the title will include one or more of the following:

Conveyance: the normal method of transfer of the title.

Discharged mortgages: in favour of previous mortgagees.

Abstracts of title: copies of previous reports on title.
Certificates of search: carried out by previous mortgagees or owners.

In addition to establishing that the prospective chargor has a good title to the property you will also need to be happy that there is nothing in the deeds which will adversely affect your mortgage. For example, if there is a mortgage form in favour of a previous mortgagee and it has not been discharged then you will have to arrange for this to be completed. There may also be some mention of *restrictive covenants* and these may have an impact on the mortgage. These have usually been created to preserve the value or quality of a property and its surrounding area and they 'run with the land' which means that they continue to affect subsequent owners. If you are providing finance so that a residential property can be extended and converted to business use, a covenant specifically prohibiting this will, of course, be relevant. Fortunately, cases affecting banking propositions are rare and it is possible to insure against losses which might arise should a restrictive covenant be enforced.

- Valuation

Valuing a property is not an exact science and prudence demands a cautious approach. Private residential property should be fairly easy to value, particularly where similar properties are for sale, but it is sensible to leave some margin for error. Commercial or industrial premises are more difficult and a professional valuation will often be sought. Properties should be revalued on a regular basis to ensure that you remain adequately secured.

- Search

A search of the Land Charges Register has to be made at the Land Charges Department using Form K15 and paying the required fee per name. There are various classes of land charge denoted A, B, C, D, E and F, and brief reference will be made of any of those registered against the names of the chargors. If you require more details then an office copy of the entry can be obtained. The main charges in which you might be interested are:

Class C(i): puisne mortgage – a legal charge where the mortgagee does not hold the deeds.

Class C(iii): general equitable charge – not protected by deposit of the deeds.

Class D(i): charges in favour of the Inland Revenue in respect of inheritance tax.

Class D(ii): restrictive covenants.

Class D(iii): equitable easements, e.g. a right of way.
Class F: a charge registrable under the Matrimonial Homes Act 1983 protecting the rights of occupation of a spouse.

There are two main reasons for searching:
– to confirm or establish the priority of your charge,
– to discover whether there is any entry registered which is likely to affect your charge.

With unregistered land first priority attaches to the possession of the deeds or the date of registration of a charge at the Land Charges Department, whichever comes first. So, if you have taken possession of the deeds, have searched the Land Charges Register and been advised that there are 'No subsisting entries', and have no notice of any other interest, you can be confident that you have first priority against the property. If, however, there is a time gap between your search and the taking of the mortgage, it is possible that an entry might be registered without you knowing. Some banks, therefore, insist on searching before and after the date of the charge. It is possibly more efficient to search only after the date of the charge to ensure you have priority and this will provide adequate protection as long as you lend no money before completing the security, a rule which should always be followed in practice. It is also advisable to search the *Local Land Charges Register*. These are kept by the local authority and record against the property such things as planning permissions and compulsory purchase orders.

● Completion of the charge form
As we have already seen, it is important that you consider the equitable interests of occupiers who must join in the charge or postpone their interests in favour of the bank for the security to be effective. The legal mortgage form will contain some specific clauses relating to property such as an undertaking by the mortgagor not to grant further mortgages or create leases and to keep the property in good repair.

● Registration
A first charge on unregistered land is the one exception referred to previously under this heading. The legal mortgagee who has possession of the title deeds has no need to register a charge and indeed cannot.

● Insurance
Whenever a charge is taken on property you need to ensure that there is a suitable insurance policy giving adequate cover against

the normal risks, and that the premiums have been paid to date.

You can then give notice to the insurance company advising them of the charge and asking for an acknowledgement. The insurance company will advise the bank if the policy is in danger of lapsing through non-payment of the premium, and the bank can take appropriate action to protect its security. Such notice will be given in respect of all industrial and commercial properties, but in some cases of private properties below a certain value (the threshold changes from time to time), some banks and insurance companies have agreed that notice need not be given and the bank's position will still be protected.

(b) Leasehold – first mortgage

The procedure is very similar – only the differences or additional steps are discussed here.

● Examination of title

As with freehold, the title is evidenced by deeds but, in this case, there will be the original lease and subsequent *assignments* drawn up each time the leasehold title changed hands. The original lease would be a *head lease*, being the first lease carved out of a freehold title, or a *sub-lease* carved out of a leasehold title. Again, a 'root of title' of 15 years should be established where possible and it is essential to read the whole lease or sub-lease noting any onerous covenants or conditions which may detract from the value of the security. The main danger is that the lessee will renege on a term or condition of the lease which will then be forfeited and the bank's security lost.

● Valuation

Valuing leasehold property can present problems not applicable to freehold because as the period of the lease expires the value reduces. For long-term leases, say 99 years, this should not present a problem, but short-term leases can be unattractive as security because of their rapidly diminishing value.

● Insurance

The lease will normally stipulate who is responsible for the insurance and may even give some instruction as to what type and level of insurance is required. Whether the lessor or lessee is responsible you need to obtain the necessary details, ensure that cover is adequate, and give notice to the insurance company as appropriate.

- Additional steps

The lease may require that the *lessor's permission* be obtained before the lease can be assigned or charged elsewhere and, in any event, notice of any assignment or charge will have to be given to the lessor. When the lease is created provision will usually be made for the payment of a *ground rent*, the amount and frequency being stipulated. Non-payment of this by the lessee could diminish the value of the security by giving the lessor certain rights against the property and it is important to ensure that payments are up to date and that receipts are exhibited in future.

(c) Second or subsequent mortgage
- Examination of title

Examination of the actual deeds is not possible because these are in the possession of the first mortgagee. To overcome this problem most lenders have a questionnaire which the chargor signs, and which is then sent to the first mortgagee for completion. This gives sufficient detail for the completion of the second mortgage and there is an assumption that the title has been properly examined where the first mortgagee is reputable such as a building society or a bank.

- Valuation

The basic process is the same but from the total value of the property you have to deduct the amount due under the first mortgage. The remaining sum is known as the *equity*.

- Completion of the charge form

When the charge form is being prepared it is necessary to enter details of the prior mortgage(s).

- Search

As a second mortgagee you would still expect to receive the answer 'No subsisting entries' because, of course, the first mortgagee will not have registered a charge.

- Registration

Registration of your charge as a Class C(i), puisne mortgage is necessary using form K1, and if you search again later, as some banks do, you can check that your charge has been registered properly.

- Insurance

The first mortgagee will normally hold the policy but you will have obtained details of this by means of the questionnaire. Notice can be given to the insurance company in the normal way.

- Additional steps

You should give notice to the first mortgagee and request again the amount outstanding. This will be included in the acknowledgement of the notice which will have the effect of fixing the amount of the first mortgagee's priority, unless there is an obligation under the first mortgage to make further advances.

2 Registered land

The same comments regarding equitable and legal mortgages apply as for unregistered land with the exception that with first mortgages the practice of some banks, as we shall see later, results in their having an equitable charge but a legal charge form.

(a) Freehold – first mortgage

- Examination of title

As we have already seen, a Land Certificate is the *prima facie* evidence of title and this is issued on registration of the land. The certificate is divided into three parts:

the property register: giving details of the property including the title number.

the proprietorship register: giving details of the type of title and the registered proprietor(s).

the charges register: giving details of all charges, covenants, and leases on the register when the Land Certificate was last updated. At the back of the certificate a copy of the plan or map of the property is included. The types of title which can be granted on registration are as follows:

Absolute title: The best possible title. Normally applicable to freeholds but can apply to leaseholds where the freehold title out of which they are carved has been registered as absolute.

Possessory title: Applicable to both freehold and leasehold titles which are only guaranteed from the date of registration. Implies some defect in the title. Can be converted to absolute for freeholds and good leasehold (see below) after a certain number of years has elapsed.

Qualified title: Applicable to both freeholds and leaseholds but rarely seen in practice. Implies some defect in the title.

Good leasehold title: As the name implies, applicable only to leaseholds. The leaseholder's title is guaranteed but not that of the freeholder who granted the lease.

- Valuation
The requirements are exactly the same as for unregistered land.

- Search
A search at the appropriate District Land Registry can be achieved either by submitting the Land Certificate for updating or by submitting a search form (94A) which, unlike unregistered land, requires the authority of the registered proprietor. Where the Land Certificate is submitted for updating it is marked with the date on which it was compared to the actual register.

Priority with registered land is governed by the date of the registration of the charge and thirty days' protection to register is granted after a search has been made. A search of the Local Land Charges Register should take place as with unregistered land.

- Completion of the charge form
This takes place in exactly the same way as described previously.

- Registration
There are two options: register the charge or lodge notice of deposit or notice of intended deposit.

The second option is attractive because no land registration fees are payable, but it is effectively an equitable charge. However, as a legal charge form usually has been completed, full registration can take place subsequently if the bank wishes to protect or strengthen its position, particularly where it receives notice from the Land Registry that an application to register a second charge has been received. With full registration the Land Certificate, the mortgage form and a certified copy have to be sent to the Land Registry with an application for registration (A4). The bank also has to certify the extent to which it is relying on the charge and a fee based on this figure has to be paid. In return the bank receives a *Charge Certificate* inside which is stitched the original mortgage form.

- Insurance
The same criteria apply as already discussed with unregistered land.

(b) Leasehold – first mortgage
The additional steps and considerations relating to obtaining the lessor's permission, giving notice, and valuation, already discussed apply here. The procedure regarding examination of the title,

searching and registering are exactly the same as for a first mortgage on registered freehold land, including obtaining the lease.

(c) Second or subsequent mortgage

- Examination of title

As with unregistered land, an examination of the Land Certificate is not possible as this is either with the first mortgagee or the Land Registry from which you will have to obtain an office copy using form A44. A questionnaire will have to be sent to the first mortgagee. A legal mortgage form can then be completed including the details of the first mortgage. If this is protected only by notice of deposit, then it must be registered before your second mortgage will be accepted for registration by the Land Registry.

- Valuation

The valuation of the equity is required as for unregistered land.

- Search

Unlike a first mortgage, where you can submit the Land Certificate for comparison, the only option you have is to search using form 94A, giving you thirty working days in which to register your charge.

- Registration

Registration is exactly the same as for a registered first legal mortgage, a *Certificate of Second Charge* being received from the Land Registry. All other steps relating to notice to the first mortgagee and the insurance company apply as for a second or subsequent mortgage on unregistered land.

3 Sub-mortgages

A sub-mortgage is a mortgage of a mortgage and can best be illustrated by the following example:

Mr Kelly, your customer, lent £20 000 to Mr Gardner a year ago and as security took a first legal mortgage over a property owned by Mr Gardner and worth £50 000. Mr Kelly finds that he now needs to borrow from you £10 000 and offers as security a charge over the mortgage from Mr Gardner.

As Mr Gardner has now reduced his debt to £15 000 this would be the value of your security and not the value of the property because when Mr Gardner repays the loan in full he has the right, as do all legal mortgagors, to have the property returned to him unencumbered by the mortgage which must be discharged. When this happens the sub-mortgage effectively ceases to exist. Sub-mortgages are infrequently seen in practice and it is not proposed to consider them in detail here. Suffice to say that, should you have to take one, you need to ensure that:

– the original mortgage has been properly and effectively taken.
– the necessary searches and registration are carried out in the same way as for a first legal mortgage. An equitable sub-mortgage is unlikely in practice.
– a legal sub-mortgage form is completed giving details of the original mortgage.
– notice is given to the original mortgagor requesting confirmation of the amount outstanding and that the repayments on the original mortgage be redirected to the bank account of the sub-mortgagor.

Sub-mortgages do suffer from the disadvantages that the value of the security diminishes as the original debt is repaid and if the original mortgage is in any way defective then so will be the sub-mortgage unless the defect can be rectified.

Advantages and disadvantages of land as security

Advantages

The list of advantages is disappointingly short but this in no way diminishes its popularity as security. The main attraction is that land will normally increase in value, although we can all quote examples where the opposite has proved the case. A further advantage is that land is immovable and cannot disappear, although some banks have found to their cost that actual buildings over which they have a charge are derelict or have been demolished, emphasising the importance of valuations.

Disadvantages

These are numerous and can be listed as follows:
- difficult to value (unless residential property)
- difficult to realise because vacant possession is required and adverse publicity can follow eviction
- can impose liabilities on the bank where the title is leasehold and there are onerous covenants in the lease
- complex charging procedures giving rise to mistakes and consequently defective security
- properties are subject to deterioration
- the equitable interests of occupiers need to be accounted for
- with a second or subsequent charge the co-operation of the prior mortgagees may need to be sought before realisation

- insurance cover needs to be maintained and increased in line with the increasing value of the property. (This problem can be overcome by index-linked cover.)

Releasing the security
1 Unregistered land
(a) Equitable mortgage

Where a memorandum of deposit or equitable charge form has been taken, this is cancelled and the deeds returned to the mortgagor against a suitable receipt. The mortgage does not form part of the chain of title and can be placed to old papers. If a charge without the deeds had been taken, a Class C(iii) charge should have been registered at the Land Charges Register and this should now be removed.

(b) Legal mortgage

The form of discharge is normally printed on or attached to the mortgage form and this should be completed and the form placed with the deeds which can then be returned to the chargor. If, however, the bank has been notified of a second mortgage, the deeds must be sent to the second mortgagee. If the bank itself is the second mortgagee then the discharged mortgage form should be sent to the first mortgagee to be placed with the deeds and the Class C(i) charge should be cancelled at the Land Charges Register. Where only part of the land is being released, as with the selling off of building plots, then a separate deed of release can be used.

With both equitable and legal charges any notices to insurance companies should be cancelled and where the charge is on leasehold land the notice to the lessor should be withdrawn.

2 Registered land
(a) Equitable mortgage protected by notice of deposit

If a memorandum of deposit or equitable charge form has been taken, this can be cancelled and placed to lapsed papers. The land certificate can then be returned to the chargor against a suitable receipt and the Notice of Deposit withdrawn from the Land Registry.

(b) Legal mortgage

Where a full legal mortgage has been taken then the charge certificate or certificate of second charge in the case of a second mortgage should be returned to the Land Registry with the application to remove the charge. Where the bank is first mortgagee the Land Certificate will be returned unless there is a second mortgage in which case the Land Registry will retain it. Where it is returned it can be handed to the chargor who must acknowledge receipt. Other notices to insurance companies and lessors should be withdrawn as for unregistered land.

Realising the security
As a legal mortgagee the bank will have several remedies open to it:
• sale of the property
• sue on the personal covenant to repay
• entry into possession
• appointment of a receiver
• foreclosure (*see* Glossary).

In practice, unless there is an alternative source of repayment, the bank will want to sell the property with vacant possession and will normally try to obtain the co-operation of the chargor in occupation of the premises. If the chargor refuses to leave, then a possession order will be applied for in court and ultimately the occupants may be evicted. Once the bank has vacant possession it will ensure that it obtains a fair price for the property, as is its duty, by employing professional estate agents to handle the sale. Where the amount realised exceeds the liability, the bank is obliged to hand any surplus to second or subsequent mortgagees or, if there are none, to the chargor. With unregistered land this will require a search of the Land Charges Register to ascertain whether any subsequent charges have been registered.

If the bank is an equitable mortgagee, the courses of action available to it will depend on whether the mortgage was under hand or under seal. If under hand, and the mortgagor refuses to comply with the undertaking to complete a legal mortgage, the assistance of the courts will be required before a sale can be achieved. With an equitable mortgage under seal the remedies are as for a legal mortgage except for the right to enter into possession of the property.

Guarantees

A guarantee is defined as a promise by one person to answer for the present or future debt of another. An alternative and well-known definition is that of Charles Dickens who said 'A guarantee is where one man who cannot pay gets another man who cannot pay to say that he will.'

A guarantee is an agreement which, like all third party security, must be evidenced in writing (The Statute of Frauds 1677 s.4) and over many years guarantors, who rarely expect to have to pay when they sign the guarantee form, have sought, sometimes successfully, to avoid liability. When guarantors have escaped liability banks have responded where possible by amending their guarantee forms to close escape routes or loopholes. To strengthen further what can often be weak security bank guarantee forms contain several clauses which seek to postpone the legal rights of the guarantor in favour of the bank. For instance, where a guarantor repays part of the outstanding debt, he acquires an equitable right to the extent of such payment in any other securities that the bank may be holding in support of the borrowing. Any further advances to the principal debtor would be subject to this equitable interest and so the guarantee form will contain a clause putting behind the bank's charge any such equitable interest. Other examples would be the guarantor being prohibited from competing with the bank in the insolvency of the principal debtor and being precluded from contesting during legal proceedings the amount of any claim against him by the bank.

Taking a guarantee

Unlike a life policy, a guarantee is not a contract *uberrimae fidei* (of the utmost good faith) but there is, nevertheless, an obligation on you as the banker to answer honestly and accurately any questions asked by the guarantor prior to the signing of the guarantee. The only rider to this is that you have a *duty of secrecy* to your customer and must have permission to disclose information to the guarantor. In practice it is likely that the principal debtor and the guarantor will be present together at the bank at some stage during the discussions and confidentiality should not be a problem. There is no onus on you to volunteer information but you must correct any misapprehension the guarantor appears to be under, as failure so to do may make the guarantee contract voidable, as will any misrepresentation of the facts, whether innocent or fraudulent.

One further preliminary you must always consider when taking a guarantee is the question of undue influence. Is the relationship between the principal debtor and guarantor one protected at law and, if so, should you be taking the guarantee? Even if it is not such a relationship, do you still need to ensure that the guarantor receives independent legal advice so that any later claim by the guarantor of undue influence can be refuted? Particular care may be necessary where the guarantor is a customer of the bank and is dependent upon the bank for financial advice. As in the case *Lloyds Bank Ltd* v *Bundy* (1975) the guarantor might successfully claim undue influence by the bank. Although the circumstances in this case were somewhat exceptional, there remains a danger and, where you are banker to both principal debtor and guarantor, giving rise to a potential conflict of interests, you should consider the question of independent legal advice for the guarantor.

A guarantee can be for a fixed or unlimited amount, the latter type being used where some flexibility is required. Despite the label 'unlimited guarantee', in practice there will be a limit to the liability in that some form of sanctioned facility will have been marked on the guaranteed account. If the balance of the account is in excess of the sum, it will represent the extent of the liability. This is relevant in two respects: the valuation of the guarantee and answers that can be given to the guarantor when the extent of the liability is requested.

Valuation

Before taking a guarantee you will need to satisfy yourself as to the financial standing of the guarantor and this is usually achieved by sending an enquiry to the guarantor's bankers requesting an opinion as to his or her trustworthiness and ability to meet a commitment under the guarantee. The amount quoted will be either the amount quoted in the limited guarantee or the amount for which the unlimited guarantee is being relied upon. If the guarantor is a customer of yours then you can make the necessary judgement. These enquiries are updated during the currency of the guarantee, usually at six or twelve-monthly intervals, to ensure that the guarantor's circumstances have not changed *to the detriment of the security*. The valuation process is made easier where the guarantee is supported by tangible security in the name of the guarantor, because the more substantial this is the less reliance has to be placed on the status report on the guarantor.

When the guarantor wishes to know the amount outstanding you should only disclose the limit of the guarantee liability. Where the balance is in excess of the limit it must not be disclosed, but the guarantor should be told that the guarantee is fully relied upon. Where there is an unlimited guarantee then the balance of the account, which represents the liability, can be disclosed. Under the Consumer Credit Act balances in excess of guarantee limits can be disclosed on written request and payment of a fee.

Signing the guarantee

Any person or entity such as a company who has legal capacity to contract can sign a guarantee. Guarantees can be completed under seal but this is rare in practice. For guarantees under hand to be effective they must be supported by consideration, but this consideration for a bank guarantee is the granting or continuing to grant overdraft or loan facilities. The guarantee form must always be signed on bank premises or in the offices of the solicitor who is giving independent advice and witnessing the signature of the guarantor. Neither the principal debtor nor the guarantor should be allowed to take the form away for signature as disputes could arise subsequently as to the circumstances surrounding the signing of the guarantee.

The one exception to this rule relates to the signing of a guarantee by a company where the form can be sent to the company for completion following the necessary resolution and appointment of signatories. Where the guarantee is to be given by more than one person, known as a *joint and several guarantee*, then all the guarantors must sign before the guarantee becomes effective against any of them.

Once the guarantee has been signed the guarantor(s) should be given a copy of the guarantee, receipt of which should be acknowledged. Thereafter, very little maintenance is required other than the renewal of the status reports on the guarantor.

Advantages of guarantees as security

As with many other forms of security, the advantages seem limited when compared with the disadvantages, but in practice this fact does not appear to have restricted the use of guarantees as security. The advantages can be simply stated as follows:

(a) There is little or no formality and the procedure is very simple and inexpensive.

(b) The upkeep is undemanding requiring only the renewal of status reports.

(c) Should the principal debtor become insolvent the bank can place any repayment by the guarantor to a suspense account and prove for the full amount of the debt in the insolvency.

Disadvantages of guarantee as security

It has often been said that a guarantee is the easiest form of security to take but the most difficult to realise and the following list of disadvantages show why this should be:

(a) The guarantee has no intrinsic value and gives no rights over tangible assets.

(b) The guarantor's financial position may deteriorate without the bank's knowledge and the six or twelve-monthly review of status may be too slow in picking this up.

(c) Guarantors never expect to pay and often refuse to do so making realisation a difficult and lengthy process.

(d) Guarantors have often escaped liability in the past and may continue to do so in the future despite the preventative action of the banks.

(e) There may be a reluctance to enforce the security where the guarantor is a valued and influential customer of the bank.

Releasing the security

Where the borrowing has been repaid by the principal debtor and you are no longer relying upon the guarantee, then the guarantor can be released from liability. However, there are two important points which must be remembered:

(a) If the guarantee had been given for a specific borrowing, then it is imprudent to look to it for any future commitment.

(b) The guarantee form should be retained by the bank.

The latter requirement is also important where the borrowing has been repaid by the guarantor, particularly if the principal debtor is subsequently found to be insolvent. In these circumstances, it is possible that the repayment could be set aside as a preference under the Insolvency Act 1986 and the monies received by the bank made available to other creditors. If this happened the bank would want, amongst other things, to resurrect the guarantee. The guarantee form states that it will at all times remain the property of the bank.

Should the guarantor wish to be released from the liability before the debt is repaid, the procedure to be followed will depend on the circumstances. If you and the principal debtor are willing to accede to this request, either because there is alternative security, or because the borrowing is considered safe on an unsecured basis, then the guarantor can be released from the liability. If you wish to continue to rely on the guarantee, then the guarantor must be referred to the clause in the guarantee form demanding notice of intention to determine the guarantee. At the end of the period of notice, usually one or three months, the account should be stopped and the guarantor advised on the amount of his or her liability.

Realising the security

If in the circumstances just described no alternative arrangements can be made, then the bank will wish to realise its security. This requires demand being made upon the guarantor preceded by demand upon the principal debtor. This procedure will also be followed where you are dissatisfied with the conduct of the account and wish to have the borrowing repaid. Where there are joint guarantors demand for the full amount will be made upon each of them. Any payments received from guarantors should be placed to a *suspense account* or *securities realisation account* to preserve your right to prove for the full amount of the debt in any subsequent insolvency of the principal debtor.

Finally, although a clause in the guarantee form ensures postponement until full repayment is obtained, you must remember that the guarantors have a right to other securities held by the bank to the extent of any repayments they may have provided.

Consumer Credit Act

In this chapter there are several references to the Consumer Credit Act and it is important to point out that special considerations apply to lending regulated by the Act, i.e. amounts of £15 000 or less to an individual, although there are exemptions. These include the issue of Forms of Agreement/Facility letters, the method of taking third party security, and withdrawal rights where land is being taken as security. You must refer to your own bank's procedures when dealing with regulated lending.

Summary

1 Security is not a substitute for the proper assessment of a lending proposition but an alternative source of repayment should things go wrong.
2 Ideally, security should be easy to take, value and realise, and should not impose any liability on the bank.
3 There are various types of security arrangement such as lien, pledge, mortgage and debenture which relate to items of security.
4 It is important to recognise the difference between first

and third party security, the latter being any instance where any party to the security is not a party to the account.

5 Third party security must always be evidenced in writing and demands some consideration of the possibility of undue influence.

6 There are several classes of relationship where undue influence is presumed and independent legal advice should be obtained, both for these and other cases where undue influence might exist.

7 Many standard clauses are common to all charge forms, but it is particularly important to understand the need for a 'continuing security' clause in relation to the 'rule in Clayton's Case'.

8 Significant differences exist between legal and equitable mortgages, both in the way they are taken but, more importantly, in the remedies they provide the mortgagee.

9 Stocks and shares are split into two main categories, namely registered securities and bearer securities – the title to the latter is transferred by delivery.

10 Life policies are contracts uberrimae fidei (of the utmost good faith) and depend upon there being an insurable interest.

11 There are two legal estates in land – freehold and leasehold.

12 There are two types of land – unregistered and registered – the documents of title consisting of a bundle of deeds and a land certificate respectively.

13 The Land Charges Department relates to unregistered land and the District Land Registries to registered land.

14 Guarantees are the easiest form of security to take but, arguably, the most difficult to realise.

Self-assessment questions

1 List *three* features of ideal security.

2 What is the main difference in the remedies available under a legal as opposed to an equitable mortgage?

3 Mr Jones has deposited a gold pocket watch with you for safe-keeping. Is this an example of:

    (a) lien

    (b) pledge

    (c) neither.

4 Company ABC has given you a debenture incorporating a fixed and floating charge on its assets. Will the stock be covered by the fixed charge or the floating charge?

5 You have taken security from Mr and Mrs Cooper in support of an account in Mrs Cooper's sole name. Is this first or third party security?

6 Who will sign the charge form in **5** above?

7 Mr Bloomfield deposits some share certificates to secure a borrowing in the name of Mr Blackbourn. Is this effective security?

8 Who are the three parties to a life policy?

9 Mr Wardle has taken out a policy on his own life for the benefit of Mrs Wardle. Is this an MWPA policy?

10 You wish to release to Mr Murgatroyd a life policy in his name which has been legally assigned to your bank as security. What happens to the form of assignment?

11 Mr and Mrs Robinson and their sons, Paul and Simon, owned a property. Both the legal estate and the beneficial interest were held as joint tenants, but Mr Robinson has recently died. In whom is the beneficial interest now vested?

12 You are completing a second mortgage over unregistered land and have just received a reply to your search of the Land Charges Register. What will it show about the first mortgage?

13 Which five items are you required to send to the District Land Registry when applying to register a first legal mortgage?

14 List three disadvantages of land as security.

15 John Stephens is 17 years old and has substantial funds following his creation of a very successful programme for home computers. He is keen to guarantee a loan for his older brother who wishes to buy a car. Is this security acceptable? If not, why not?

10
Review and control of accounts

Objectives

After studying this chapter you should be able to:
1 explain the purpose of reviewing accounts;
2 spot adverse trends in the run of an account;
3 take early action to remedy the situation.

Introduction

Why do we bother to review accounts? If we apply the principles of CAMPARI (Chapters 6 and 7) and assess the customer's proposition realistically then, surely, we should leave it to run by itself without interference? Easily said, but there will be many a banker with stories to tell about the dangers of not monitoring lendings, with the benefit of hindsight. You constantly need to gather information about an account to have an early indication of any adverse trends.

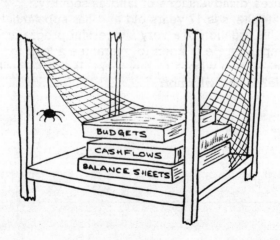

Sometimes a customer is less than honest and uses the funds borrowed for a purpose other than that agreed. Mary Jones may say, for instance, that she wants to buy a hi-fi unit, but you discover later that she has spent the money on gambling. Lending the money is only the beginning. It is most important that you review all borrowings regularly and control those that appear to be getting out of hand. So, what are the sort of things you need to look for? This chapter recommends some guidelines to help you.

Personal and small business accounts

Anticipatory limits

Never ignore the smaller lendings. They have a habit of becoming bigger ones! Many banks today operate *anticipatory limits* which, without prior agreement, gives a customer the opportunity of overdrawing on current account up to a certain percentage of their regular salary income. The internal limits marked tend to be based on the debit turnover through an account, and enable the customer to anticipate up to 50% of monthly salary income.

Such a system helps the customer by providing them with immediate and flexible facilities and helps the bank to reduce the costs of handling this type of account. There is a temptation, however, for the bank officer to let the computer 'do all the work' and, providing the account stays within the anticipatory parameters, to take no further action. In that case, how do you identify that the balance is never improving beyond a certain figure and a solid core of borrowing has developed? This places the banker in a fire-fighting position, having to deal with a problem later than they should, which increases the risk of the borrowing becoming a bad debt.

These limits should not be given to students who do not have regular salaries, nor to minors because recovery may be precluded by law (*see* Chapter 7). Any excesses over the marked limit need to be investigated without delay.

Agreed limits

From time to time the bank will agree with its customers specific overdraft limits for a given length of time to meet short-term needs. A lending record card is raised, briefly outlining the terms of agreement. A diary note is made to review the situation periodically to make sure that the terms are being followed and the borrowing is repaid in time. If the customer fails to honour the agreement then the bank officer will need to make contact to establish the reasons why.

If a customer is over committed, or funds previously expected are no longer forthcoming, then the bank and customer must agree an alternative course of action to repay the borrowing. One method is to transfer the overdraft to a loan account with agreed regular reductions being made. The bank must then control and monitor that borrowing to ensure that the revised terms are fulfilled. If the bank officer diarises too far ahead before carrying out such a review, and maybe if the current account has an anticipatory limit, a situation could arise where the loan is reducing but the overdraft is rising again. Back to square one!

Bank charges printouts

Your bank's computer system will produce extremely useful and varied information to assist you in monitoring the trends on your customers' accounts. Quarterly or half-yearly you will receive a printout of details which form the basis of the commission and interest which will be charged to the accounts. Such details include the number of debit and credit entries, highest and lowest balances for the period, average balances, turnover through the account, and the interest rate applicable. This information will help you to identify unusual features, like the development of a progressively worsening overdraft balance, known as 'hard core', or a particularly high turnover through a personal account.

Some banks produce additional computerised details of borrowing accounts, either monthly or bi-monthly. These printouts show rising trends, hard core borrowing, excesses over agreed limits, dormant borrowings. Any report highlighting the financial history of an account is invaluable in assisting the control of lendings. Early action by the bank may avoid a recovery situation.

Ledger sheets examination

Periodically the lending officer may wish to review a customer's bank ledger sheets or microfiche to look for signs of pressure on the account. For example, does the current account fluctuate well between an agreed overdraft limit and credit? Has the balance been distorted by exceptional items, like a large debit in respect of the deposit on a new home for instance, or a large credit from the sale of, say, a car? There may be a hard core developing, in which case it may be appropriate to transfer that element of the borrowing to a loan account with regular reductions agreed.

Looking at business accounts you may wish to query why turnover through an account is either rising or falling, or indeed why there is any change in the character of the account. Some businesses are seasonal, of course, like ice cream sales people, and you will need to make allowances for this type of change. But take care always to investigate, especially when turnover is falling. One reason may be that the customer is using cash and carry companies and avoiding paying cash into the bank by using the money in direct payment for supplies received. Regular payments may be made out of the account, which could be to other financial institutions. It would be prudent to check the purpose and extent of this other borrowing to keep abreast of your customer's total commitments. Some borrowers overreach themselves considerably and face financial ruin if the problem is not nipped in the bud at an early stage.

Vouchers examination

Obviously it is impractical to examine every voucher that passes through a bank account but, from time to time, you should examine the range of entries. You may decide to look at all entries in excess of a certain amount perhaps, or every item for an account which already gives you cause for concern. But what can these entries tell you?

Debits
You could spot that a business account pays a lot of money to one particular supplier. That could mean that the supplies are dominated by that one creditor, which may cause problems for your customer concerning pricing, timing of deliveries, or the supplier having their own problems. A review of cheques can show a customer's habits and activities; payments made to gambling houses on the one hand, or to building society savings on another. Round amount payments to suppliers need investigating. If the lending has just been granted then you could check whether the debits passed through the account correspond with the purpose for which the customer asked to borrow.

Credits

These provide a banker with a ready source of knowledge concerning income; monthly salary payments, dividends, etc. Are all the credits from one debtor? The same dangers apply with relying on one debtor as they do with relying on one creditor – they may prove unreliable. Never depend on just the ledger balance. It may disguise an uncleared effects position, i.e. uncleared cheques, which, if withdrawn, could place the bank at risk. Any large or unusual entry on any account should be scrutinised and investigated. As bankers, we are required by law to disclose any known instance of customers using their accounts to 'launder' cash, that is to try to hide ill-gotten funds from illegal dealings such as in drugs.

Lending records

A brief note needs to be kept of the terms of lending agreed with both personal and business customers. Any member of staff in the branch then has a point of reference when considering whether to lend more money or to return a cheque unpaid for lack of funds. A diary system is required so that the account can be reviewed regularly to ensure that it is following the agreed terms and is on the right track. At such times the records should be updated with any other relevant information; the personal customer may have married, meanwhile, or had a baby. The business customer may have changed their terms of trade. All of these examples may have an effect on the customers' ability to honour their commitments.

Unpaid cheques

These days, unless we are already checking every entry through a customer's account because of concern over the borrowing, we do not know that an account has gone 'out of order' until the following morning when the computer printout is received. The sheer volume of entries passing through banks preclude us from checking them all. Because of that fact, the clearing banks have an agreement to rely on the 'rule of inadvertence' which provides that, where a cheque is paid by mistake when there are insufficient funds on the account, the cheque may be returned unpaid the following business day. If the cheque is above a certain figure, currently £50, then the collecting bank must be advised by telephone so that they are on notice on non-payment and can pass the necessary entries to debit the payee's account before funds are withdrawn.

Normally each day a branch receives a computer printout showing details of accounts which need to be referred due to overdrafts, excesses, uncleared effects, etc. The decision taken by the drawer's bank depends on the previous track record. All the principles of CAMPARI need to be considered (*see* Chapter 6) and there are certain additional checks which need to be made:

- Whether there are funds on other accounts.
- Another lending officer may have agreed an overdraft or loan which has not yet been processed.
- There may be an account with a similar name to which your customer's credit has been placed in error.
- Look at the ledger sheets and paid vouchers to see whether there have been items posted to the account in error, like postdated cheques.
- There may be a credit in the day's work which has not yet been posted to the account.
- There may be funds due from, say, a sale of stocks/shares.
- A cashier may have forgotten to take out of the customer's paying-in book the credit slip, which should reflect in the branch's internal 'overs in tills' account.
- The cheque may have been issued under the cheque guarantee scheme, in which case the bank cannot return it for lack of funds.
- If a cheque has been cashed under an open credit arrangement it cannot be returned unpaid.
- The security and safe custody register may show evidence of background funds, e.g. life policy with a surrender value, stocks and shares, property.

Once these checks have been made and the principles of CAMPARI applied then you are in a position to determine whether you will pay the debit or return it for lack of funds. The answer on such unpaids depends on the item concerned. If a cheque, then it will be 'refer to drawer' or 'refer to drawer, please represent', or 'uncleared effects'. If a direct debit, then 'refer to debtor'. Do not treat the situation lightly; your action may affect the good standing and reputation of your customer. It is advisable to make arrangements to meet the customer in an attempt to clarify the situation and to find an acceptable solution.

A review of the unpaid register will reveal any trends of regular unpaids on particular accounts. In such cases it may be considered appropriate to close the account.

Other points for consideration

You may find that you are being asked to answer enquiries from other financial institutions regarding the status of your customer. You may wish to investigate the reasons behind such an enquiry. You may also be faced with receipt of a notice of a further charge being taken against security held at the bank, in favour of a third party lending institution. Again, you would wish to investigate why the customer is seeking to borrow outside the bank and the terms involved.

Case study

Until recently, the account of your customers, Mr and Mrs Finnegan, ran smoothly with no problems. There is a regular monthly salary credit of £800 received direct to the account from Mr Finnegan's job at the local engineering firm. During the past few weeks, however, increasing overdrafts have begun to appear and the highest debit balance has now reached over 50% of his net salary. Regular payment orders are:

Mortgage	£350
Rates	£ 70
Heat, light, water	£ 60
Car loan	£100
TV hire	£ 12
	£592

Upon further investigation, you notice from the ledger sheets that the mortgage payments have recently increased from £280 per month. The car loan balance stands at £900. There is a cheque for £65 in respect of the telephone bill in today's clearing.

What would you do?

Well, before returning the cheque for £65 unpaid, you will need to carry out the various checks highlighted above on unpaid cheques. Assuming that there have been no errors or mis-posts, you must then decide whether you will wish to pay an overdraft up to nearly £500 when the salary credit is only £800 and regular payment orders total nearly £600. In any event, you may wish to interview Mr and Mrs Finnegan to establish the reasons for the overdraft and to confirm their total commitments. There may be cash forthcoming from an outside source but, failing that, it may be prudent to set up a loan with an agreed repayment programme – perhaps amalgamating the borrowing with the existing car loan.

Can the new loan repayments be afforded when there is only £200 per month left to service all other expenses including food? If not, it may be necessary for an asset to be sold (stocks and shares, life policy with a surrender value, etc). Is security available? Have the customers moved house recently causing a temporary cash flow problem? In both the bank's and the customers' best interests we would wish to help them through and provide certain disciplines for repayment – current account to stay in credit, for instance, during the currency of the loan. There is no need to take drastic action if, after an interview with the customer you find, for instance, that he is due for an increase in salary shortly. However, only you can decide when you have the full facts available to you.

Summary

Customers are only human and sometimes they fight shy of contacting the bank when they run into financial difficulties. If you are to help them to overcome their problems then you need to be alert to the danger signs. Remember to monitor:

- Ledger sheets for unusual items.
- Computer statistics to identify worsening trends and uncleared effects.
- Vouchers, both debit and credit, for dominant features in debtors, creditors, round amounts.
- Lending records to check that the borrowing follows the agreed terms.
- Unpaid cheques registers.

Review, control and vigilance will reduce or prevent a deteriorating position and avoid the necessity for placing the account on your 'accounts at risk' report.

Self-assessment questions

1 A hard core borrowing is one where there are:
   (a) Regular excesses over the agreed limit
   (b) Few substantial credit balances
   (c) Progressively worsening overdraft balances
   (d) Overdrafts plus loans.

2 Ledger sheets are examined for:
   (a) Number of entries passing through an account
   (b) Breakdown of commission charges
   (c) Range of highest and lowest balances
   (d) Unusual trends.

3 The rule of inadvertence enables a bank to return a cheque unpaid late:
   (a) When payment has been stopped
   (b) For lack of funds
   (c) When it is postdated
   (d) If over £500.

4 If a cashier forgets to take the credit slip out of a customer's paying-in book, it will be shown on the:
   (a) Customer's account
   (b) Overs in tills account
   (c) Shorts in tills account
   (d) Refer list.

5 Round amount cheques to suppliers can be reviewed by examination of the:
   (a) Vouchers
   (b) Computer statistics
   (c) Lending records
   (d) Unpaid cheques register.

11
Bad and doubtful debts

Objectives

This chapter is intended as a guide to help you to:
1 recognise the causes and warning signs for doubtful debts;
2 know when to make formal demand;
3 discuss the benefits of employing debt collectors and tracing agents;
4 explain in outline the stages towards legal proceedings for recovery.

Introduction

Bank statistics show that debts are more likely to be classified as 'doubtful' in recovery terms through banks not applying the principles of regular review and control (*see* Chapter 10) than through unforeseen outside circumstances or fraud. Bankers have many options for spotting problem accounts which, if handled correctly, could help the customer to repay their financial obligations in the long term. Regrettably, warning signs are quite often overlooked until the position is critical and by then it may be too late to take appropriate remedial action. The debt then becomes 'bad' and may have to be written off in the bank's books. This does not please its senior managers or shareholders.

Causes

There are five principal reasons why debts fail:
1 The lending officer's failure to apply the canons of lending when assessing a proposition (*see* Chapter 6, CAMPARI techniques).

'Hello, is that the Bank? Don't worry about the overdraft – I'm just setting off with the cash now.'

2 The lending officer's failure to monitor the borrowing regularly.

3 The lending officer's failure to exercise firm control after noticing a deteriorating position.

4 Unforeseen circumstances beyond the customer's or bank's control, e.g. exceptional storm damage.

5 Fraud by the customer.

The first three points tend to recur most often. Even though a debt may become bad as a result of unforeseen circumstances, it may well be the case that insufficient attention was given to such contingencies when assessing the proposition to lend in the first place.

Warning signs

As a creditor and a banker you have the opportunity of privileged information because you can see all the entries passing through the bank accounts of your personal and business customers. You may spot a large credit which, on investigation, tells you that the business customer has sold a capital asset at short notice, an item which you would expect them to keep to produce profits for the business. The customer may be paying into the account late to meet the issue of cheques presented. Do they exceed their agreed overdraft limit without reference to you and with insufficient explanation? The customer may be paying 'round' amounts to creditors to keep them sweet. For example, paying off £200 per month towards an invoice payment of £657.25, instead of paying the debt as it falls due. Some wily birds deliberately make technical errors on their cheques, e.g. out of date, words and figures differing, in the hope that the bank returns the cheque unpaid for the technicality, thus giving a few more days breathing space. Similarly, customers will place 'stops' on cheques to certain creditors without good reason. Always ask *why* the stop instructions are being given.

Is the personal customer anticipating their salary on an increasing scale? If you check the computer statistics for the account you may recognise the development of a 'hard core' in the borrowing, that is when the overdraft never seems to improve beyond a certain figure. For instance:

John Smith's Account

Month	Max debit balance	Min credit balance	Average balance	Limit
Feb	6824 Dr	3462 Dr	5023 Dr	10 000
Mar	9712 Dr	3523 Dr	4723 Dr	10 000
Apr	9998 Dr	3987 Dr	5554 Dr	10 000

John Smith's account looks as if it is developing a hard core of nearly £4000. The volume of debts passed over the account may be much higher than you would expect for the type of business. It is important also to check for any 'uncleared effects' in the balance, when the customer is using funds before the bank has received value for them in the banking system. Great care must be taken in these circumstances. It is very dangerous to pay funds against uncleared effects – whether or not the account is in debit. Banks lose hundreds of thousands of pounds through customers playing the banking system against them and using bank funds to finance accounts on uncleared effects until they have enough money suddenly to withdraw it all. This is known as 'cross-firing'.

Rather than transferring to another bank, some customers just open a second bank account and leave the account at your bank to become dormant. Any changes in the frequency of funds in or out of the account must be investigated without delay. There will be occasions perhaps outside your customer's control, like a loss of job. Early action by the bank can help the customer to overcome such difficult temporary situations in the long term.

Some customers are, of course, dishonest and will use the funds for a purpose other than that sanctioned. That does not mean to say that the bank will not recover the lending but it is another warning sign to show that the customer is playing games with their finances. However, if we do not take the necessary and effective action in any potentially doubtful lending situation we could be faced with having to take legal action for recovery.

Stages of recovery

Problem accounts fall into two categories. *Doubtful* debts are those where it looks as if repayment will be protracted at best and all of the borrowing may not be recovered. If after taking appropriate action there comes a point when it is unrealistic or a waste of time to continue pursuing recovery, and there is no security available, then the debt becomes classified as *bad* and will have to be written off in the bank's books. Let us look at the various stages in the process.

Stage 1

First, it is vital to check any security held in support of the borrowing. It inevitably seems that whenever the bank wishes to recover the debt it finds that the security has not been perfected. Bank records need to be checked for the background to the borrower; for example, ledger sheets, safe custody registers, regular payment authorities, unpaid cheques register, credits, paid cheques, etc.

Second, we need to establish contact with the debtor. Your own bank will have a best practice for determining how many times you would write in such circumstances to obtain the debtor's realistic proposals and to inform them of your intentions and course of action. We need to find out whether the customer is unemployed to help us determine what may be realistic in those circumstances. A follow-up visit, either at the bank or at the customer's home, tends to be very useful and helps to persuade the customer to face up to the situation. A visit to the customer's home also helps the lending officer to assess their present life style and maybe to size up the availability of more security. Care must be taken, however, that the customer has no excuses for suggesting that the banker is placing them under duress. For that reason it is recommended that two bank representatives make such visits. It may be considered hazardous to make a personal visit in which case the task could be given to a firm of debt collectors on a 'no success, no fee' basis.

Stage 2

Having assessed the situation through contact with the customer, we may determine it necessary to issue a Form of Demand which is required if the bank intends to pursue legal action through the courts. If the borrowing is 'regulated' under the Consumer Credit Act, then a Termination Notice or Default Notice must precede the bank's own Form of Demand. Again, your bank's own practice probably will be to proceed under the guidance of your regional control office. If you have been unable to make contact with the customer, then you may need to consider making a search through a credit reference agency to confirm the debtor's current address, details of their previous commitments and repayments programme, and to discover other claims provided by credit institutions or the courts.

Stage 3

The next stage is for the bank to obtain confirmation of the debtor's means. A Sworn Statement of Affairs is given under oath in front of a solicitor or commissioner for oaths certifying the debtor's assets, liabilities, income and expenditure. In the event that the debtor refuses to provide such a statement, it may be considered prudent to appoint investigators to determine the debtor's means. The customer will be asked to attend an oral examination (see below) at which stage the investigators' findings may highlight assets which the bank may be able to seize and sell to reduce the debt.

If contact with the customer has been lost, the bank could appoint a tracing agent, many of whom work on a 'no luck, no fee' basis. If they are successful, the fees tend to be relatively cheap at £25/£30.

Stage 4

It may be that the debt remains outstanding for a long time with no repayments forthcoming. It is quite possible that the interest accruing on the debt may reach such significant levels that the total borrowing becomes too much for the debtor to afford to repay. If such is the case, then it may be feasible to agree with the debtor some sort of compromise; for example, ceasing further interest charges. However, it is important for the bank to establish that the debtor does repay the maximum they can afford from both income and assets. Your local control office will advise you on the action to take to protect the bank's position.

Further security may be available and should be obtained wherever possible. If, on the other hand, the debtor owns a substantial equity in, say, a home, it may be more realistic to all concerned if they sell and move into a smaller property. This would generate funds to reduce or repay the borrowing. The bank will wish to see a Sworn Statement of Affairs detailing the debtor's current position before making any repayment settlement. The appropriate wording can be provided through your regional office or a local solicitor. It usually includes clauses protecting the bank in the case of fraudulent statements made by the debtor and failure to honour agreed reductions.

Legal proceedings

There will be the occasion when the debtor refuses to co-operate and the bank finds it necessary to take legal action to recover. Before such action is taken, however, the bank needs to consider the impact of the costs involved – solicitors' fees, court fees, etc. The first step will be to send a solicitor's letter to the debtor informing that there will be fourteen days before proceedings commence. A strict timetable of events must then be followed to ensure that the bank's reputation is maintained.

Judgment

Judgment (as in law) is the legal recognition of the amount owed by an individual. If the bank holds security under one of its standard legal charge forms, then it will be able to realise the security without needing to obtain judgment. However, if the security is insufficient to repay the borrowing, and if the bank wishes to pursue its legal remedies against the debtor, it must obtain judgment. Judgment needs to be obtained against each and all parties to ensure that the bank is able to realise jointly owned assets plus all 'regulated' borrowing in accordance with the Consumer Credit Act 1974.

The County Court deals with all 'regulated' borrowings, plus small debts up to £5000. The High Court issues judgments for any amount *excepting* 'regulated' borrowings. Although obtaining judgment through the High Court may be a little more expensive, it may give a psychological advantage to the bank if it is felt that the debtor may ignore County Court proceedings. The bank must bear in mind whether it will wish to obtain an Attachment of Earnings Order (see below) because such an order may be granted only in the County Court. The bank must remember that the debtor may be successful in persuading a court to allow payment by instalments which, in some instances, are pitifully low.

As soon as judgment has been obtained, the bank has the opportunity of having the debtor examined as to means – assets, liabilities, and so on, known as an oral examination. The bank can insist on sight of relevant documents and papers to prove the position. Sometimes this type of examination encourages the debtor to offer repayments to avoid the next step of legal action. We must remember, however, that at all times the bank refers back to its objectives of maximising the return to the bank.

Some common remedies

Listed below are some of the common remedies available to a bank to enable it to recover the debts which have gone bad:

Attachment of earnings order

Regular payments are deducted from the debtor's salary by their employers and routed via the court through the bank's solicitors. Such action is feasible only where there is a regular income which is the most likely source of repayment.

Charging order

The Charging Order Act 1979 provides a creditor with the right to obtain a Charging Order on any beneficial interest under a trust and any interest in:

- land (legal, equitable and beneficial interests)
- certain securities (government stocks, registered stocks and shares)

- funds held in court

The Order acts like an equitable mortgage under hand (i.e. in writing) but gives a charge only against the individual debtor. There is no power of sale and the bank would need to apply to the court for action.

Garnishee order

This order enables a creditor to obtain money owed to the debtor by a third party, for instance, credit balances in a bank account. (Remember, a bank is its customer's debtor.) Obviously, speed is of the essence to freeze the account before the debtor removes the funds. Trade debts can be garnisheed, although we may ponder on the feasibility and advisability of so doing if the trade debtors happen to be customers of the bank.

Levying execution

If a customer defaults on a loan for a consumer durable, e.g. a car, then we may wish to seize that car to sell it and reduce or repay the borrowing. Such an execution may be obtained over a wide range of assets but, quite often, the debtor claims that they are owned by the spouse and the bailiff or sheriff will have problems in proving otherwise.

Receiver by way of equitable execution

This remedy is available for use on assets not covered by a charging order and gives the bank rights over the sale proceeds of an asset when it is sold, a life policy for example.

Bankruptcy proceedings

If all else fails and as a last resort, the bank would take legal action to recover the borrowing by petitioning to make the debtor bankrupt. This happens in particular when the bank is suspicious that the debtor has made dishonest statements or transfers of assets. Once the bankruptcy order has been made by the court all the debtor's assets are vested in a trustee and will be shared amongst the creditors. Under the Insolvency Act 1986 a petition must be presented within four months of a statutory demand for repayment being made, hence our previous comment concerning the necessity to follow a strict timetable of events.

Voluntary arrangements

Subject to the agreement of more than three-quarters of the creditors, a debtor may enter into a scheme of Voluntary Arrangement. Under the Insolvency Act 1986 the debtor may offer partial satisfaction of the debts and, providing that the debtor's proposals are approved, the arrangement will be binding on *all* creditors. Such an arrangement does not affect a secured creditor's rights to enforce any security held, e.g. a bank holding a charge on specified property. The charge cannot be avoided.

Corporate customers

Poor management is the most common cause of business failure. Regrettably, the smaller business tends to suffer most. While the skills of developing the product, be it bedroom furniture or bicycles, are handed down from generation to generation, the management tends to overlook the fact that, as it grows, it needs to be more financially aware. Proper records must be kept of outstanding debtors, stockholdings, etc., to monitor trends. The company may be able to sell as much as it can produce but if it does not have the management skills to control the business and to pay its own debts as they fall due it will fail.

Sometimes, when the chief executive dies, it is discovered that no other person has any idea how to manage the company. No management succession – no business! A common failing is where the 'one-man band' grows and becomes successful to such a degree that staff must be employed. Consequently, management interpersonal skills like team building and delegation, are needed but not always inherent in that type of entrepreneur.

Irresponsible management is another factor in company failure. The principals spend more time on travel and entertainment than on paying attention to the variances in the business figures. Up-to-date financial information is essential to the management of a company. Profitability is the name of the game. If profits are not made, cash flow will eventually suffer and there will not be funds to pay the bills.

The rapidly changing environment catches many otherwise competent managers off guard, particularly where there is heavy competition, a volatile market, social attitudes to the product. Any business which tries to expand or diversify without sufficient capital to finance the plans is in trouble. The procedure for obtaining a judgment against a company is similar to obtaining a judgment for an individual. There are, however, many other legal considerations which must also be taken into account, but it is not intended to cover them in this book.

Summary

In terms of RECOVERY we need to take account of:
- Our   Responsibility to shareholders
- The amount of   Effort needed to obtain recovery
- The debtor's   Circumstances – we need to be firm but sensitive to an individual's case
- Our   Objective for the recovery
- The prior need to Verify our approach
- The necessity to   Evaluate our approach
- The need to be   Realistic – is it cost effective to pursue?

We must maximise the return to the bank in the most efficient and cost effective way, whilst being mindful of any social responsibilities we may have towards the debtor's circumstances. Recovery is the name of the game.

Self-assessment questions

1 Examination as to means is called:
   (a) default notice
   (b) oral examination
   (c) means test
   (d) credit reference search.
2 The County Court deals with:
   (a) all 'regulated' borrowings plus small debts up to £5000.
   (b) all 'regulated' borrowings plus debts in excess of £5000.
   (c) only small debts up to £5000.
   (d) any amount except 'regulated' borrowings.
3 Creating uncleared funds and attempting to draw against them is called:
   (a) levying execution

(b) hard core lending

(c) regulated borrowing

(d) cross-firing.

4 An attachment of earnings order may be granted only in the:

(a) High Court

(b) County Court.

5 A garnishee order:

(a) enables the bank to seize and sell the debtor's assets

(b) gives the bank rights over the sale proceeds of an asset

(c) enables a creditor to seize funds owed to the debtor by a third party

(d) provides a creditor with rights over a beneficial interest in land.

12
Interpretation of financial statements

Objectives

After studying this chapter you should be able to:
1 identify the strengths and weaknesses of financial statements for risk assessment purposes;
2 identify from financial statements effective measures of safety, liquidity, and profitability;
3 examine trends in the key financial criteria;
4 measure the past performance of a business using financial statements;
5 define the purpose and content of budgets and cash flow forecasts for both the customer and the bank;
6 test the validity of projections and the assumptions on which they are based;
7 explain the need to monitor actual performance against that projected and describe the methods which can be used;
8 construct a funds flow statement and explain its use as an assessment tool.

Introduction

When considering propositions from business customers you must attempt to establish the level of risk and in so doing need to examine both the track record of the business and its future prospects. In looking back you need to scrutinise the annual reports of the business which include the profit and loss account, the balance sheet and the source and application of funds statement, more simply described as the funds flow statement. These not only paint a picture of the past performance of a business but also give an indication of what might be possible in the future. In looking forward you will depend upon the budgets and cash flow forecasts produced by the customer who will have made certain assumptions about the future of the business. These assumptions need to be tested to verify how realistic the projections are and one of the most effectie ways of testing is to compare the projections with the past performance of the business. But perhaps the most important thing to remember is that any assessment of financial statements, be they balance sheets or budgets, is likely to be insufficient and ineffective unless you know something about the business and the industry it is in. Historic financial statements only reflect how successfully or otherwise a company or business has managed to cope with the environment in which it has had to operate.

Before discussing in detail how we interpret financial statements and use them in the risk assessment process, it is important to understand fully their basic structure. This understanding will enable you also to appreciate their strengths and weaknesses.

'Wow! You really want us to write your cashflow forecast?'

Financial statements

From your study of *Introduction to Accounting* you will be familiar with the structure and content of financial statements and will be aware that these are drawn up in accordance with two sets of rules:

(a) The laws of the land and in particular the *Companies Acts* for incorporated businesses.

(b) *Statements of Standard Accounting Practice (SSAP)* as laid down by a joint committee of the accountancy institutes in the UK.

All registered companies are obliged to have their accounts audited annually by qualified auditors but this rule does not apply to sole traders, partnerships or other unincorporated businesses. These will, however, be required to produce some record of activity, and assets and liabilities so that the Inland Revenue can assess any tax liability. It is usual also for bankers who are lending money to such businesses to insist that audited accounts be produced at least each year so that a proper review of the facility can take place. These requirements of the Revenue and the banks have given rise to the long held belief amongst bankers that many businesses produce at least two sets of accounts, one for the Revenue showing as little profit as possible to eliminate tax payments, and one for the bank showing an impressive profit performance in order to enhance borrowing capabilities. This may or may not be true but it does highlight the first of the *limitations or weaknesses in financial statements* which are as follows:

(a) Despite statutory obligations and the imposition of SSAPs, manipulation of the information is possible as many of the rules provide for a wide variety of interpretations.

(b) The balance sheet only shows the position on one day in the trading year – a balance sheet drawn up the following day may paint a very different picture.

(c) The figures, being historic, are to a greater or lesser extent always out of date.

(d) While they can be a guide to the future, they concentrate on the past.

(e) There are many things that they cannot tell you about a business such as the nature of its markets, the quality of its staff or the fierceness of the competition.

Having said this, the financial statements remain the best and usually the only source of financial information available on most businesses, and give a good indication of the trading record.

Balance sheet

Balance sheets show on a given day the assets and liabilities of the business, or the resources available to the business and the means by which these are being funded. They are presented usually in a vertical format as shown below, but because more than one method of presentation is acceptable most banks will attempt to standardise the format for interpretative purposes by extracting the information on to their own 'spreadsheet'.

Balance Sheet

Fixed Assets

Freehold Premises		150
Plant and Machinery		50
Motor Vehicles		40
		240

Current Assets

Cash	20	
Debtors	1050	
Stock	700	
		1770

Current Liabilities

Tax	10	
Creditors	1300	
Hire Purchase	40	
Bank Overdraft	120	
		1470

Net Current Assets/(Liabilities)	300
	540

Financed by

Share Capital	200
Retained Profit	340
	540

You must be aware that while some of the items in the balance sheet represent an accurate statement of the value or amount outstanding this does not apply to all of them. For instance, the freehold premises may well appear at their original cost whereas the current market value is greatly in excess of this figure. These true amounts must be considered when you are analysing the figures looking for trends and calculating ratios.

Profit and loss account

The profit and loss account is not just a snapshot like a balance sheet but more a record of activity, giving the sales or turnover for the period in question, the cost of those sales and the resulting gross profit (or loss). From this is then deducted (or added) the overheads and other expenses of running the business, the residual amount representing the net profit (or loss). It should be possible to identify how the profit is made, but you must be aware that extraordinary or exceptional items can distort the picture. For instance, a manufacturing company may sell part of its premises at a profit one year, but this is a transaction which will not be repeated on a regular basis, and you should exclude this profit when making comparisons between one year and the next. As profit is ultimately the only source of repayment for bank borrowing, its consistency and quality is very important to the banker.

Profit and Loss Account

		£000
Sales		150
less Cost of Sales		70
Gross Profit		80
Salaries	30	
Rent and Rates	8	
Distribution	5	
Heat, Light, Water	6	
Depreciation	11	
		60
Net Profit		20
(before Interest and Tax)		
Bank Interest	4	
Tax	2	
		6
		14

Statement of the source and application of funds

The funds flow statement seeks to show how funds have moved into and out of the business over the period in question. In its simplest form it is merely a record of the movement in the balance sheet items between one year and the next but can be presented in such a way as to be much more informative. Many bankers now see the funds flow statement as the crucial financial document when assessing a company's performance because it shows whether a business consumes or generates cash.

Source and Application of Funds

Net Profit (before Interest and Tax)	67 000
add Depreciation	35 000
Adjustment for Other Items not involving the movement of funds	2000
Working Capital Variation (*see* below)	1000
	105 000
less Interest Paid	25 000
Tax Paid	10 000
	70 000
add Disposal of Fixed Assets	4000
less Capital Expenditure	30 000
Cash Available for Dividends	44 000
Dividends Paid	5000
Cash Available for Investment	39 000
Investments/Acquisitions	6000
Cash Surplus/(Deficit)	33 000
Financed by/Applied to	
(Increase)/Decrease in Debt	23 000
Increase/(Decrease) in Cash	10 000
	33 000

Working Capital Variation
Stocks (Increase)/Decrease	(2000)
Debtors (Increase)/Decrease	(21 000)
Creditors Increase/(Decrease)	24 000
Other Variations	
Working Capital Surplus (Deficit)	1000

From the Source and Application of Funds statement you can see that the company generated funds amounting to £102 000 (£67 000 + £35 000) from its normal trading operations and this was more than sufficient to cover the purchase of capital equipment amounting to £30 000. The need to fund higher levels of stocks and debtors (£2000 + £21 000) was offset by the ability to obtain a further £24 000 from creditors. Finally, the company was a net generator of cash to the tune of £33 000 and this was used to reduce debt and increase cash balances.

Notes to the accounts

The notes to the accounts are as important as the accounts themselves because they define the basis on which the accounts are produced and also give more detail of individual items in the balance sheet, profit and loss account and the funds flow statement. It is particularly important that you notice any change in accounting policies because these may have the effect of distorting the information and this fact needs to be taken into account when you are trying to interpret the figures. The example below will illustrate this.

The profits for The Manipulation Co Ltd read as follows:

	Year 1	Year 2	Year 3
	20 000	25 000	28 000
After depreciation of	15 000	20 000	16 000

The profits show an improving trend which would please most bankers. However, the notes to the accounts in Year 3 state that depreciation policy has changed, resulting in a lower depreciation charge. This means that the profit in Year 3 has been calculated differently to Years 1 and 2 and any analysis of the trend of the profit which ignored this fact would be flawed.

Interpretation

The financial statements are a source of information which should help you assess risk and make a lending decision by providing some answers to the questions raised by the application of the canons of lending as follows:

(a) *Character and ability*

- Do the audited accounts provide evidence that the proprietors have managed the business successfully over a period of time?
- Is this business profitable and how does the profitability look when compared to that of other businesses in the same industry?

(b) *Margin*

- What is the level of risk involved and what should the return be to reflect this?

(c) *Purpose*

- Do the balance sheet and funds flow statement show a need for the advance?
- What will be the impact on the balance sheet of an increase in the lending?

(d) *Amount*

- Does the amount appear sufficient?
- How does the amount being borrowed or requested compare with the proprietors' investment in the business?

(e) *Repayment*

- Profit is the ultimate source of repayment: is it sufficient both to service and repay the borrowing?
- Is the repayment programme realistic?
- Are profits turned into cash or consumed elsewhere?

(f) *Insurance*

- What assets does the business own and are they suitable/available as security?
- Are asset values accurate?
- If the lending is unsecured what is the net worth of the business? Is it sufficient to protect the bank's position should things go wrong?

Selection of key criteria

Interpreting financial statements is an art rather than a science and bankers subject to the same experiences and training will still approach the subject differently. But there are certain ground rules which need to be observed:

(a) If trends are to be identified then more than one year, and preferably a minimum of three years, need to be examined.

(b) You need to ensure that you are comparing like with like before drawing any conclusions. This means that allowance must be made for any year where accounts have been constructed differently to the norm.

(c) Conclusions should not be based on the movement in one figure or ratio but supporting evidence should be sought. If this is not available then questions should be asked of the proprietors.

(d) Key criteria or measures of performance should be selected and used as a framework for interpretation.

Although approaches to interpretation will vary in detail, most bankers will agree on the important areas which are *safety, liquidity and profitability*, although not necessarily in this order. Within each of these areas there are key ratios or financial relationships which seek to measure risk or performance and you need to understand how these are constructed, what makes them move one way or another, and what is their significance.

Which of these you use in practice will depend upon several things, not least your personal preferences.

Safety

There are two main questions you need to ask about safety:

(a) What is the net worth or net tangible asset value of the business, also known as the surplus?

(b) How does the surplus compare with borrowed money in the business, including the bank's, known as the gearing?

Surplus

The first question has been asked traditionally by bankers as part of a 'gone concern' approach to risk assessment which says that if everything goes wrong how much of a buffer is there (the surplus) before the bank's money is at risk. If the business makes a loss, then the surplus reduces and will continue to do so as long as losses are incurred. Losses are likely also to create an increased demand for bank assistance as the business is not generating its own funds to finance future trading or capital expenditure.

The surplus represents the amount of cash that would remain if all the tangible assets of the business were sold at their balance sheet values and all liabilities repaid. If you wish to examine this figure in isolation, which bankers still do to get a feel for the size and strength of the business, then there are certain items which may have a bearing on the surplus and which must, therefore, be taken into account.

(a) *Hidden reserves* Where the current market value is greater than the balance sheet value of an asset, then the surplus will be understated. Conversely, some assets may appear at greater than their actual value and the surplus will be overstated, an example being debtors where insufficient deductions have been made for bad and doubtful debts.

(b) *Amounts due to directors* Directors may have provided loans to the company or may have left in the company for cash or tax purposes undrawn remuneration. While these amounts are not fixed capital, they can be counted as part of the surplus. It is possible in practice to ensure that these sums remain in the business by arranging for the directors to sign letters of postponement in favour of the bank.

Looking at the size of the surplus in isolation will not tell you very much other than whether it is increasing or decreasing. What is more important to ascertain is why it is moving one way or the other. Has the business been retaining profits over a period and so building up the surplus or has it been revaluing assets thereby creating a capital reserve and an increase in the surplus?

A comparison of two companies will illustrate this:

	Steady Growth Ltd	Miscellaneous Ltd
	£	£
Surplus	100 000	100 000
Comprising:		
Opening Share Capital	10 000	10 000
Capital Reserve	–	20 000
Capital Issue	–	30 000
Retained Profits	90 000	40 000
	100 000	100 000

It could be argued that Steady Growth Ltd provides greater reassurance to the banker given that it is its consistent profit record which has enabled it to grow, whereas Miscellaneous Ltd has had to raise fresh capital and has included a capital reserve following a revaluation of assets. If you are comparing the quality of the growth in the surplus then Steady Growth Ltd is the more attractive company. How often and quickly will Miscellaneous Ltd be able to raise capital in the future? When is the next asset revaluation?

Gearing
Gearing is a term used to describe the amount of borrowed money in a business, the relationship of debt to equity, or *leverage* as the Americans call it. It follows that a company with a substantial amount of borrowed money in relation to the surplus is highly geared and a company with limited borrowing commitments is lowly geared. There are no hard and fast rules as to what level of gearing is acceptable because this will vary from business to business, but banks traditionally start to get edgy when the ratio exceeds 1:1. UK banks are deemed to be much less generous with gearing levels than their other European or American counterparts.

There are several ways in which gearing can be measured and you can use one or more of them as the need arises:

$$\text{Gross gearing} = \frac{\text{Total borrowing}}{\text{Surplus}}$$

$$\text{Net gearing} = \frac{\text{Total borrowing} - \text{Cash}}{\text{Surplus}}$$

$$\text{Potential gearing} = \frac{\text{Actual proposed borrowing limits}}{\text{Surplus}}$$

$$\text{Gearing (total liabilities)} = \frac{\text{Total liabilities}}{\text{Surplus}}$$

When using any of these ratios you must remember that the surplus may be distorted by an undervaluation or overvaluation of assets, and if you include amounts due to directors as capital it will dramatically change the ratio. For example:

Surplus	50 000
Borrowed money including	
£20 000 due to directors	40 000
Gross gearing ratio	0.8:1

Now assume that the £20 000 due to directors is treated as capital:

Surplus	70 000
Borrowed money	20 000
Gross gearing ratio	0.29:1

It is also important to note that the first three ratios do not include trade creditors so that where borrowing from banks and other institutions is being reduced at the expense of trade creditors the gearing ratio will improve but the total exposure of the company may increase. What you really need to know is whether the gearing trend is up or down and why. An ever increasing reliance on borrowed money makes a business more vulnerable because the supply of funds may dry up and interest charges will have a progressively greater impact on profit margins. Because of this you must be just as concerned about a company's ability to service its debt as you are about the comparative size of that debt.

There are two elements to servicing a debt; one is covering the cost or interest charge and the other is meeting repayments as and when they fall due. The measure of ability to cover the cost is *'interest cover'* and this is calculated as follows:

$$\frac{\text{Profit before interest and tax}}{\text{Interest paid}} = \text{Times covered}$$

The result is the number of times the interest is covered, the more the better as far as the bank is concerned. It follows that a highly geared company will pay more interest and may find it more difficult to earn sufficient profits to provide an acceptable level of cover. Furthermore, the highly geared company is more susceptible to increases in interest rates and unless profits are improved in these circumstances the interest cover will decline.

If you wish to analyse further the impact of interest charges it is often enlightening to compare the profit margin before and after interest. For example, if relevant margins are:

$$\frac{\text{Profit before interest and tax}}{\text{Sales}} = 15\%$$

$$\frac{\text{Profit before tax}}{\text{Sales}} = 10\%$$

it is obvious that the interest charges are eroding one third of the profit margin or to put it another way, for the first four months of the year the company is working for the bank! One general word of warning is appropriate here. When you are comparing one percentage with another, do not fall into the trap of misreading any movement. For instance, it would be easy in the previous example to say that interest had reduced the margin by 5% rather than 33⅓%. In practice, interest cover of 1:1 is the absolute minimum but even 2:1 is considered low. What you want to see is sufficient cover and a rising trend.

There is a school of thought which maintains that cash flow provides a more accurate measure of interest cover than profit, although the aggregate cash flow for a period of 3 or 4 years should be used to iron out any wild fluctuations. The justification for this is that interest can be paid only out of cash and the calculation would be as follows:

<u>Aggregate cash flow before interest and tax</u>
Aggregate interest paid

Generating sufficient cash to cover interest is one thing, but the business will also be required to repay any borrowing. An overdraft is supposed to be a fully fluctuating short-term facility funding cash shortages arising out of the normal trading process, but medium- or long-term loans will have an agreed repayment programme. To measure a company's ability to meet these longer-term commitments you can use the following:

<u>Medium and long-term debt (including current portion)</u>
Operating cash flow (after interest and tax)

This will produce a period of years to repayment and the shorter this is the better. It might be interesting to compare this period with the repayment period agreed with the customer.

Liquidity

Liquidity is an overused word in the context of balance sheets and running a business, and there are several views as to its meaning. For the purpose of this discussion liquidity simply means *the ability of the company to meet its debts as and when they fall due*. This in turn means having either sufficient cash or lines of credit available to meet commitments as they arise. While profit is vital for the future health of a business, access to cash or credit is often more important. It has been known for profitable companies to go into liquidation for a lack of cash. Liquidity has been measured traditionally by calculating the liquid or working capital surplus or deficit as follows:

Current Assets − Current Liabilities

Alternatively, it is expressed as a ratio known as the *current ratio*:

Current Assets
Current Liabilities

No conclusions about the trend in the liquid surplus or deficit or the current ratio can be drawn without some analysis of their constituent parts. For instance, in this next example you might be tempted to say that Water is more liquid than Milk:

	Water Ltd	Milk Ltd
Liquid surplus	20 000	10 000
Current ratio	2:1	1.5:1

If you now look at the example below you will see a breakdown of the current assets and liabilities and it may be more difficult to decide which company is more liquid.

	Water Ltd	Milk Ltd
Current Assets		
Cash	3000	10 000
Debtors	7000	15 000
Stock	30 000	5000
	40 000	30 000
less		
Current Liabilities	20 000	20 000
Liquid Surplus	20 000	10 000

75% of Water Ltd's current assets is tied up in stock, whereas over 80% of Milk Ltd's assets are in cash or debtors.

Liquidity is also dependent to some extent on the nature of the business. For instance, large retailers such as supermarkets can manage very happily without working capital because their terms of trade allow them to do so. They buy in bulk on credit from their suppliers but sell for cash and have few if any debtors. Manufacturers on the other hand have to finance stocks of raw materials, work in progress and debtors and have a need for working capital. Unfortunately, this need often increases in line with an increase in turnover unless they can manage their assets and liabilities more efficiently.

There are slightly more refined measures of liquidity than the one we have just examined and these are:

1 *Liquid ratio* calculated as follows:

$$\frac{\text{Cash} + \text{Quoted Investments} + \text{Debtors (Quick Assets)}}{\text{Current Liabilities}}$$

2 *Acid test ratio* which is:

$$\frac{\text{Current assets capable of conversion into cash within one month}}{\text{Current liabilities which have to be met within one month}}$$

Again the constituent parts must be examined before conclusions can be drawn and any statements made about trends. This examination may include an analysis of the trends in the individual items and some assessment as to how successfully they are being managed by the proprietors. The items which may need to be examined, the measures used and the questions which might be asked, are listed below:

1 Debtors: the average amount of credit being given is calculated as follows:

$$\frac{\text{Debtors}}{\text{Sales}} \times 365 = \text{Number of days given}$$

You will have to be careful where the period in question is not a full year and some banks prefer to use an average figure for debtors and sales, adding together the opening and closing figures and dividing by two. Where the length of time given is increasing you will want to establish the reasons, one of which may be poor credit control. Comparisons can also be made with similar business and any standard terms of trade for the industry. If the period is reducing then cash will be generated automatically because the company is financing a shorter period of credit but if it is achieving the reduction by offering discounts for early payment, then the calculations must be carefully made because it may be cheaper to borrow, pay interest, and wait for the debtors to pay in full.

You will also need to be happy that there is a good spread of debtors rather than a small number whose failure could seriously affect the business. Remember also that the period calculated is only an average and there will be extremes either side of this. If a large proportion of sales are for cash then the actual period of credit given will be longer than calculated unless you eliminate cash sales from your calculations. If the period is increasing significantly then you may decide to ask the customer for an aged list of debtors to establish in more detail what proportion of the debtors is good.

2 Stock: the average rate at which the stock turns over is calculated as follows:

$$\frac{\text{Stock}}{\text{Cost of goods sold}} \times 365 = \text{Number of days}$$

If a Cost of Goods Sold figure is not available the Sales figure will suffice and, as with Credit Given, an averaging method can be used. There is rarely a full audit of the stock by the auditors, who take the figure given to them by the proprietors or directors but satisfy themselves that there is an adequate stock control and valuation system. It is possible, therefore, for the valuation to be inaccurate and if this is the case many other items and measures are affected. In fact, because the stock valuation has a direct impact on the calculation of the gross profit, the net profit and ultimately the surplus, there are very few key figures or ratios that will not be affected. Consequently, if you have need to question the stock valuation you must be fully aware of the repercussions for other measures of performance and risk.

You will want to know whether stock levels are increasing or decreasing in line with turnover. Where you have details of the composition of stock as between raw materials, work in progress and finished goods, you may need to examine these figures individually as they relate to the total and each other. Increasing stock levels require financing and, as such, will consume cash, although this can be mitigated by persuading suppliers of raw materials to extend further credit. Conversely, more efficient stock management will result in lower stock levels being necessary and cash will be generated. Again, it must be remembered that the rate of turn calculated is only an average and may disguise some out-of-date or unsaleable stock. Where the turnover period is lengthening significantly, then the management must be questioned as to possible reasons. They may be stocking for a particular contract or to meet a particular market, or it may be that they have missed a market and are stuck with the stock. In addition to comparing one year to the next, comparisons can be made with typical turnover periods for similar businesses and products.

3 Trade creditors: the average amount of credit being taken is calculated as follows:

$$\frac{\text{Creditors}}{\text{Cost of Goods Sold}} \times 365$$

Previous comments concerning averaging and substituting the sales figure apply here. Although the purchases figure might give you a more accurate answer, this is not often available. As with all of these calculations, the important point is that you are consistent in the method so that trends can be revealed rather than being precisely accurate in the arithmetic. The questions you might want to ask about creditors are similar to those for debtors. Are the creditors well spread or are there unusually large amounts outstanding to a small number of creditors, any one of whom could bring pressure to bear and ultimately petition for the bankruptcy or liquidation of the business? Particular care must be taken to ensure that preferential creditors, such as HM Customs and Excise for VAT, are included in any analysis and are paid up to date. If the period of credit taken is lengthening it may be the result of improved terms negotiated with suppliers or merely because the business has cash flow problems and is unable to pay creditors on the due day. Where a company is managing its creditors more efficiently and taking advantage of extended credit its cash flow will improve. An added advantage of this policy is that less borrowing is required and consequently less interest is paid. The business person needs to balance the cash savings that might be earned from discounts for early payment against potential interest charges and must ensure that creditors' forbearance is not abused.

Where there is a worsening trend and this is matched by a deterioration in the bank account, evidenced by excesses and unpaid cheques for instance, it is likely that there are serious cash flow problems. You must also realise that where credit from suppliers is taken in preference to bank borrowing you must not be misled by an apparent improvement in the *gearing ratio*.

Furthermore, previous comments concerning cash transactions apply here in that where the proportion of cash purchases included in the cost of goods sold increases, the period of credit taken will be understated.

Exhibit 12.1

Purchases *including* cash transactions	125 000
Creditors	15 000

$$\text{Period of credit taken} = \frac{15}{125} \times 365 = 44 \text{ days}$$

Purchases *excluding* cash transactions	110 000
Creditors	15 000

$$\text{Period of credit taken} = \frac{15}{110} \times 365 = 50 \text{ days}$$

Where the terms of trade remain the same but the turnover increases you should see a rise in the level of debtors, creditors and stock. *See* Exhibit 12.2. The increased debtors and stock will consume cash because they have to be financed and, although some of the need will be met by the increased credit taken, the balance will have to be found from retained profit, and where this is insufficient, from further borrowing.

Exhibit 12.2

Consistency Ltd

	Year 1 £000s	% sales	Year 2 £000s	% sales	Year 3 £000s	% sales
Sales	802		865		995	
Debtors	240	30	260	30	298	30
Stock	176	22	190	22	219	22
Creditors	166	21	182	21	209	21
Cost of goods sold	487		528		607	
Credit given	109 days		110 days		109 days	
Credit taken	124 days		126 days		126 days	
Stock turn	132 days		131 days		132 days	

If you calculate the liquid surplus (debtors + stock – creditors) for each year for Consistency Ltd and divide it by the sales you will see the amount of working capital which is required for each £ of sales.

	Year 1 £000s	Year 2 £000s	Year 3 £000s
Liquid Surplus	250	268	308
Divide by sales =	£.30	£.31	£.31

It follows, therefore, that if sales increase in Year 4 by, say, £100 000, all else being equal, there will be a need to fund a further £31 000 of working capital. If the increase in turnover is coupled with a fall in profits, then the borrowing requirement will increase. This measure is not scientific but can be very useful as a guide to future requirements and as a check against a customer's forecast of borrowing needs. You must exclude from the calculation extraneous current assets and liabilities and concentrate on just debtors, stock, and creditors, known as the *net working assets*.

Overtrading
Most but not all businesses have a need for working capital, but whether the amount is adequate will depend on the nature of the business, the terms of trade, and the level of turnover. Where there is insufficient working capital to support the level of sales, then there is a danger that the business may be overtrading and unless this is controlled the business will fail. If sales continue to outstrip the resources available to the business more and more reliance is placed upon outside sources of finance, the bank and the suppliers, and ever increasing pressure is exerted on debtors to pay up because cash becomes a very scarce commodity. If overtrading does exist it will be apparent from the balance sheet in the following ways:

(a) Dramatic increases in turnover and current assets and current liabilities but without any increase in the surplus or liquidity.

(b) A disproportionate increase in finance provided from outside the business resulting in a deterioration in liquidity evidenced by worsening liquid and acid test ratios.

(c) Credit taken period lengthening but period of credit given reducing.

(d) Gross profit margin falling because stock is being sold at reduced prices to raise cash.

There will be corroborating evidence in the way the bank account is conducted in that there will be pressure on limits, constant excesses, returned cheques, requests to pay cash against uncleared funds, and cheques being issued in round amounts representing part of the debts to creditors to keep them quiet.

The signs of overtrading are fairly easy to spot but the solutions are more elusive. Depending upon the severity of the problem, a controlled retrenchment with an injection of capital may help, but it is likely that the bank will have to advance further monies in the short term to enable the business to trade out of its difficulties.

Cash flow
As has already been mentioned, it is more important to examine the composition rather than the amount of the liquid surplus to establish a more accurate view of liquidity, but perhaps the truest test of liquidity is the quality of the cash flow. You need to ascertain whether a business consistently produces a positive cash flow and how it does it. If, over time, a business generates profits from normal trading and reinvests these in the business, then it is financing its own activity and growth. Where, however, profitability is inconsistent and inflated in some years by occasional profits from such things as the sale of fixed assets, then the quality of the profit and consequently the cash flow is questionable. Because it is quality and consistency you are looking for as a guide to the future it is necessary to analyse the cash flow over a number of years. This can be done using a simple model (*see* Figure 12.1) which enables you to establish the proportion

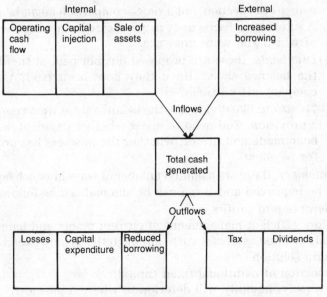

Fig. 12.1

of cash traditionally provided internally and externally and how this is dispersed or applied. By expressing each source and application as a percentage of the total it is possible to recognise patterns or trends which will be useful for forecasting.

Other current assets and liabilities

An examination of items under this heading should only be necessary where the amounts are substantial or there have been significant movements between one period and the next. Some examples and the sort of questions which might arise are:

(a) *Cash and Bank:* compare with previous years and investigate any substantial fall. An examination of the funds flow statement may elicit how the cash has been employed.

(b) *Quoted investments:* what is the current market value? If this is substantially different from the balance sheet value the surplus will be affected and ratios may need to be recalculated.

(c) *Hire Purchase/leasing:* which are the corresponding assets and what are the monthly or annual commitments? Assets acquired on hire purchase or leased will not be available to other creditors on liquidation.

(d) *Bank overdraft:* this will not agree precisely with the account balance on the same day due to cheques and credits in the course of collection, but a rough comparison might be useful. A substantial discrepancy may indicate borrowing elsewhere of which you were unaware.

(e) *Dividends:* these are proposed but not paid at the date of the balance sheet. Have they now been paid? Can the company afford them?

(f) *Taxation:* like dividends, the balance sheet item represents a provision. You need to know whether payment has now been made and, if not, whether the business has provided for payment.

In summary, there are a limited number of ways in which liquidity can be improved and these can be summarised as follows:

- Retention of profits.
- More efficient management of current assets and liabilities.
- Sale of fixed assets for cash, although this is only ever a short-term solution.
- Injection of additional fixed capital.

Conversely, liquidity will deteriorate where a business:

- incurs losses

- mismanages its current assets and liabilities
- purchases fixed assets using cash or short term financing.

Profitability

Profitability is the ability of a business to earn a profit over a period of time and must be distinguished from the figure for profit. This is merely a measure of how successfully or otherwise the business has exercised this ability. Although the profit figure is the starting point for any calculation of cash flow, the comment has already been made that profitable companies can fail for a lack of cash.

It is a fact of life that profit rarely equals cash but, despite this, it is profit which, in the long term, will ensure the continued existence and health of a business. Profit can be calculated in a variety of ways all permitted by accounting conventions, and it is vital that before drawing any conclusions you ensure that you are comparing figures which have been arrived at by similar methods. It is also necessary to establish which profit it is you are talking about. Is it gross profit or net profit before interest and tax (PBIT) or net profit after interest and tax, and have extraordinary or exceptional items been excluded or included?

Before attempting to measure profitability it is advisable to pay some attention to the actual figures for profit or loss. A rising or falling trend should be apparent immediately and a comparison can be made with the movement in turnover. You can then try to discover more precisely how the profit has been earned or the losses incurred. Are profits from trading or are they largely attributable to extraordinary items? In short, what is the quality of the profit? Are the profits being retained in the business or being dissipated on dividends or excessive drawings?

Let us now look at some measures of profitability and examine how these might be applied to the task of assessing the performance of the business.

$$\text{Gross profit} = \text{Sales} - \text{Cost of goods sold}$$

$$\text{Gross profit margin} = \frac{\text{Gross profit}}{\text{Sales}} \times 100$$

If the gross profit margin remains constant, then the gross profit should rise or fall proportionately to sales. Analysing movements in the margin, therefore, will be more fruitful and informative than merely looking at the gross profit figures. It can also be useful to compare the gross profit margin across similar businesses, although there will often be good reasons for any disparity. An improving trend in the margin is to be welcomed and, as long as overheads are controlled, will result in an enhanced net profit. Where the trend in the margin is downwards you must not automatically assume that disaster is around the corner.

A business person may as a matter of policy reduce prices and, therefore, margins to improve sales. If the ultimate outcome is a higher gross profit, then there can be little cause for complaint. However, there may well be some cause for concern where the margin is falling and questions may have to be asked of the customer. The deterioration could be caused by one or more of the following:

- Failure to pass on higher material or production costs.
- Poor buying decisions.
- Increased competition on prices.
- Pilferage, wastage, returned goods.

We saw earlier that the stock valuation has a direct bearing on the calculation of gross profit and any distortion here will also distort the gross profit and the margin. Because full stocktaking and valuation is a time-consuming and expensive business it has been known for business proprietors to simplify the process using an assumed gross profit margin. For example, if the customer is convinced that he is earning a gross margin of 40% the calculation would be as follows:

Sales		£250 000
less Cost of sales		
Purchases	£160 000	
+ Opening stock	£ 30 000	
	£190 000	
− Closing stock	£?	
Gross profit @ 40%		£100 000

The gross profit figure is assumed and it is a simple matter to work backwards to the closing stock which will be £40 000. It may well be that the opening stock was calculated in the same way, it being the closing stock for the preceding period. However, this is not a consistency in approach that you should welcome. Suffice to say that when you are examining the financial statements and the gross profit margin is the only constant factor – beware!

$$\text{Net profit margin} = \frac{\text{PBIT}}{\text{Sales}} \times 100$$

This is a widely used measure of performance and is comparable across companies in similar industries. The fact that a business works on very low margins need not cause alarm because there are some sectors of industry which work on a basis of high turnover and low margins, for example supermarkets. What is more important is any trend in the margin and whether it compares well with similar businesses. If you compare the trends in the gross and net margins you may be able to isolate problems. Where the gross margin is constant or improving but the net margin is declining this may indicate a lack of control of costs or exceptional increases in overheads. A detailed profit and loss account may not be included in the annual report, and if you are concerned or have queries, then a copy should be obtained from the customer.

$$\text{Return on capital employed} = \frac{\text{Net income}}{\text{Capital employed}} \times 100$$

Some explanation of the terms used may be necessary here. Capital employed can be defined in different ways, but in its simplest form it is the proprietors' stake in the business or surplus to which is added medium and long-term liabilities. Net income is PBIT plus other income such as investment income. This measure illustrates the return on the capital investment in the business and can be compared with previous years, with similar companies and with other forms of investment. Using this definition of capital employed it should be obvious that if a company switches long-term funding to short-term and net income remains the same, the margin will improve. This is one of the reasons some banks include short-term borrowing in the calculation of capital employed.

$$\text{Return on total assets} = \frac{\text{Net income}}{\text{Total assets}} \times 100$$

The argument in favour of this measure is that the managers of a business have the total assets at their disposal and it is their task to maximise the return on these. In this context it could be considered a true test of their competence.

Other factors

Having covered the key areas of safety, liquidity and profitability, it is appropriate to look at some items which, while not falling under one of these headings, are nevertheless important.

Auditors' certificate
Public companies are obliged to produce audited accounts within seven months of their year end and private companies within ten months. Even these periods make the information very much out of date by the time the bank receives a copy, but if the auditors' certificate is dated outside these periods then this may give cause for some concern.

More importantly, you want to see an unqualified report from the auditors and if there is a qualification its significance and impact needs to be understood and acted upon. On occasions, where the auditor is unknown or unfamiliar to you, a status enquiry may be appropriate.

Capital commitments
In the notes to the accounts companies must state the capital expenditure commitments that existed at the date of the balance sheet. This can be compared with actual expenditure on an annual basis, and if the amount is substantial you may wish to ask whether it will need funding and how the company proposes to do this.

Contingent liabilities
A variety of items can appear under this heading such as guarantees and performance bonds, but in recent years there has been a growth of off-balance sheet financial instruments which will also be included. The fact that these are not on the balance sheet should be considered when gearing ratios are being calculated.

Consolidated accounts
When dealing with a group of companies it is important that you obtain a copy of the consolidated accounts and not just those of the holding company or the individual companies. Where you are dealing with an individual company and the accounts show an investment in a subsidiary or associate company, it would be

advisable, where the amounts are significant, to obtain balance sheets for the subsidiary or associate. The same rule would apply where there is evidence in a balance sheet of inter-company indebtedness.

Budgets and cash flow forecasts

All of the financial statements we have looked at so far concentrate on the past and record past activity or history. They will give you some means of estimating likely future performance and, therefore, risk, but a more detailed view of the future of a business is needed in practice. Every business, no matter how small or unsophisticated, should make some attempt to plan its future, setting itself objectives and yardsticks by which the achievement of those objectives might be measured. Once the longer-term aim has been established then a strategy can be formulated and out of this the more detailed planning will be born. Some companies aim simply at a stated return on capital employed and everything else they do evolves from this. There is no guarantee that budgeting and cash flow forecasting will ensure success, but the lack of any attempt to plan ahead will increase the chances of failure. For the smaller business the planning process does not need to be sophisticated but the management must think ahead and try to establish where the business is going. This process will help identify possible problems, assess the need for resources such as personnel, equipment, and cash, and allow the setting of targets or objectives. The planning process should follow clearly defined steps which are:

(a) Set objectives and policies.
(b) Consider the options for achieving the objectives.
(c) Choose one or more of the options and act on them.
(d) Measure the performance of the business against the plan.
(e) Identify and analyse significant variances.
(f) Alter actions or the plan as necessary.
(g) Continue to monitor performance.

If the plan proves to be unrealistic a new plan and strategy may have to be considered.

Out of the planning exercise will come one or more budgets depending on the size of the business and its complexity. For the larger companies each division or department may have to develop its own plan, budget, and cash flow forecast in the context of the overall objectives of the company. From these individual budgets will be produced master profit/loss and cash budgets for the company. In the smaller business the proprietor is likely to produce one profit budget – sometimes called an *operating budget* – which will attempt to forecast sales, the cost of sales and the overheads. Alongside this will run the cash budget or cash flow forecast which attempts to predict the cash inflows and outflows of the business, at the same time identifying the borrowing requirement at any given time. This highlights the essential difference between profit budgets and cash flow forecasts. A business may be predicting in its operating budget sales of £20 000 in January, but if half of these are on 60 days' credit only £10 000 cash will be received immediately, the balance being received in March. The cash budget will show, therefore, £10 000 sales income in January and a similar amount in March.

It is essential here to illustrate the other major differences between operating budgets and cash budgets which are as follows:

(a) *Capital expenditure.* Because this involves the conversion of one asset (cash) or a liability (borrowing) into another asset it is not taken into account when the profit or loss is being calculated. It follows that it must not appear in the operating budget but must be included in the cash budget.

(b) *Value added tax.* When sales are invoiced any VAT due is included in the total amount but is excluded when the sales are recorded in the books of the business. However, the full amount of the invoice is recorded against the name of the purchaser as a debtor. When the debtor makes payment it will include the VAT. It follows, therefore, that budgeted sales do not include VAT but the cash income from these sales does. The same rule applies to materials purchased and costs incurred which appear in the operating budget *exclusive of VAT*, but in the cash budget *inclusive of VAT*. You must also remember that forecasted VAT settlements have to be included in the cash budget.

(c) *Timing differences.* When calculating a budgeted profit for a particular period you have to include only those sales and costs which will relate to that period, whether payment for them has been made or not. With a cash flow forecast you must include only items for which cash will either be received or paid by the business.

(d) *Loan or hire purchase repayments.* These represent cash flows only and will not appear in an operating budget.

(e) *Non-cash items.* There are some items which are included in the profit calculation but do not involve the movement of funds and the best example is depreciation which is treated as an overhead but no cash actually leaves the business. This is why it is always added back to profit when cash flow is being calculated. Such items will appear in an operating budget but not in a cash flow forecast.

Bearing all of these points in mind, an operating budget and cash flow forecast can be prepared. The period which the budgets should cover can vary but 6 months or 12 months forward would be normal. Examples of a simple operating budget and cash flow forecast are shown in Exhibit 12.3 and 12.4. You will see in both cases that actual figures can be recorded as they occur and comparisons can then be made with the budgeted figures and the differences analysed. One important item is missing from the examples and that is the list of assumptions upon which the budgets were based. You must always ensure in practice that this list of assumptions is received otherwise you will not be able to judge the validity of the projections.

Assumptions

We have seen that when a budget is being prepared the past performance of the business is a useful guide but there will be a need for some astute gazing into the crystal ball when predicting future trends. The need is not for absolute accuracy but for realistic judgments about what is likely to happen based on certain properly considered assumptions. Perhaps the most difficult item to predict is sales turnover and the business person must take a view based on the following considerations:
- economic and market outlook
- the rate of inflation
- the views of existing customers
- the strength of the competition
- the orders in hand
- the past performance and recent trends.

Assumptions arising out of these considerations must accompany the budget and you can then test these against your assessment of past performance and your view of the future economic climate. A similar approach can be made to the budgeting of production costs and overheads, although these should present fewer problems. However, forecasts of requirements for additional personnel, capital equipment and premises will have to be made but these can be tested against the historic relationship

Exhibit 12.3 Operational Budget

Month	1		2		3		4		5		6	
	Budget	Actual	Budget	Actual	Budget	Actual	Budget	Actual	Budget	Actual	Budget	Actual
Sales: Home												
Export												
A Total sales												
Direct costs:												
Materials												
Wages/salaries												
Stock (increase)/												
decrease												
B Cost of goods sold												
C Gross profit (A – B)												
Overheads:												
Production												
Selling & distribution												
Administration												
Finance charges												
D Total overheads												
E Net profit (before tax) (C – D)												

Exhibit 12.4 Cash flow forecast

Enter month	Month 1		Month 2		Month 3		Month 4		Month 5		Month 6	
	Budget	Actual	Budget	Actual	Budget	Actual	Budget	Actual	Budget	Actual	Budget	Actual
Receipts:												
Sales :(inc VAT)												
– Cash												
– Debtors												
Other trading income												
Loans received												
Capital introduced												
Disposal of assets												
Other receipts												
A Total Receipts												
Payments:												
Cash purchases												
Payments to creditors												
Principals' remun- eration												
Wages/salaries (net)												
PAYE/NIC												
Capital items												
Transport/packaging												
Rent/rates												
Services												
Loan repayments												
HP/leasing payments												
Interest												
Bank/finance charges												
Professional fees												
Advertising												
VAT												
Corporation tax etc												
Dividends												
B Total Payments												
Opening bank balance												
C Total												
D Closing bank balance (A – C)												

to sales. The projected costs of raw materials and other stocks should be based on anticipated price rises linked to an appropriate inflation rate or prior notices received from suppliers. A business should be able to forecast accurately the amount of its wages and salaries bill and will have a reasonable idea of likely movements in the costs of electricity, gas, rates and insurance.

When the cash budget is being prepared assumptions will have to be made about such things as future terms of trade, likely tax payments, discounts to be allowed or received, and the level of dividends. When the cash budget has been completed and borrowing requirements identified, likely interest charges can be calculated based on an assumed level of interest rates.

Try to ensure that the budget and cash flow forecast is submitted prior to any meeting with the customer so that you can examine these, listing any queries you have and preparing questions about the underlying assumptions. Only in this way will you be able to assess the validity of the predictions and identify possible problems. The following are some examples of the questions you may wish to ask about specific items in the budget and cash flow forecast:

Sales
- Is the business dependent upon one product?
- Could technology make this customer's products obsolete?
- What is the future pricing policy and will the products remain competitive?

Materials
- Are these readily available and is there a dependence on one supplier?
- Is the quality likely to be consistent?
- What are the optimum stocking levels?

Personnel
- Have the full costs of employing people been included?
- If additional skilled labour is required is it available?
- Are there likely to be any industrial relations problems?

Cash flow forecast
- How realistic are projected terms of trade and has any allowance been made for delays in receipt of funds?
- Is there any provision for bad debts?
- Have all items of proposed capital expenditure been included?

Once the budgets have been properly examined and the questions satisfactorily answered a balanced judgment of the proposition should be possible. In practice, many of the smaller businesses present only a cash budget without an operational budget. While this in itself is insufficient reason to decline a proposition, it calls for careful scrutiny because the cash flow forecast should be based on an operational budget, however simple or unsophisticated. The operational budget will contain many of the basic assumptions underlying the cash flow forecast and these will be required if any sound judgment of the borrowing requirements is to be made.

Monitoring

When any agreed facility is up and running the budgets should constitute a working document both for the business and the bank. Your view of the risk will determine the frequency and format of the submission of actual figures, but whenever these are received you will expect the customer to have analysed any variances and, where these are significant, to have provided some explanation and proposed action. Do not forget that the budgeted figures were predictions and some variance is inevitable. In addition to ensuring that actual figures are plotted against the budget as a means of monitoring performance there are steps which can be taken to ensure that the business continues to progress satisfactorily.

These may include:
- Receipt of interim profit and loss accounts and balance sheets.
- Monitoring of debenture cover figures.
- Aged lists of debtors and creditors.
- Comparison of cash flow forecast with actual borrowing activity.

Remember that with the last of these the peak requirements shown in the cash budget are usually struck at a month end and will not reflect mid-month positions in excess of these figures, and allowance for this should be made when limits are marked.

Finally, a further benefit accruing from the production of budgets and cash flow forecasts is the opportunity to use these to forecast a profit and loss account, balance sheet and funds flow statement for the end of a given period. Comparisons can then be made between the historic and projected financial statements and likely trends in ratios and key figures established.

Summary

1 When assessing risk it is necessary to examine the past performance of a business, using this as a guide to the future.

2 Historic financial statements have inherent weaknesses in that they are out of date, static, concentrate on the past, and do not cover all the relevant information.

3 To be effective, interpretation of financial statements is dependent upon more than one year's figures, a consistency in construction and supporting evidence.

4 Key criteria should be selected and these will usually include safety, liquidity and profitability.

5 The audited accounts may not present the true position as balance sheet values might be understated or overstated, and this must be taken into consideration when calculating ratios.

6 Profit does not equal cash and some profitable businesses have failed for want of cash. However, profit is essential for the long-term health of a business.

7 A consistency of method in calculating ratios is more important than inherent accuracy if meaningful trends are to be revealed.

8 An understanding of the constituent parts of a financial relationship or ratio is necessary to make sense of any movement therein.

9 In addition to comparisons year on year for a particular business, reference to similar businesses or industry norms should be made where possible.

10 Overtrading has certain tell-tale signs but need not necessarily lead to disaster.

11 Analysis of cash flow is important to a banker because this represents the source of repayment or the measure of ability to repay.

12 All businesses must make some attempt to plan ahead and to translate these plans into a budget and cash flow forecast, however unsophisticated.

13 Include in budgets all items relating to a particular period whether payment will be made or not.

14 Include in cash flow forecasts only those items for which cash will be paid or received during the period.

15 It is vital to ensure that all relevant assumptions

accompany budgets and cash flow forecasts and that those assumptions be tested.

16 Actual figures should be plotted against the budget figures and significant variances analysed and explained.

Self-assessment questions

1 Stumped Limited

Accounts for the year ending 31 December

Fixed Assets

Land and buildings		64 708
Fixtures and fittings		10 700
Motor vehicles		6 760
		82 168

Current Assets

Cash	590	
Debtors	59 443	
Stock	208 993	
	269 026	

less Current Liabilities

Creditors	142 252	
Bank	32 830	
Tax	8 171	
Amounts due to Directors	20 000	
	203 253	

Net Current Assets	65 773
Net Tangible Assets	147 941

Financed by:

Share Capital	10 000
Capital Reserve	28 617
Retained profit	109 324
	147 941

Sales	614 185
Purchases	548 150
Cost of Sales	501 176
Gross Profit	113 009
PBIT	17 708
Interest Paid	5 009

Using the figures provided calculate the following:
  (a) Net gearing ratio
  (b) Current ratio
  (c) Liquid ratio
  (d) Credit given period
  (e) Stock turnover period
  (f) Credit taken period
  (g) Gross profit margin
  (h) Net profit margin
  (i) Interest cover

2   Using the figures in Question 1, recalculate the net gearing ratio assuming the land and buildings are understated by £10 000 and the amounts due to directors are to be treated as capital.

3   Will cash flow improve or deteriorate where:
  (a) the period of credit given reduces
  (b) the period of credit taken increases
  (c) the rate of stock turn slows down
  (d) the depreciation charge increases

4   Should projected capital expenditure appear in an operational budget?

5   What will an analysis of a funds flow statement tell you?

6   What are the danger signals in financial statements which might suggest overtrading?

7   What do you need from a customer before examining a budget and cash flow forecast?

8   In what ways can a business generate cash?

9   How can you measure very roughly the future working capital requirements of a business?

10   If the bank borrowing in a balance sheet is substantially higher than has been seen on the bank account, what might this imply?

13
Alternative sources of finance

Objectives

After studying this chapter you should be able to:
1   identify sources of finance available to the customer other than bank overdraft or loan;
2   discuss the benefits and drawbacks of each alternative.

Introduction

Sometimes a customer prefers not to, or cannot for some reason, borrow by way of overdraft or loan from a High Street bank. The smaller business, in particular, has difficulty in raising finance for long periods since the number of people willing to supply funds over such a length of time is limited. During periods of credit restraint banks may be reluctant to provide funds for other than short-term situations. If such is the case, are you in a position to help them? Well, if there is not a product which your bank can offer to satisfy the customer's needs, you may be able to provide a service by directing them to alternative sources of finance. The most common of those which you will encounter to help the individual and small business are outlined in this chapter.

Factoring

Administrating and accounting for the debts owed to a company, i.e. its 'receivables', can be time-consuming and sometimes costly, particularly in the collection of bad debts. Factoring companies can remove the burden of the administration by taking on the duty of sending out invoices, chasing outstanding debts and, if necessary, taking action to recover bad debts. The factor may offer an alternative facility, known as *invoice discounting,* where it actually purchases without recourse the book debts of the company less a discount charge. Thus, the company receives immediate net cash but fulfils the usual administrative tasks itself pending sale. There is a third option available which encompasses the factor taking care of both the administration and accounting work and the purchase of the book debts. In this latter situation the factor will determine the amount of credit the company may allow to each debtor. It may be that the factor is acting in a similar capacity to a number of other companies with the same debtor, and the factor would wish to limit the credit risk to which it may be exposed. Certainly, because of this greater knowledge, the factor is able to lend far more than a bank against anticipated income. Usually, up to approximately 80% of funds are advanced to the client company by the factor pending reimbursement from the debtors; the remaining 20% is paid over once it has been received by the factor company.

The complete factoring service provides:
- the administration of the company's sales ledger
- credit control over the agreed percentage of debtors
- full cover for the company against bad debts
- payment to the company of collected debts.

Hire purchase

Chapter 7 on Personal Borrowers outlined the banks' own in-house personal loan finance for purchases of consumer durables. Quite often, though, a customer can obtain finance at the point of sale. Say, you were shopping in a department store and saw a sofa which you wanted to buy. The store may have an arrangement with a finance house, sometimes a wholly owned subsidiary of a bank, to provide an immediate instalment credit loan for you as an hire purchase contract. Such a contract is an agreement to hire with an option to purchase as the last instalment is paid. Until that final payment has been made the furniture will belong to the finance house, although, as explained in Chapter 7, you will have certain rights to protect your interests under the Consumer Credit Act 1974.

The contract may be one of *conditional sale* which means that you are legally bound to complete payment for the purchase of your furniture, at which stage you become the owner. These days you may be asked instead to sign a *credit sale* agreement which gives you immediate ownership of the furniture and you then pay for it by regular instalments. The hire purchase companies may be prepared at times to provide fixed loans at very favourable rates for, say, showroom extensions or additional outbuildings. Generally, finance houses link their lending to the Finance House Base Rate which is calculated on an agreed formula based on the inter-bank three-month rate. Hire purchase facilities tend to be available for periods from six months to three years for normal consumer durables.

Stocking loans

Some sellers of expensive consumer durables, like cars, have the opportunity of borrowing from the finance houses which provide point of sale finance to the consumer at the dealer's premises. The manufacturer will send the cars to the dealer but will invoice the finance house. The finance house pays for the consignment and sets up a *stocking loan* for the dealer, on which interest will be charged. As each car is sold the dealer pays the finance house

'Beryl! The next time a customer asks for a stocking loan, don't offer him your fishnets!'

which may then provide instalment finance to the ultimate purchaser, if required. This type of facility is normally granted on a revolving basis at an agreed level so that the dealer may purchase more cars from the manufcturer as sales are made.

Leasing

If, for some reason, you do not wish to *purchase* an asset by means of instalment credit, you can decide to *lease* the asset instead. By paying a rental charge over an agreed period of time you will have the exclusive use of, say, a car as a lessee but the car belongs always to the lessor, the leasing company. Even though the vehicle is of your own choice you have no option to purchase under a *financial lease* arrangement. At the end of the initial leasing period you may have the option to renew at a much reduced, nominal rent. There is a second type of lease arrangement, called an *operating lease*. In this latter case, the lease is granted for an agreed term and, on expiry, the car is sold in the second-hand market to a third party. Part of the sale proceeds will be returned to you as a refund of rentals. This type of lease can be terminated voluntarily at any time if you pay agreed termination rentals.

This type of facility can improve your cash flow. There is no deposit to pay 'up front' and no burden of capital purchase cost. Rental payments are tax deductible if you are using the car for business purposes. The lessor is responsible for maintenance of the asset, but the lessee must ensure against fire, theft and other normal business risks. To summarise the two types:

(a) *Finance lease* – covers the capital cost of the asset plus the cost of financing the lease over an agreed term. The period of rental depends on the estimated life of the asset.

(b) *Operating lease* – the lease term covers only part of the estimated life of the asset, which is then sold and the proceeds split.

Franchising

Nowadays there is a trend towards franchising. The franchisor, a firm like Wimpy's hamburger food chain for instance, may provide funds towards the purchase of suitable premises and equipment to a franchisee. The franchisee, the person(s) who will run the business, pays a licence to the franchisor for the use of the 'name' plus, perhaps, any facilities provided. The franchisee is financially and legally independent of the franchisor, although there is always the risk to the franchise network through the failure of the franchisor themself. So, providing that the franchisee can raise sufficient capital, they will receive the back-up support and guidance of the franchisor's network to set them on the road towards a potentially highly successful business.

3is

This financial institution, known previously as ICFC, was formed by the Bank of England and the large clearing banks with the objective of providing finance for small to medium-sized companies for development and expansion. As a form of security for its lending to a company 3is sometimes arranges for an equity stake in the business, with a representative taking a seat on the board to observe and be involved in decision making. 3is provides a range of services, like leasing and hire purchase finance, and loans for terms between seven and twenty-five years against acceptable security. It is also involved in the Government's sponsored Small Firms Loan Guarantee Scheme which is available between two and seven years.

Agricultural Mortgage Corporation

The AMC was introduced originally by the Bank of England and other banks in 1928 to provide long-term funds at favourable rates, specifically for farmers. Providing that the farmers can show a reasonable degree of success and are prepared to offer as security the freehold agricultural land, facilities can be available for up to forty years. There is further help for farmers available from the Agricultural Credit Corporation (ACC) which normally guarantees a bank overdraft, subject to the farmer's agreement that securities held by the bank are held to back up the guarantee. Loans can be used for capital improvement, for working capital, or even to repay money borrowed from other sources. Tenant farmers may borrow, providing that the purpose is for the purchase of the farm, which can be taken out as security.

Government aid

During the past few years successive governments have provided schemes to assist small businesses by way of grants and loans. Special facilities are available in areas of high unemployment. One of the best known of these options is the Small Firms' Loan Guarantee Scheme and those eligible to apply are sole traders, partnerships, co-operatives or limited companies who are either already trading or starting in business. Currently (October 1988), loans are available up to £75 000 over seven years, and the Government guarantees a proportion of the loan, presently 80% in assisted areas. Certain activities are excluded from the scheme, for example nightclubs, house and estate agents, travel agents; a prospective borrower would need to check that they do not fall within one of the excluded activities. Some of the development agencies have been particularly successful in helping to regenerate the economy and to improve the local environment.

Summary

Type of service	What it is for	Term
Factoring	Debtor administration and accounting.	Revolving.
	Collection of book debts.	Advances subject to limit on credit given to debtors.
	Purchase of book debts.	
Hire purchase	Finance at point of sale for purchase of consumer durables.	Usually 6 months to 3 years.
Stocking loans	Bulk purchase of expensive consumer durables by retailers.	Revolving within agreed limits.
Leasing	Loan rather than purchase of moveable assets.	Agreed term over (i) life of asset

		(ii) fixed period pending sale of asset.
Franchising	Business start up finance and support from large retailing network.	Subject to agreed term of licence.
3is	Development and expansion finance for small to medium-sized companies.	Medium-term: 2–7 years. Long-term: 7–25 years.
AMC	Finance for farmers for capital improvements, working capital, etc.	Up to 40 years, secured by freehold.
Government aid	Financial incentives and assistance for industry.	Depending on scheme, e.g. Small Firms' Loan Guarantee Scheme 2–7 years.

Self-assessment questions

1 Which type of service provides collection for a company's debtors?
  (a) Credit sale
  (b) Factoring
  (c) Finance house
  (d) Conditional sale.
2 Finance House Base Rate is calculated by reference to:
  (a) Clearing bank base rate
  (b) Inter-bank one-month rate
  (c) Bank of England rate
  (d) Inter-bank three-month rate.
3 A conditional sale contract gives the purchaser ownership of the underlying asset:
  (a) Immediately
  (b) Half-way through the agreed term

(c) At the end of the agreed term

(d) Never

4 Stocking loans are provided to sellers of consumer goods by:

(a) Finance houses

(b) Leasing companies

(c) Factoring companies

(d) The Government

5 An operating lease means that the asset will be:

(a) Chosen by the lessor

(b) Written-off during the agreed term

(c) Sold part-way through its estimated life

(d) Re-leased at a nominal rent

Answers to self-assessment questions

Chapter 1

1 An international money order.
2 The receipt of the goods may be delayed due to the time it would take for the payee's bank to collect the proceeds of the cheque.
3 (a) An international payment order.
  (b) The overseas bank may well require references and specimens of the customer's signature.
4 A telegraphic transfer.
5 By means of banker's draft.
6 (a) There is an exchange risk when converting to the local currency.
  (b) Collection of the proceeds will take time and can be expensive.
  (c) The cheque might not be paid.

Chapter 2

1 Nostro.
2 Vostro.
3 In UK: debit customer account sterling equivalent of US$5000
                credit mirror account US$5000.
    In USA: debit nostro account of UK bank $5000
                credit exporter $5000.
4 In Japan: debit customer yen equivalent of US$5000
                credit mirror account US$5000.
    In USA: debit nostro account of Japanese bank US$5000
                credit nostro account of UK bank US$5000.
    In UK: debit mirror account US$5000
                credit exporter with sterling equivalent of US$5000.

Chapter 3

1 Subtract the premium rate from the spot rate
(result = 1.6429).
2 The bank's profit margin.
3 Apart from the normal canons of lending to be applied,
whether the customer has income due *in Italian lire* for the
equivalent amount.
4 In two working days' time.
5 The telephone and telex links worldwide.
6 Commercial and note rates.
7 3.8985. Bank sells *low,* buys *high.*
8 Forward contracts, currency accounts, currency options,
financial futures contracts.
9 Between spot and certainly by the three-month end date.
10 To buy the underlying currency.

Chapter 4

1 Economic reports on countries and industries. Status reports
on prospective buyers and suppliers. Names of potential customers
or suppliers.
2 It is a document issued when goods are transported by sea and
is a receipt for the goods, evidence of the contract of carriage,
and the document of title to the goods.
3 A receipt for goods delivered to an airline.
4 The buyer.
5 The exporter ships the goods and sends the relevant documents
direct to the importer and awaits payment as agreed.
6 A guarantee given to an importer that an advance payment
will be returned to the importer should the goods not be shipped.
7 Any two of the following:

   (a) It is possible to obtain credit.
   (b) More convenient than a documentary credit.
   (c) The exporter will normally be responsible for the
   charges.
   (d) Payment can be deferred pending arrival of the goods.
   (e) A produce loan becomes a possibility.

8 Under a transferable credit the original beneficiary can make
the credit available to one or more third parties.
9 Any two of the following:

(a) The exporter is no longer dependent upon the creditworthiness of the importer.

(b) If the credit is confirmed by a bank in the exporter's country, country risk is eliminated.

(c) If irrevocable, the credit cannot be cancelled without the express agreement of the exporter.

(d) The documents will not be released until payment or a commitment to pay has been made.

(e) There is the possibility of raising finance through discounted bills.

10   90%.

11   With recourse.

12   A trust letter or trust receipt.

Chapter 5

1   Purchase them and advance funds against the invoice value up to 80%.

2   The Bank of England.

3   Forfaiting.

4   Daily.

5   Demand.

6   Profit.

7   Time and amount.

Chapter 6

1   (c).

2   (c).

3   Before lending.

4   The amount introduced by the customer which establishes their commitment to the proposition and lessens the risk to the bank.

5   Ask the customer, visit the home, check the run of the account and standing order payments, and credit reference agencies.

6   Profit and a return to the shareholders on their investment. It also measures the risk involved.

Chapter 7

1 (c).
2 (d).
3 (b).
4 (a).
5 (d).

Chapter 8

1 (c).
2 (b).
3 (a).
4 (b).
5 (d).
6 (c).
7 (d).
8 (b).
9 (a).
10 (c).

Chapter 9

1 Easy to take, easy to value, stable or increasing value, and easy to realise.
2 A legal mortgage has a power of sale which can be exercised without reference to the mortgagor or the courts.
3 (c) Neither. It is subject to a contract of bailment, the bank being the baillee and the customer the baillor.
4 The floating charge.
5 Third party.
6 Both Mr and Mrs Cooper.
7 No, unless it is evidenced in writing as it is third party security.
8 The proposer, the life assured and the beneficiary.
9 Yes.
10 It must be handed over with the policy as it now becomes part of the permanent title to the policy and will be required by the assurance company on surrender/maturity.
11 Mrs Robinson, Paul and Simon.
12 'No subsisting entries.' The first mortgage will not be registered as priority is gained by possession of the deeds.

13 The Land Certificate
   The original and a copy of the charge form
   The application form (LA4)
   A letter certifying the extent to which the charge is being relied upon
   The scale fee.
14 Difficult to value and realise.
   Complex charging procedures.
   Properties are subject to deterioration.
   Equitable interests of occupiers can intervene.
   Can impose liabilities on the bank where the title is leasehold.
15 No. John Stephens is a minor and has no legal capacity to contract.

Chapter 10

1 (c).
2 (d).
3 (b).
4 (b).
5 (a).

Chapter 11

1 (b).
2 (a).
3 (d).
4 (b).
5 (c).

Chapter 12

1
(a) $\dfrac{\text{Total borrowing} - \text{Cash}}{\text{Surplus}} = \dfrac{32\ 830 + 20\ 000 - 590}{147\ 941}$

$$= 35\% \text{ or } 0.35{:}1$$

(b) $\dfrac{\text{Current assets}}{\text{Current liabilities}} = \dfrac{269\ 026}{203\ 253} = 1.3{:}1$

(c) $\dfrac{\text{Quick assets}}{\text{Current liabilities}} = \dfrac{590 + 59\ 443}{203\ 253} = 0.29{:}1$

(d) $\dfrac{\text{Debtors}}{\text{Sales}} \times 365 = \dfrac{59\ 443}{614\ 185} \times 365 = 35$ days

(e) $\dfrac{\text{Stock}}{\text{Cost of goods sold}} \times 365 = \dfrac{208\ 993}{501\ 176} \times 365 = 152$ days

(f) $\dfrac{\text{Creditors}}{\text{Cost of goods sold}} \times 365 = \dfrac{142\ 252}{501\ 176} \times 365 = 104$ days

(g) $\dfrac{\text{Gross profit}}{\text{Sales}} \times 100 = \dfrac{113\ 009}{614\ 185} \times 100 = 18.4\%$

(h) $\dfrac{\text{PBIT}}{\text{Sales}} \times 100 = \dfrac{17\ 708}{614\ 185} \times 100 = 2.9\%$

(i) $\dfrac{\text{PBIT}}{\text{Interest paid}} = \dfrac{17\ 708}{5009} = 3.5$ times covered

2   The surplus of £147 941 will increase by £10 000 + £20 000 = £177 941 and total borrowing will reduce by £20 000. The calculation is: $\dfrac{32\ 830 - 590}{177\ 941} = 18\%$ or $0.18{:}1$

3   (a) Improve.
   (b) Improve.
   (c) Deteriorate.
   (d) It will make no difference as depreciation is not a cash item and is added back to profit when cash flow is calculated.
4   No, but it should appear in the cash flow forecast.
5   Whether a business generates or consumes cash, and how it does it.
6   A rapid increase in turnover without a similar increase in working capital, a reducing period of credit given but increasing reliance on outside creditors including the bank, declining margins, and rapidly deteriorating liquidity.
7   A list of the underlying assumptions.
8   By making a profit, raising capital, selling fixed assets, and more efficient management of current assets and liabilities.
9   By dividing the working capital by the sales and applying the result to projected increases in turnover.
10   The business is borrowing elsewhere.

Chapter 13

1 (b).
2 (d).
3 (c).
4 (a).
5 (c).

Glossary

Advance payment guarantee Guarantee to the buyer that, if the exporter fails to complete the contract, any advance payments can be reclaimed.

Airmail transfer *See* international payment order.

Articles of association Rules and regulations which govern the internal procedures of a company and the powers of the directors and officials.

Assignment The document used to transfer the title to unregistered leasehold land.

Bailment Holding an item in trust upon the understanding that it shall be returned when requested.

Bankers draft A draft drawn by a bank upon itself. Sometimes known as an **international draft** when used for overseas payments.

Bill of exchange, defined by the Bills of Exchange Act 1882 as: An unconditional order in writing addressed by one person to another, signed by the person giving it, requiring the person to whom it is addressed to pay on demand or at a fixed or determinable future time a sum certain in money to, or to the order of, a specified person or to bearer.

Buyer credit Finance facility used for high-value export contracts for capital goods whereby a UK bank lends direct to the overseas buyer or to a bank in the buyer's country.

Buying rate The rate at which a bank agrees to buy from its customer a specified amount of one currency in exchange for another currency. With a few exceptions, a bank will always buy currency at a rate higher than that at which it will sell.

Call money Deposits which are lent 'at call', i.e. repayable on demand, or when called.

Call option   An option to buy a specified currency, e.g. a Yen call is an option to buy Japanese Yen (currency contract).

Charge certificate   The document issued by the Land Registry as evidence of a legal charge on the land.

Closing rate   The exchange rate at the close of a bank's business, and the rate quoted in the financial press the next day. Due to trading on markets in different zones, these rates may not apply when business opens the following day and should be taken as a guide only.

Collection   Cheques/bills. The process by which a bank sends a cheque or bill of exchange to the bank on which it is drawn for payment.

Convertible currency   A currency which may be readily exchanged for (converted into) another currency without undue restriction.

Conveyance   The document used to transfer the title to unregistered freehold land.

Counterparty   The other name (i.e. customer or bank) with whom a deal has been concluded.

Cover   (a)   To arrange forward contracts to protect against exchange rate fluctuations.
(b)   To lay off funds in the market.
See also hedge.

Currency account   A bank account maintained in any currency other than sterling.

Currency basket   A group of currencies weighted to provide an index of value, e.g. SDR, ECU.

Deal   A transaction, either foreign exchange, deposit or loan, entered into with a counterparty.

Debenture   A written acknowledgement by a company of a debt which, in the case of a debenture to a bank, includes a fixed or floating charge on the assets of the company.

Discount   A margin added to a spot exchange rate, reflecting the cheaper forward value of one currency against another. *See also* premium.

Drawdown   The actual payment of a loan to a customer; the drawdown date may be much later than the date on which the loan was agreed.

ECGD Export Credits Guarantee Department. Government insurance operation providing cover against the risk of non-payment for exported goods or services.

ECGD comprehensive bank guarantee Guarantee given to a bank as security for finance made available to an exporter for goods covered by ECGD Comprehensive Insurance.

ECGD comprehensive insurance Insurance against risk of non-payment for goods exported on a continuous and repetitive basis with credit terms of less than five years.

Endowment policy A life policy payable at a fixed future date or on death before that date.

Entry into possession The right of a legal mortgagee to occupy or collect the rental income from the mortgaged premises.

Equity The proprietors stake in a business, i.e. share capital and reserves or the owner's share of an asset such as the value of a house after deduction of any outstanding mortgage.

The word is also used in respect of stocks and shares, described as 'equities'.

Equity linked policy A life policy where a proportion of the premiums are invested in unit trusts.

Eurocurrency A deposit in any major market currency held outside the country which issued the currency.

Exchange risk The extent to which an asset receivable in a foreign currency has not been matched by a liability payable in the same currency.

Exotic currency A currency not readily quoted in international markets and infrequently dealt in.

Extension An arrangement with a customer to prolong an existing forward contract; this will involve a compensation deal. *See also* rollover.

Fixed rate currency A currency which has a fixed rate of exchange within narrow limits against another currency.

Foreclosure A remedy available to a legal mortgagee requiring the consent of the Court, by which a mortgagor is deprived of the right to redeem the property – the equity of redemption.

Forward contract A legally binding contract between a bank and the customer where the customer agrees to receive or deliver foreign currency from or to the bank. The bank undertakes to sell to or buy from the customer a specified amount of currency at a specified rate on a fixed date (fixed forward contract) or, at the customer's option, within a specified period (option forward contract). No cash is exchanged at the time a contract is taken out, but both parties commit themselves to a currency exchange at the agreed rate on the maturity date or the option take-up date.

Forward cover   The arrangement of a forward foreign exchange contract to protect a buyer or seller of foreign currency at a future date from unexpected adverse fluctuations in the exchange rate between now and that date.

Freehold   One of the two legal estates in land, this represents absolute ownership.

Ground rent   An annual payment made by a lessee to a lessor as a condition of the lease.

Hedge   Action taken to reduce exchange exposure.

International bankers draft   *See* bankers draft.

International money order   An order drawn by a bank in sterling or US dollars in favour of a specified beneficiary. Used for small international settlements (e.g. maximum £500/US$1000).

International payment order   Sometimes known as an **airmail transfer.** A method of transferring funds internationally, appropriate payment instructions being sent by one bank to another in writing.

Joint tenancy   A form of co-ownership of land where, upon the death of one of the co-owners, the title rests in the survivors.

Land Certificate   The document of title to registered land.

Leasehold   An interest or estate in land for a specific period of time.

Letters of postponement   These are usually in respect of directors' loans to their company and have the effect of ensuring that the loans cannot be repaid without the permission of the bank.

Lien   The right of a creditor to retain possession of the debtor's property until such time as the debt is repaid.

MWPA policy   A policy issued under the Married Women's Property Act 1882 which creates a trust in favour of the beneficiaries.

Margin (a) An amount added to (discount) or deducted from (premium) a spot exchange rate to determine the forward rate.
(b) An amount added to or deducted from market rates in order to provide for profit.

Marking name The name in which American and Canadian type certificates are held to improve their transferability and acceptability.

Memorandum of association The document which determines the objects and powers of a company.

Memorandum of deposit The name given to the form used by banks when taking a charge over stocks and shares.

Middle price The average of the buying and selling price for a currency (also referred to as 'middle rate').

Mortgage A conveyance of a legal or equitable interest in property as security for payment of a debt or discharge of some obligation.

Mortgage protection policy A life policy used to repay a mortgage on the death of the mortgagor.

Net tangible asset value *See* net worth.

Net worth The net value of a business. This can be calculated by taking the total of the tangible assets at balance sheet values and deducting all liabilities except share capital and reserves.

Nominee company The phrase used to describe the company into whose name stocks and shares are transferred by a bank consequent upon taking a legal charge. It can also be used by individuals or organisations who, for a variety of reasons, do not wish shares to be held in their own names.

Nostro account A local bank's account with a correspondent. *See also* vostro account.

Open account business Business transacted on credit terms, where no security in the form of bills of exchange or promissory notes is obtained from the buyer (i.e. on trust).

Operating cash flow This is calculated by adding back to the net profit any non-funds items such as depreciation and then adjusting the figure for any increment in working capital. It is the cash generated from ordinary trading by a business.

Option contract A forward exchange contract which gives the customer the right to settle at any time within two specified future dates.

Performance guarantee Guarantee to the buyer that the supplier will carry out the terms of the contract.

Pledge The deposit of a chattel – i.e. any tangible, movable article of property – as security for the payment of a debt.

Premium A margin deducted from a spot exchange rate reflecting the dearer forward value of one currency against another. *See also* discount.

Promissory note defined by the Bills of Exchange Act 1882 as: An unconditional promise in writing made by one person to another signed by the maker engaging to pay on demand or at a fixed or determinable future time a sum certain in money to, or to the order of, a specified person or to bearer.

Put option An option to sell a specified currency, e.g. a US dollar put is an option to sell US dollars.

Quoted company A company whose shares are quoted on a recognised stock exchange.

Recourse agreement Agreement signed by the exporter in favour of ECGD, undertaking to reimburse ECGD any sums paid by them under the bank guarantee.

Rollover (a) Extension of a forward contract.
(b) The renewal of funding (with an additional revision of the interest rate) for a loan (usually medium term) at the end of an agreed period.

SSAP Statement of Standard Accounting Practice. The accountancy profession imposes standards on its members and makes recommendations on specific accounting or auditing procedures.

SWIFT Society for Worldwide Interbank Financial Telecommunication – a system for rapid transfer of funds internationally between member banks.

Selling rate The rate at which a bank agrees to sell to its customer a specified amount of one currency in exchange for another currency. With a few exceptions, a bank will always sell currency at a rate lower than that at which it will buy.

Short date A value date between the spot date and one month.

Spot deal An exchange contract for settlement on the spot value date (normally two business days after the contract date).

Spread The difference between a bank's buying and selling price for a currency. This is the margin on which foreign exchange dealers make a profit.

Spreadsheet Manual or computerised means of standardising the format of accounting information used by most banks.

Stake The amount of capital introduced by an individual, or a proprietor of a business, towards the purchase of an asset.

Stock transfer form The document used to transfer the title of stocks and shares from seller to buyer.

Sub-mortgage A mortgage of a mortgage.

Supplier credit Finance for the sale of capital goods whereby a UK bank lends direct to a UK supplier in order that the supplier may extend credit to an overseas buyer.

Surplus *See* net worth.

Surrender value The value of a life policy if it is surrendered before the maturity date.

Swap deal A simultaneous spot sale and forward purchase of a currency (or vice versa).

Tenancy in common A form of co-ownership of land allowing for the interest of a deceased co-owner to pass to heirs.

Tender guarantee Guarantee to the buyer that the UK exporter will comply with the conditions of the exporter's tender and enter into a contract if it is accepted.

Ultra vires An act which is outside the power of a company, exceeds the authority of the officers, and cannot be ratified by the shareholders.

Value date The date on which settlement of a foreign exchange contract takes place.

Vostro account A correspondent bank's account with a local bank. *See also* nostro account.

Whole life policy A life policy payable only on death.

With profits The phrase used to describe those life policies which participate in the profits of the assurance company.

Working capital variation   The movement in the working capital over a period, usually between one year end and the next.

Appendix
Banking Operations – UK Lending and International Business

Model paper (May 1988)

Answer *five* questions: *two* from Section A, *three* from Section B.

The number in brackets after each question indicates the marks allotted. Where questions are subdivided, the figure shown after each subdivision indicates the number of marks allotted to that part of the question.

In awarding marks the examiner will look for answers which show (a) an appreciation of the significance of the question and (b) a reasoned practical approach to the problem.

Tabulated answers (i.e. statements in listed note form) are acceptable.

Silent electronic calculators may be used in this examination. Whether or not candidates use them, it is in their interest to show the basic figures from which their calculations are made.

Time allowed: three hours.

Section A

1 Answer all parts (i)–(x) of this question. Each part is divided into (a) and (b), both of which must be answered.
For (a), write the number of the part (e.g. (i)(a), (ii)(a) etc.) and one of A, B, C or D.
For (b), brief answers only are required.
(i)(a) In documentary credits operations, what do the banks themselves deal in?

A the goods to which the documents relate.

B the documents to which the goods relate.

C the Euro Currency market.

D the International Chamber of Commerce.

(b) What is meant by the expression 'confirmed'? [2]

(ii)(a) A factoring service can provide

A the ability to predict cash flow more accurately

B a collection/delivery system between buyer/seller

C a monthly statement showing a customer's foreign exchange deals

D travellers cheques and currency on demand.

(b) State one drawback of a factoring service from the customer's point of view. [2]

(iii)(a) When a forward contract is arranged for one month at an agreed date covering an exchange risk, at what stage is the rate fixed?

A At end of the contract in one month's time.

B Three days after the contract is agreed between Bank and customer.

C At the half-way stage (i.e. in 15 days' time).

D At the beginning of the contract.

(b) What service, other than a forward contract, can a customer use to provide limited cover for exchange loss? [2]

(iv)(a) What is the most beneficial method of settlement so far as an exporter is concerned?

A Open account.

B Advance payment.

C Documentary collection.

D Documentary letter of credit.

(b) Give one reason for your answer to (a). [2]

(v)(a) When demand is made under a performance guarantee, which party to the guarantee undertakes to pay the sum claimed?

A The buyer of the service given.

B The seller of the service given.

C The issuing bank.

D The beneficiary bank.

(b) What is the purpose of a performance guarantee? [2]

(vi)(a) Exchange rates are usually quoted on the London Market as, e.g. £1 = Swiss Francs 2.44–2.46. Which figure does a bank use to sell currency today?

A The mid-price figure.

B The lower figure.

C The higher figure.

D An average of the two figures.

(b) What represents the difference between the buying and selling rates? [2]

(vii)(a) What is the most beneficial method of settlement so far as an importer is concerned?

A Open account.

B Advance payment.

C Documentary collection.

D Documentary letter of credit.

(b) Give one reason for your answer to (a). [2]

(viii)(a) When a UK exporter, dealing on documentary collection terms, wishes to retain control of documents until he is paid or has the importer's undertaking to pay, he achieves it by

A sending the documents with the invoice for the specified amount

B withholding shipment until payment is received

C sending the documents to the buyer by surface mail

D instructing his bank to present the documents to an overseas bank for presentation and payment/acceptance by the buyer.

(b) What extra safeguard does an exporter have where goods are shipped by sea? [2]

(ix)(a) In trade terms, FOB means

A full on board

B fault on buyer

C free on board

D favour of bank

(b) In such a case, who is responsible for paying transport and insurance costs? [2]

(x)(a) What are '*nostro*' accounts?

A Our account in a bank in an overseas country in the home currency of that country.

B Our account in the UK reflecting a Vostro account in the home currency of an overseas country.

C An overseas bank's account in its own country.

D Our account in a bank in an overseas country in a currency other than sterling or the home currency of that country.

(b) What are *nostro* accounts for? [2]

[Total marks for question – 20]

2 The directors of your importing customers, Cuddly Toys Limited, have called to see you because they have been asked by a new supplier abroad to set up in his favour a documentary credit for goods supplied.

(a) Outline to the directors the five main parties to a documentary credit and describe briefly the respective roles. [10]

(b) Explain briefly what questions you should consider before a documentary credit facility is granted to Cuddly Toys Limited. [10]

[Total marks for question – 20]

3 (a) Your personal customer, Mr Angelo Ginitto, asks for advice on the best methods of remitting money to Italy to support an aged relative.

Outline briefly two alternative ways you can suggest to him, stating the principal benefits and drawbacks to him of each method. [5]

(b) Mrs Jill Jones and her husband will be on holiday for three weeks in Portugal. They are flying out to Lisbon where an hotel has already been booked for the first three nights. After that they plan to hire a car and travel north, stopping at hotels en route. Apart from the air fares, they expect that the total cost will be approximately £1500 and have asked your advice on the safest way of making payments whilst they are travelling.

Briefly recommend a solution for them, highlighting at least one advantage and one disadvantage of your suggestion. [5]

(c) The directors of Busy Hands Limited have their first opportunity to export their embroidered linen to West Germany. However, the buyer has insisted on being invoiced in deutschmarks.

The directors are concerned that they will not know until much later exactly how much sterling they will receive. They are worried about calculating the amount of profit on the transaction.

What advice can you give them to help them in their difficulties? [10]

[Total marks for question – 20]

Section B

4 (a) Your customer, Malcolm Smith, has been frequently exceeding his overdraft limit of £500 recently. This morning, when you check the computer print-out for last night's closing balances, you notice that Mr Smith's account is £675 overdrawn. Upon investigation, you discover that three cheques, each for £50, were cashed earlier in the week at the local casino, guaranteed by cheque card.

What action will you take? Give reasons to support your decision. [5]

(b) You are surprised to note that a current account in the name of Mrs Joan Brook has gone overdrawn to £300 without any prior arrangement. The account is not one with which you are familiar. Before deciding whether or not to return cheques for lack of funds, you will need to make a number of checks concerning the account. State briefly *five* of the checks you will make.   [5]

(c) A chargor may give an equitable mortgage over land by depositing the deeds with intent to charge. Why is this method not recommended in practice?   [5]

(d) As security for a loan of £5000 to your customer, John Gordon, you hold a first legal charge over his home. The charge form contains the usual 'continuing security' clause.

Today, you receive notice from the Eastern Finance Company of a second mortgage in their favour. What effect does this have on your security and what action will you take to protect the bank's position?   [5]

[Total marks for question – 20]

5 Joe Biggs is a personal customer who has banked at your branch for several years and maintained a wholly satisfactory account. Now in his mid 30s, he has worked in the greengrocery business since leaving school. He approaches you for help in setting up his own business.

Outline by way of brief notes the items you would expect him to cover in a business plan *before* you can consider his request to borrow money.   [20]

6 (a) Your long established customer, Mr Brian Hay, wants to borrow money from the bank to build an extension to his home. Your branch manager has invited you to join the interview.

What are the three main characteristics of a good banking advance? What factors will you take into account when considering Mr Hay's request?   [10]

(b) Control of working capital becomes a crucial element in the financial control of a business.

(i) Suggest three ways in which management may improve a company's cash flow and the possible effects of each method.

(ii) Which two financial ratios measure the impact of management actions on cash flow (liquidity)? How are they calculated?   [10]

7 Answer all parts ((i)–(xi)) of this question. Where parts are divided into (a) and (b), both must be answered.

For (a), write the number of the part (e.g. (i)(a), (ii)(a) etc) and one of A, B, C or D.

For (b) brief answers only are required.

(i)(a) What does a company's Memorandum of Association state?

A The history of the business.

B The experience and responsibilities of its managers.

C What sort of business it is and what it will do.

D Details of the percentage of ownership of connected companies.

(b) In what document would you expect to find the extent to which directors of the company may borrow money? [2]

(ii)(a) What is the most *versatile* form of bank borrowing for a small business?

A Overdraft.

B Term loan.

C Leasing.

D Factoring.

(b) Give reasons for your choice in (a). [2]

(iii)(a) When reviewing and controlling advances, how would you recognise that a 'hard core' is developing?

A Frequent excesses over agreed limit.

B High turnover through account.

C Increase in number of debit entries.

D Borrowing never drops below a certain figure.

(b) What action could you take if you recognised the existence of a hard core of borrowing? [2]

(iv)(a) Which of the following possibilities could be indicated by a sharply rising turnover on an account?

A Overtrading.

B A last minute provision to meet cheques.

C A reduction in the number of credits to the account.

D A change in the terms of credit given.

(b) What further investigation would you make before contacting the customer to discuss any potential adverse trend? [2]

(v)(a) The term 'bridging loan' applies to

A house purchase and sale solely

B the purchase of any asset where repayment is to come from a source other than the sale of the asset being purchased

C the interest charges which accrue before the sale of a customer's property is achieved

D the shortfall when the housing transaction is complete and the bank is left with an unwanted residual loan.

(b) Briefly state one advantage to a customer in obtaining a bridging loan for the purchase of a new home. [2]

(vi)(a) If a small retail business shows debtors of £20 000 and annual sales of £240 000, how many days' credit is given?

A 21 days.

B 7 days.

C 30 days.

D 14 days.

(b) Please show your calculation of the answer.　　　　　　[2]

(vii)(a) In Question 7(vi), if two-thirds of the annual sales are received in cash, how many days' credit is given on the remaining sales?

A 91 days.

B 62 days.

C 30 days.

D 45 days.

(b) Please show your calculation of the answer.　　　　　　[2]

(viii)(a) When dealing with a bad and doubtful debt of £10 000, what is it necessary to obtain before other legal remedies can be pursued?

A Solicitor's letter to debtor.

B Appointment of tracing agents.

C Interview with debtor.

D Judgement.

(b) What benefit is it?　　　　　　[2]

(ix) How can the bank obtain an Attachment of Earnings Order?

A Through the County Court.

B By direct agreement with employers to pay monthly sums from the earnings.

C By appointment of debt collectors.

D Bankruptcy of the customer.　　　　　　[1]

(x) A bank advance for a business to purchase trading stock will

A increase the fixed assets of the business

B increase the current assets of the business

C increase the trade creditors of the business

D reduce the outstanding liabilities of the business.　　　　　　[1]

(xi)(a) If the bank holds a standard mandate for an overdrawn joint current account in the names of Paul Martin and Geoffrey Brown with either to sign, how many rights of action has the bank to recover the borrowing in the event of the death of one of them?

A Two.

B Three.

C One.

D Four.

(b) Give the name of each of the parties to the actions to justify your answer to (a) above.　　　　　　[2]

[Total marks for question – 20]

Model answers

Section A

(i)(a) B

(b) There were some weird and wonderful answers for the meaning of 'confirmed'.

When a documentary credit is 'confirmed', the beneficiary can look not only to the applicant for payment, but also will hold an undertaking from the advising bank to honour documents drawn in accordance with the terms of the credit.

(ii)(a) A

(b) Several students suggested that the drawback was the expense of using factoring services, which might have hurt some of the companies' feelings! All things are relative in terms of expense; for example, market conditions, convenience, etc.

Factoring companies tend to be very selective, and stand between the company customer and its bank. Consequently, pressure may be exerted on debtors without reference to the company customer, thereby potentially damaging the relationship with the latter. A percentage only of the debt due is released immediately, normally 80%, with the balance paid after receipt from the debtor, and a charge is made for the service.

(iii)(a) D

(b) It was disappointing that very few candidates recognised ECGD, for the syllabus requires a basic knowledge of the services of this organisation.

ECGD can provide a limited cover for exchange loss through their foreign currency contracts endorsement.

Marks were allocated where students mentioned currency options. However, currency accounts would not be recommended in this instance.

(iv)(a) B

(b) Stating that advance payment means payment in advance is not sufficient in itself to grant a mark in section (b) of this question.

An exporter would prefer to receive payment in advance of shipping goods abroad which will remove any credit or exchange risk for him and, dependent upon how far in advance payment is made, the funds could assist him in the manufacture of the goods concerned. In addition, his costs will be fixed and there will be no need to carry forward any exchange risk.

(v)(a) C

(b) Several candidates misunderstood the background of this service and how it can help suppliers of services overseas.

A performance guarantee is issued by a bank to ensure performance of a contract in accordance with a seller's contractual obligations.

(vi)(a) B

(b) Many candidates described what this difference is *called* but not what it *represents.*

The difference between the buying and selling rates represents the bank's profit on currency deals.

(vii)(a) A

(b) Several students read the question as being the *safest* method, when the examiner had asked for the most *beneficial* method.

Dealing on open account gives more flexibility to an importer who would be expected to settle on payment date within agreed terms of trade. As a result, no additional documentation is involved and, therefore, no further bank charges arise.

(viii)(a) D

(b) Generally well answered.

When goods are shipped by sea, the documents will normally include a set of bills of lading, which represent documents of title. The buyer will not be able to obtain the goods without at least one of the 'original' bills of lading.

(ix)(a) C

(b) Generally well answered.

The buyer is responsible for paying transport and insurance costs. (The seller arranges for goods to be loaded on board a named vessel advised by the buyer.)

(x)(a) A

(b) Knowledge of the settlement procedures between banks was very poor.

A UK bank must maintain accounts with other banks overseas in order to carry out international transactions. Actual debit/credit entries are passed over the *nostro* account in the centre where it is maintained, and a mirror account is held in the UK showing a reflection of that account for reconciliation purposes.

2(a) A basic knowledge is required not only of the five main parties to a documentary credit, but also the 'proper' names. When dealing abroad, customers will be faced with such expressions and we need to help them to identify the various people with whom they will be dealing. Marks were given if the understanding of the respective roles was sound and the descritpions clear.

The five main parties to a documentary credit are:

- *The applicant:* the customer at whose request the bank establishes the credit, and to whom the bank looks for reimbursement.
- *The issuing bank:* the bank which issues the credit on behalf of the applicant.
- *The beneficiary:* the person in whose favour the credit is issued.
- *The advising bank:* Normally, the issuing bank's correspondent in the beneficiary's country, through whom the credit is routed.
- *The confirming bank:* Normally, the beneficiary would rely on the undertaking of the issuing bank. If he is concerned as to the financial standing of either the issuing bank or the country concerned, he may request the applicant to have the credit 'confirmed' by the advising bank through the issuing bank.

The advising bank (by confirming the credit) would undertake, in addition to the issuing bank, to honour documents drawn in accordance with the terms of the credit. The advising bank would then have no recourse to the beneficiary if they were unable to reimburse themselves on the issuing bank.

(b) Most students found this part of the question difficult and it appeared beyond their own level of understanding. The question was not intended to be based on the CAMPARI principles; instead the examiner was looking for the type of information provided in a bank's own brochures so that it may determine the background to the credit.

Before granting documentary credit facility, a banker needs to consider:

- *Standing of customer:* basic canons of lending and company balance sheet analysis.
- *Cash cover:* whether full or partial cash cover should be held in support of the facility.
- *Exchange risk:* if the credit is expressed in foreign currency, a forward contract may be advisable.
- *The goods:* Nature of goods (e.g. whether perishable, warehousing, duty payable, etc). It is important that the commercial integrity of the proposed beneficiary (the overseas supplier) is satisfactory. A status enquiry may be necessary.
- *Control over goods:* our security position can be improved if the bank has control over the goods, and the terms and conditions in the application form incorporates the right of the bank to sell the goods if the customer fails to provide funds.
- *Insurance of the goods/shipping costs:* Check who is responsible for insuring the goods and the contract of carriage.

- *Supplier's terms of credit:* If the supplier grants a period of credit before payment, then the documents will be released against acceptance of drafts drawn on either the advising bank or issuing bank. The applicant will be able to collect the goods, thereby releasing what may be the bank's security before the draft matures for payment by the applicant.
- *Import licence:* certain goods need import licences for entry into the UK. This is the responsibility of the customer and information is available from the Department of Trade.
- *Type of credit:* the terms of the credit must be in accordance with Uniform Customs and Practice, whether irrevocable (i.e. cancellation of, or amendment to the terms of the credit are subject to the agreement of all parties to that credit) or revocable (theoretically instructions can be given to the advising bank for the credit to be cancelled or amended at any time before presentation of the documents).

3   Most candidates answered this question very well, although few took account of the number of marks allotted to each part. Hence, Part (a) might have taken three pages of the answer book, and Part (c) half a page.

(a) Generally well answered. However, students must remember that SWIFT is not a method of remitting funds, it is only a means of so doing.

Alternative methods of remitting funds abroad are:

- *Telegraphic transfer:* payment instructions are sent by authenticated message from a bank in the UK to a correspondent bank overseas. It is the fastest method for a remitter to arrange for payments of funds to a beneficiary, in sterling or foreign currency. However, it costs more than other methods, particularly if the cable is at urgent rate. The SWIFT system may be used.
- *International payment order:* instructions are sent bank-to-bank by air mail. This method is simple and cheaper than telegraphic transfer because there are no cable costs, although the delivery of instructions is slower.
- *Draft/international money order:* a bank cheque drawn on a foreign correspondent bank in favour of a named payee. The cheque is posted by the customer to the beneficiary who receives immediate credit as soon as it is paid into their bank account. This method is very cheap and simple, and more personal to the parties concerned.

SWIFT is a communications service for messages which would otherwise have gone by mail, telex or cable.

(b) Again, a good knowledge of alternatives was shown. Regrettably, however, very few candidates gave the suggested *solution* which they would recommend and which was asked for in the question. Some candidates also seem unaware that their bank can issue travellers cheques in currency.

When travelling abroad, customers have various alternatives for making payments:

- *Travellers cheques*: can be issued in sterling or foreign currency. Immediate replacement if lost/stolen. A minimum handling fee is normally charged by banks on each exchange of travellers cheques, which is subject to currency fluctuations. Not acceptable at several retail outlets.

- *Foreign currency*: Cost is fixed at date of purchase. Ready cash – therefore greater flexibility. No immediate replacement if lost/stolen: (may be covered under customer's insurance policy). It might be more beneficial for customers to exchange their sterling abroad at more advantageous rates.

- *Eurocheque and cards*: uniform Eurocheque card and cheque available for local use in European countries, and used like a UK cheque book. Can prove expensive with a minimum fixed fee for each encashment. There is a ceiling limit to the amount of each daily encashment. May be encased only at banks or used for payment of goods and services at shops displaying the 'EC' signs.

- *Credit cards*: Simple to use, customer needs only the plastic card. Several weeks' extended credit may be available dependent upon date of purchase. Widely accepted world-wide. Can be expensive if customers take borrowing on the card.

Mr and Mrs Jones could make use of any/all of these alternatives for their holiday.

(c) Most candidates picked up the benefits of a forward exchange contract, although some stated that the contract was between the exporter and importer rather than the bank and exporter. Opening a currency account would not normally be appropriate unless a company had both income and expenditure in the currency concerned; there would be a need still to change back into sterling at some time in the future and it could be necessary at a time when the exchange rate is poor.

An exchange risk exists whenever a party to a transaction has to be involved in currency other than their home currency in that the rate of exchange may move unfavourably against the home currency.

A forward contract is a firm and binding undertaking between the customer and the bank to buy/sell a certain amount of a specified currency at a fixed exchange rate either:

- at a particular date in the future ('fixed contract');
- or during a specified period in the future – the customer chooses when to utilise the contract within the period ('option' contract).

Forward rates are *not* determined by forecasts of future exchange rate movement but by interest rate differentials between the two currencies concerned. The currency with the lower interest rate will be at a 'premium' against the other; conversely, the currency with the higher rate of interest will be at a 'discount' to the other.

Exchange rates are calculated by taking the *spot* rate and adding or subtracting the 'forward margin' for the currency/period of contract. A premium is deducted and a discount is added to the *spot* rate to determine the rate for the contract.

Hence, the directors of Busy Hands Limited would be recommended to enter into a forward contract which will then fix the amount they will receive from the German buyer, so that they can calculate the amount of profit on the transaction.

Section B

4(a) A lack of knowledge was displayed by most candidates with very few knowing the special requirements for cheques issued at gaming sessions – despite a recent article in *Banking World*. Some students were determined to close a customer's account because gambling was illegal and frowned upon.

A new agreement was reached between the banks and the British Casinos Association in 1987 that in future three guaranteed cheques to a maximum of £150 (formerly two cheques) may be accepted during any one gaming session. Accordingly, the bank is unable to return any of the cheques unpaid.

Malcolm Smith should be interviewed to be 'read the Riot Act' and to discuss his financial position, budget, and ability to repay the debt over a reasonable period. It should be pointed out to him that, in effect, he is defrauding the bank in the misuse of his cheque guarantee card and may be guilty of an offence under s. 15 of the Theft Act 1968 (which states that '. . . a person who by any deception dishonestly obtains property belonging to another, with the intention of permanently depriving the other of it . . .' is guilty of an offence). The branch may need to recover the cheque book and guarantee card for the time being. (Cases: *Regina* v *Charles* (1976); *Regina* v *Lambie* (1981).)

(b) Any five of the under-mentioned checks would be pertinent:

- that no overdraft or loan facility has been granted by a colleague;
- whether any funds are due, e.g. proceeds of sale or securities;
- security and safe custody registers for evidence of worth;
- whether any funds on deposit/savings accounts, etc.;
- customer's statement of account record and paid vouchers to ensure that there have been no mis-posts and that no post-dated cheques have been paid by mistake;
- that no credit has been received in the inward credit work or over the counter during today;
- accounts in a similar name, where a credit may have been misplaced;
- the internal 'overs in tills account' for an outstanding credit because the relevant slip has been left in customer's paying-in-book by mistake;
- that the cheque(s) have not been issued against the cheque guarantee facility.

(c) There was a most disappointing display of lack of knowledge in this part of the question. There is evidently some confusion about the difference between equitable and legal charges; some students felt that equitable meant a charge against an individual, whereas legal meant a charge against land.

The method of obtaining an equitable charge over land by depositing the deeds with intent to charge is not recommended because:

- It may be overcome by prior equities.
- There is no power of sale.
- Court application is required to recover the debt.
- There is no benefit of the usual charge form clauses.
- It is difficult to prove that there was an intent to charge.
- If the borrowing is by a company it must be registered within 21 days.

(d) This part of the question was very badly answered. Clayton's case represents part of a banker's 'Bible' and falls in the category of *must know*. There appeared to be no understanding or appreciation of the requirements with answers ranging from the comment that there would be no affect at all on the bank's security to the comment that the bank will need to obtain alternative security because the present charge is now ineffective.

Notice of a second mortgage would determine the continuing

nature of the security. If no action is taken, the rule in Clayton's case will operate and the security in respect of any advances made by the bank to Mr Gordon subsequent to the date of receipt of notice will rank after the second mortgage.

The account(s) covered must be broken to defeat the rule in Clayton's case.

Any further lending granted to Mr Gordon to be secured by the home will rank after the building society advance.

5   Those candidates who had taken the initiative of obtaining a copy of any of the major banks' brochures produced for customers to help them to complete a business plan achieved good marks. Many other candidates appear to have attempted the question as a last resort and tried to gain marks by referring solely to the principles of lending, even though the question clearly stated *before* consideration of the request to borrow money. It might surprise some candidates to learn that approaches for help do not always mean a request to borrow money; a banker's role is also to give guidance.

A business plan check list should include:

(a) *Objectives:*
Customers' specific plans for the future (business/personal);
contingency plans in the event of failure.

(b) *The business:*
If buying an established business with a trading history, the accounts for previous years' trading are required;
present financial position.

(c) *Management:*
What help customers might need in running the business, and their responsibility and experience.

(d) *Market:*
Level of competition;
how large a share of the market;
advertising/marketing needs.

(e) *Products:*
How costs are calculated;
advantages of *own* product over *competitors'*.

(f) *Pricing:*
How the selling price is calculated;
whether competitive.

(g) *Suppliers:*
Whether adequate suppliers available;
acceptable quality.

How much credit available (Note: remember – customer is

probably selling mostly for cash unless he supplies to restaurants, etc.)

(h) *Physical resources:*

Premises availability and adequacy;

machinery/vehicles required;

how costs are to be financed.

(i) *Profit and cash forecasts:*

Validity of assumptions;

risks;

survival possibility of business if sales are, e.g. 20% less than planned.

(j) *Outside finance required:*

How much is required for fixed assets/working capital;

for how long is borrowing to be required;

how finance is to be repaid.

6(a) This part of the question was very well answered and covered in detail the points to consider, which are briefly as follows:

The three main characteristics of a good banking advance are *safety, liquidity, profitability.*

Considerations to be made when appraising the potential lending are:

- character;
- ability to repay;
- margin;
- purpose of advance;
- amount required;
- repayment terms;
- insurance/security requirements.

(b) Candidates need to improve their understanding concerning cash flow. For example, paying off creditors regularly does *not* improve cash flow in the context of current assets in relation to current liabilities. Neither does an increase in overdraft or loan improve those ratios; in fact, the opposite is the case. Capital items might improve *cash* balances in the short term. The request for stating the possible effects of each method was not covered at all by some candidates. Some students spent far too much time on factoring hoping to pick up extra marks.

The answers to the second half of this part of the question were mixed, with many guesses being a feature.

(i) Four ways in which management may improve a company's cash flow:

- A reduction in days outstanding to credit customers (debtors).

However, prompt settlement discounts should not be offered unless the cost of discount is lower than the cost of bank borrowing.

- An extension of day's credit taken from suppliers (creditors). The customer must avoid antagonising suppliers or losing valuable discounts.
- A reduction in stock levels will improve the cash flow through the delay in cash outflow on stock replacement.
- Employment of a factoring service for debtor collection.

(ii) The two financial ratios which measure the impact of management actions on cash flow are the *current ratio* and *acid test*.

They are calculated:

$$\text{Current ratio} = \frac{\text{current assets}}{\text{current liabilities}}$$

$$\text{Acid test} = \frac{\text{current assets capable of conversion into cash within one month}}{\text{current liabilities which have to be met within one month}}$$

7 As a multiple-choice question similar to Question 1, part (a) of each question had only one right answer. Accordingly, if students failed to gain a mark for that part of the question, with one or two exceptions part (b) would be wrong also:

(i)(a) C

(b) The Articles of Association.

(ii)(a) A

(b) A small business may overdraw up to the limit agreed. Interest is charged only day by day, and the amount borrowed varies and goes down whenever payments in are made.

(iii)(a) D

(b) Several students mentioned the need for an interview but did not state with what objective.

The bank could transfer the hard core element to loan account with arrangements made for regular reductions.

(iv)(a) A

(b) Not well answered. The request was for investigations *before* contacting the customer, so that the bank could make sure of its facts prior to a meeting.

The bank must make sure that the balance is not distorted by unusual/exceptional items (e.g. the purchase of a capital item paid through the account). The company could also be cross-firing.

(v)(a) B

(b) Many candidates did *not* read the question! Despite that, several picked up a mark for part (b).

The main advantages of a bridging loan to a customer are:

He will not have to wait for the sale proceeds before completing the purchase.

Since effectively it will be a cash transaction for the purchase, he may be able to use that as a bargaining point with the vendor.

He may be able to obtain tax relief on the bridge over borrowing.

(vi)(a) C

(b) Credit given $= \dfrac{£\ 20\ 000}{£240\ 000} \times 365$ days $= 30$ days

(vii)(a) A

Those candidates with the ability to think it through achieved full marks for this part of the question. Nerves may have played a part for some candidates who managed to calculate two-thirds but used the wrong numbers for the equation.

(b) ⅓ of annual sales of £240 000 = £80 000

Credit given $= \dfrac{£20\ 000}{£80\ 000} \times 365$ days $= 91$ days

(viii)(a) D

(b) Obtaining judgment gives a legal recognition by the courts over the debt, thereby paving the way for the bank to pursue other legal remedies for recovery of the debt.

(ix) A

Answers were mixed and candidates need to have a basic knowledge of the correct facts.

(x) B

It was pleasing to note that most candidates gave a correct answer.

(xi)(a) B

(b) This part of the question was not at all well answered. It is absolutely vital that all students are aware of these mandate positions. It was appalling to note that a lack of knowledge and experience by candidates led to comments like 'If one of them is dead, surely only the remaining one is in a position to repay.' Other candidates suggested that each party was responsible only for half of the debt.

In the event of the death of either customer, the bank has a claim against:

Paul Martin (or his estate)

Geoffrey Brown (or his estate)

Paul Martin and Geoffrey Brown jointly (and/or their respective Estates)

A bank mandate where an account may operate with either party to sign incorporates joint and several liability giving the bank rights of action against the parties jointly and against each individual separately.

Overall, candidates performed better in Section A of the Paper than in Section B and therein lies the need to obtain more practical experience in the area of UK lending.

Index